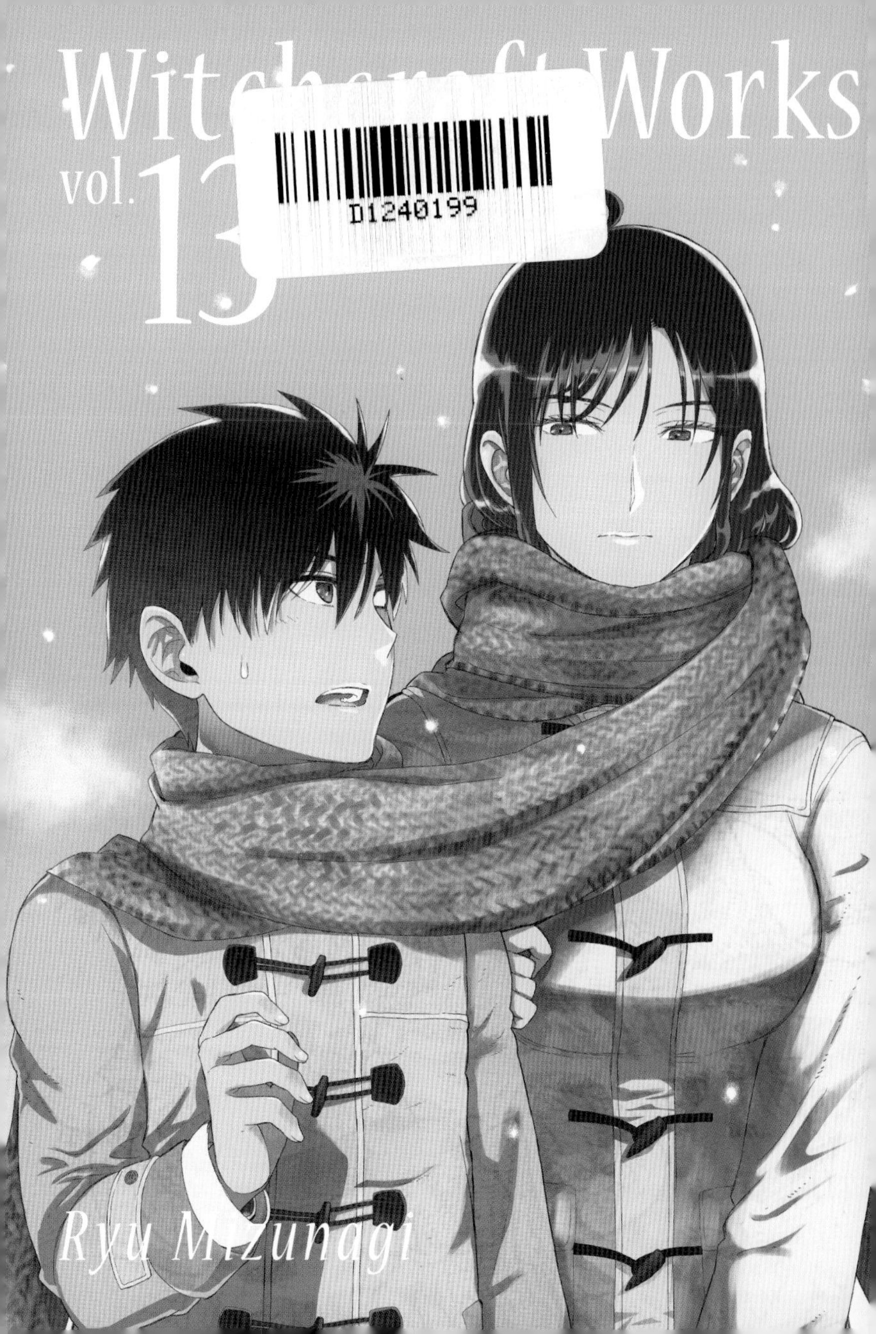

Witchcraft Works
vol. 13
Ryu Mizunagi

CONTENTS

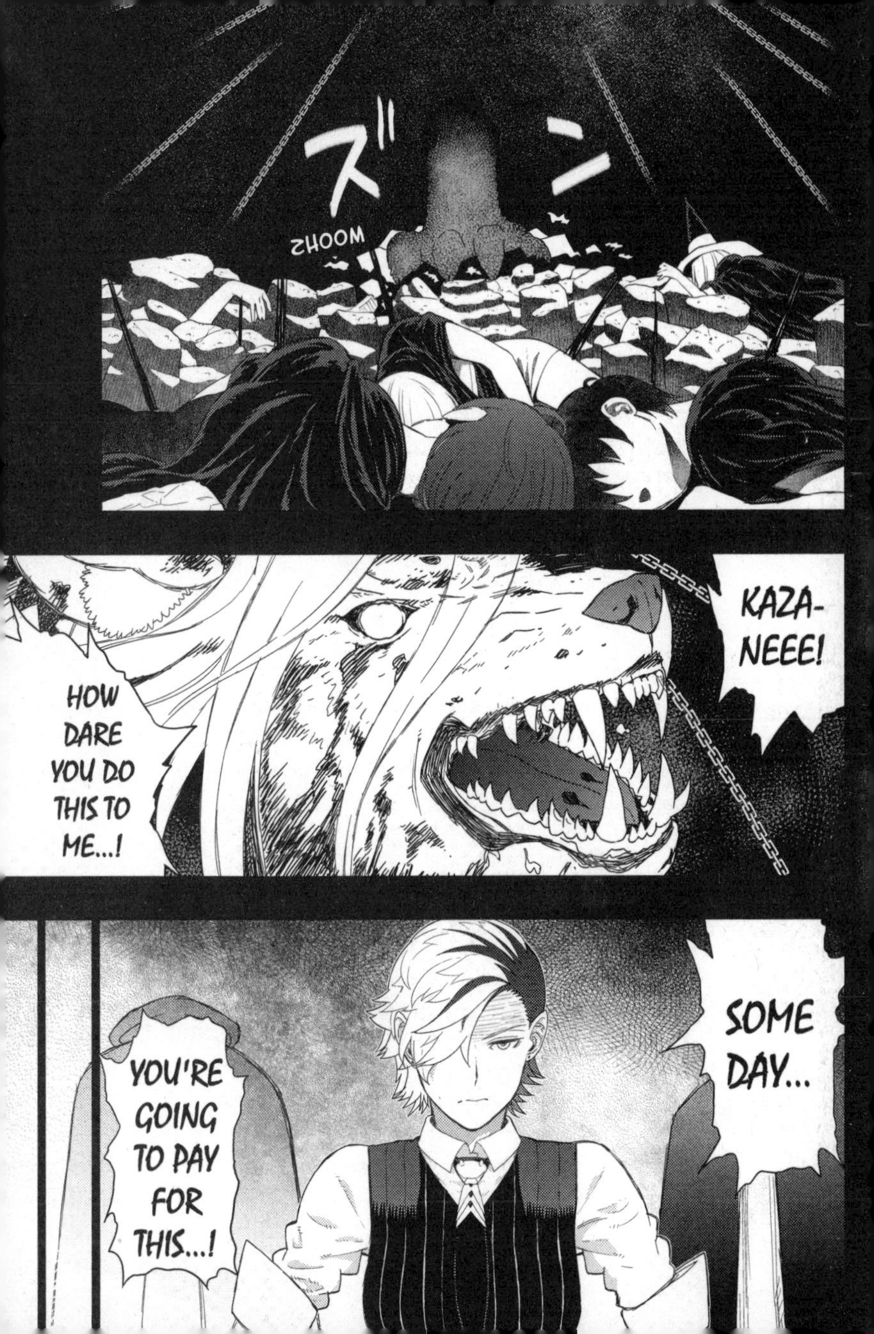
ズン
ZHOOM
KAZA-NEEE!
HOW DARE YOU DO THIS TO ME...!
SOME DAY...
YOU'RE GOING TO PAY FOR THIS...!

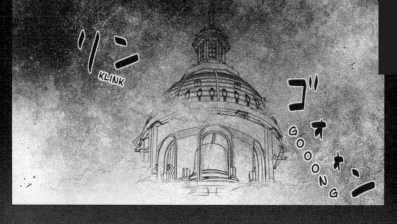

リン
KLINK

ゴオオーン
GOOOONG

HM...?
WHERE...
AM I?

In
times
of
pain...

THIS
LONG,
BEAUTIFUL
HAIR...

CHAPTER 71 Kagari and Cohabitation

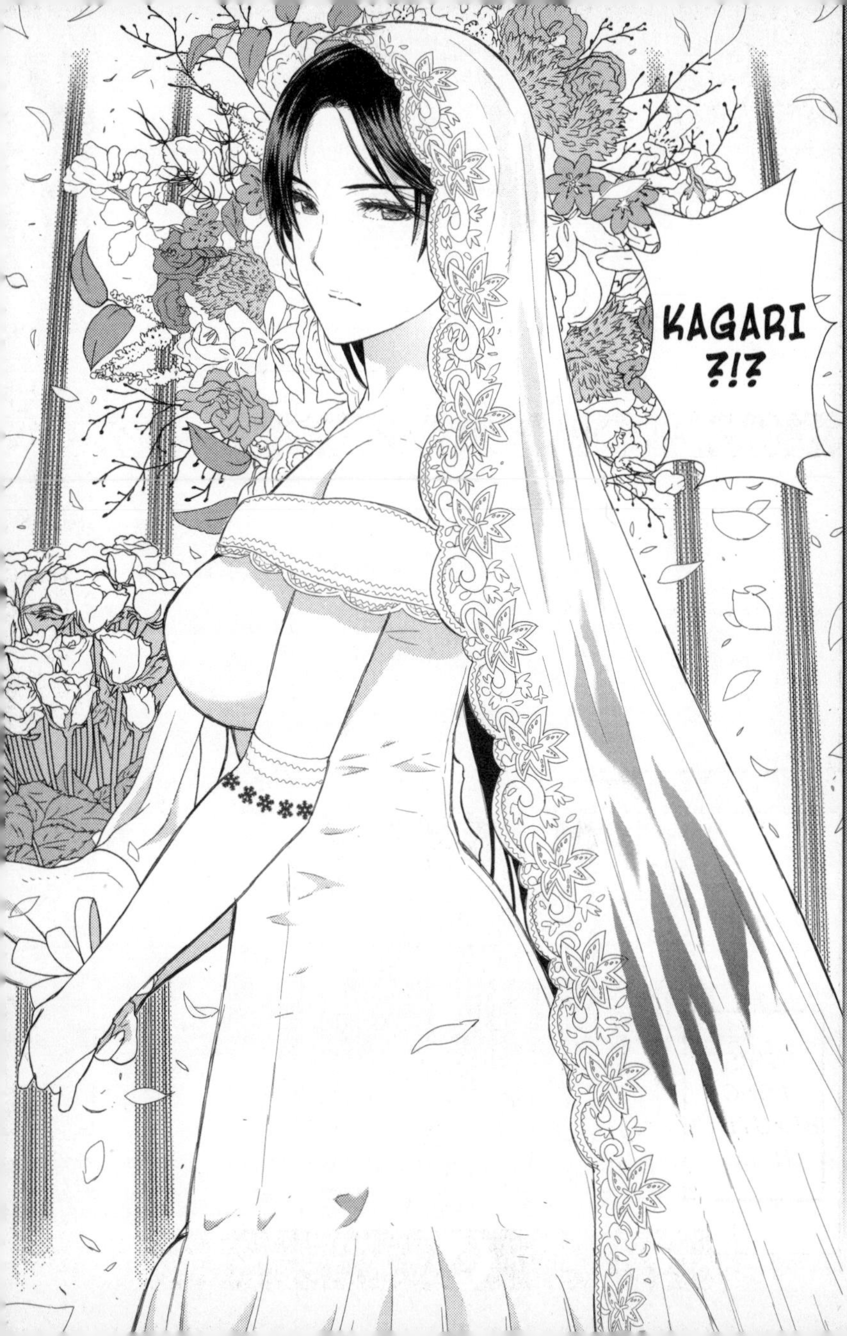
KAGARI ?!?

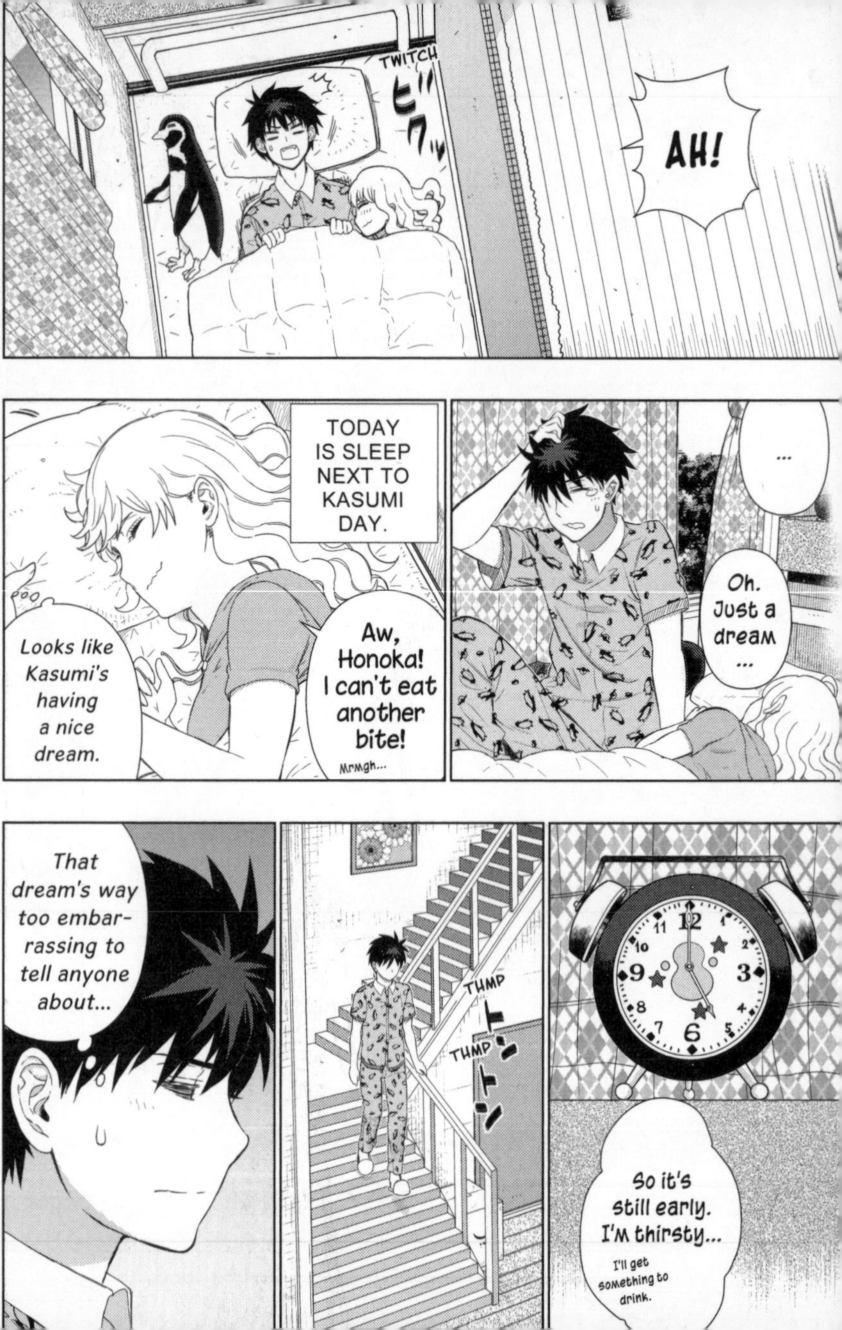
AH!
TWITCH
ビクッ
...
Oh. Just a dream ...
TODAY IS SLEEP NEXT TO KASUMI DAY.
Aw, Honoka! I can't eat another bite!
Mrmgh...
Looks like Kasumi's having a nice dream.
So it's still early. I'm thirsty...
I'll get something to drink.
THUMP
THUMP
That dream's way too embar-rassing to tell anyone about...

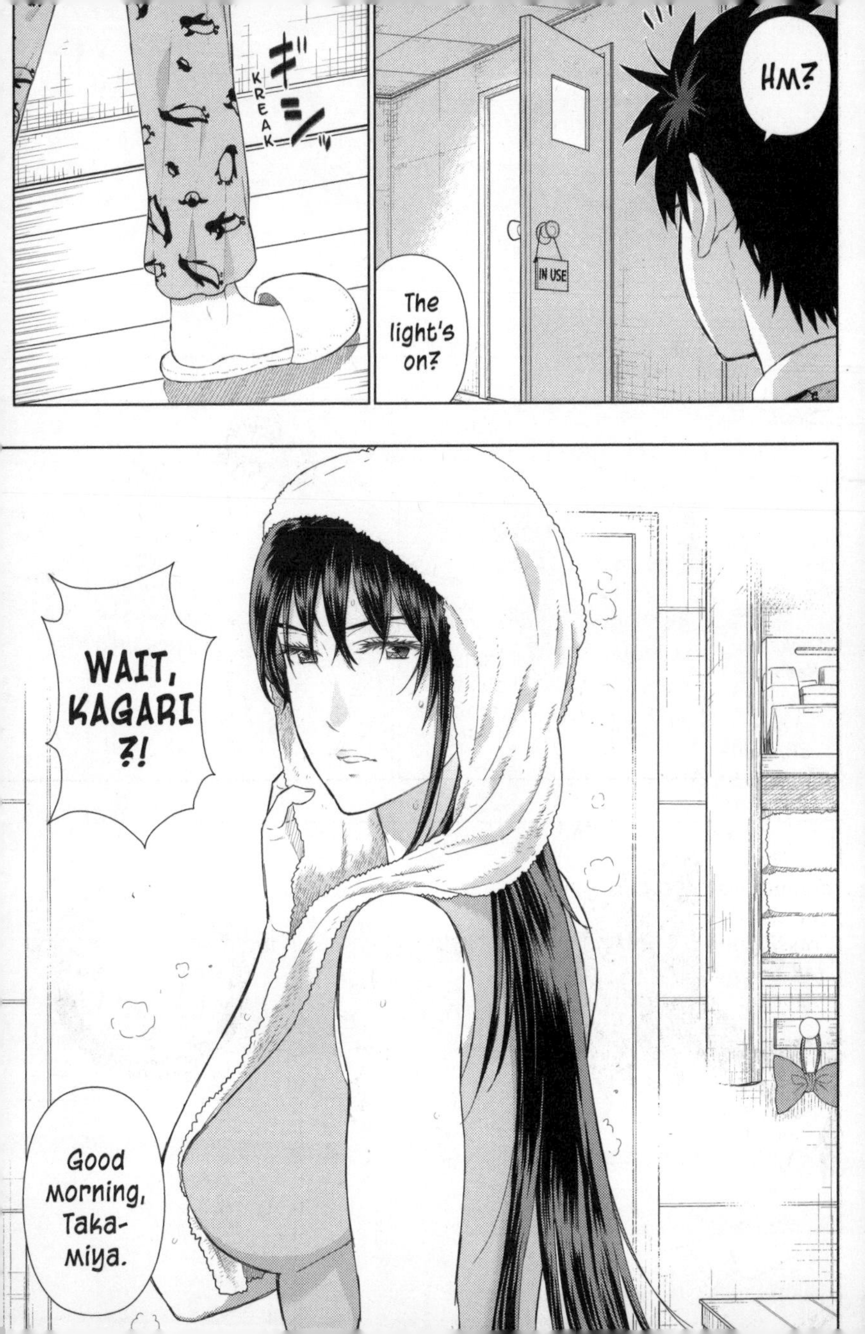
HM?
IN USE
The light's on?
KREAK
WAIT, KAGARI?!
Good Morning, Taka-miya.

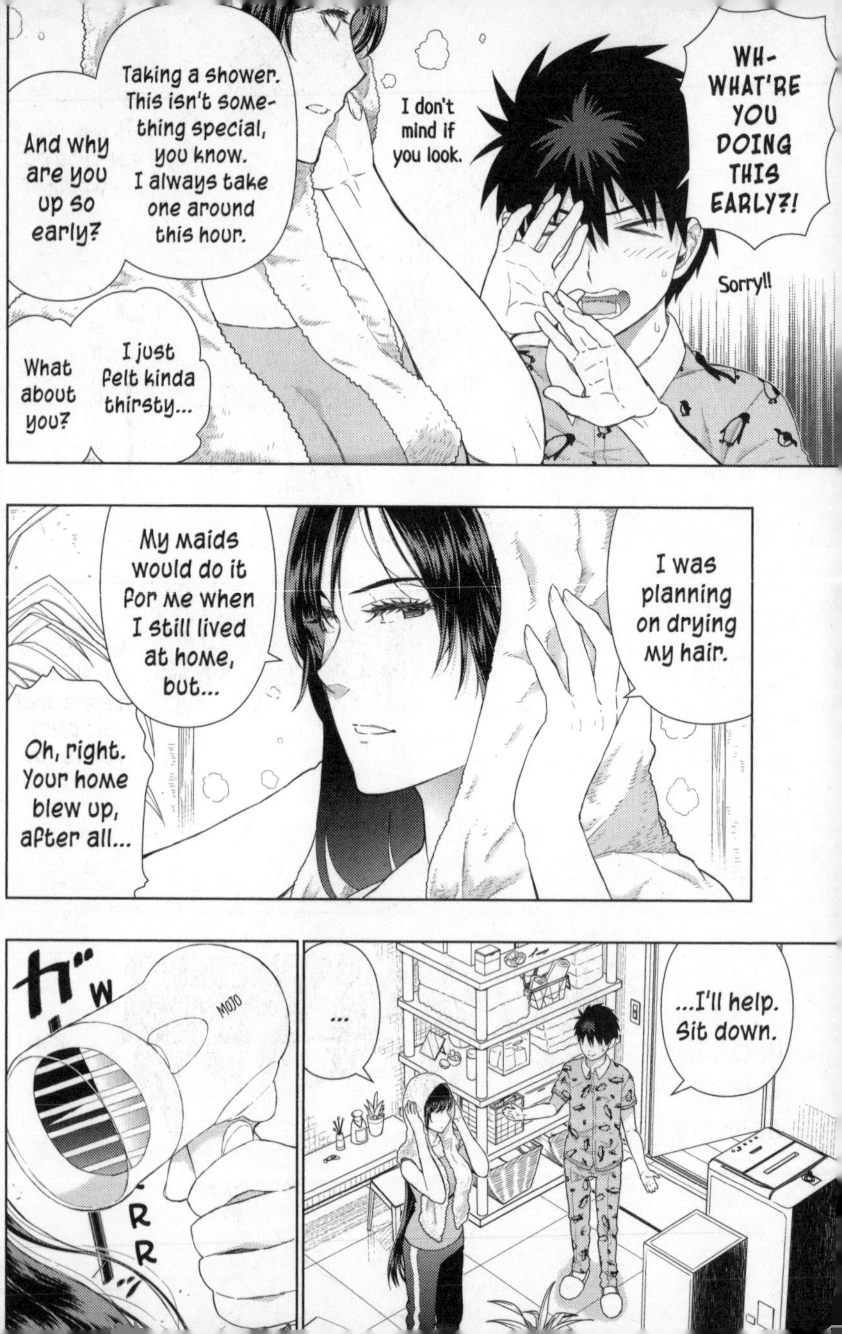
WH-WHAT'RE YOU DOING THIS EARLY?!
Sorry!!
I don't mind if you look.
Taking a shower. This isn't some-thing special, you know. I always take one around this hour.
And why are you up so early?
I just felt kinda thirsty...
What about you?
I was planning on drying my hair.
My maids would do it for me when I still lived at home, but...
Oh, right. Your home blew up, after all...
...I'll help. Sit down.
...
ガ
WRRR
MOJO

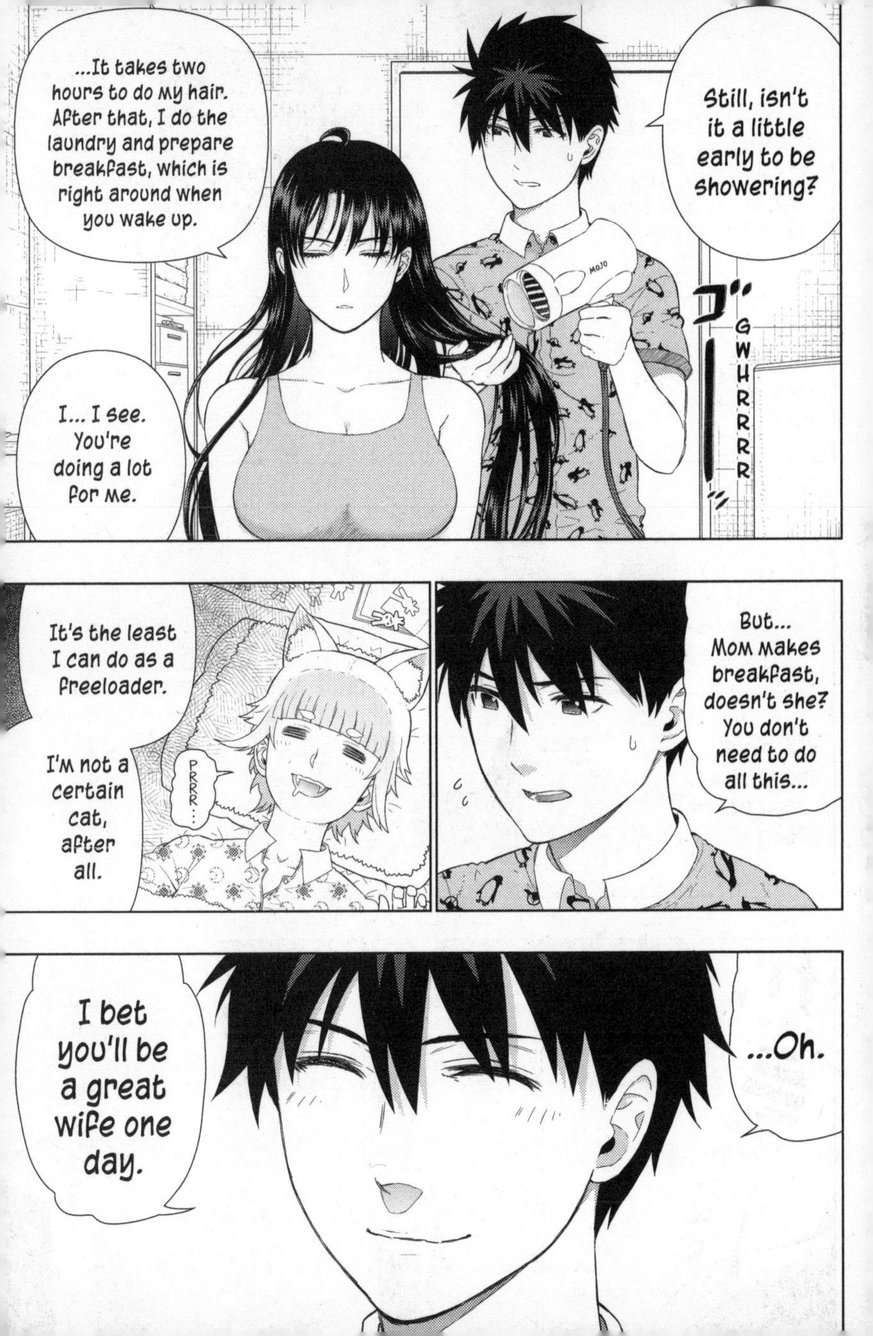
Still, isn't it a little early to be showering?
...It takes two hours to do my hair. After that, I do the laundry and prepare breakfast, which is right around when you wake up.
MOJO
GWHRRRR
I... I see. You're doing a lot for me.
But... Mom makes breakfast, doesn't she? You don't need to do all this...
It's the least I can do as a freeloader.
PRRR...
I'm not a certain cat, after all.
...Oh.
I bet you'll be a great wife one day.

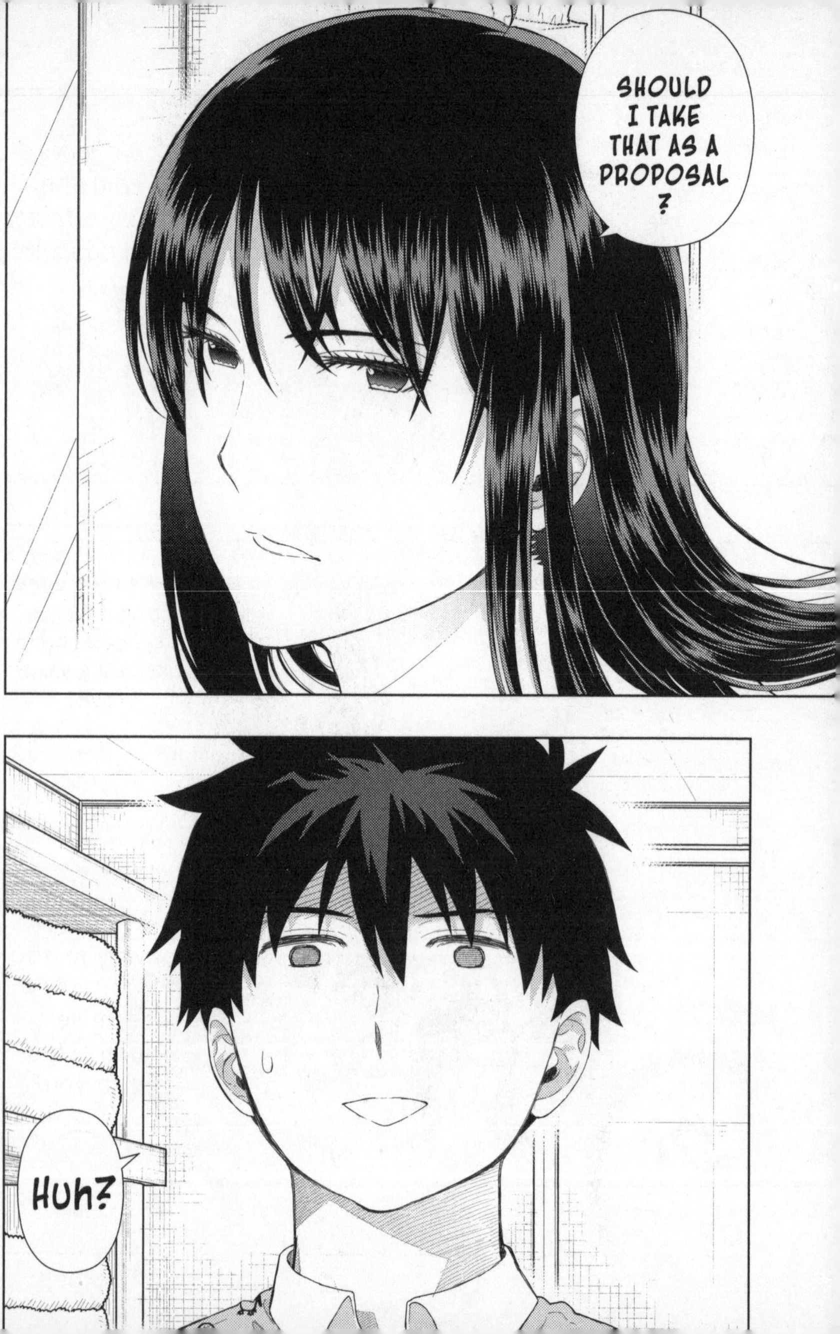
SHOULD I TAKE THAT AS A PROPOSAL?
HUH?

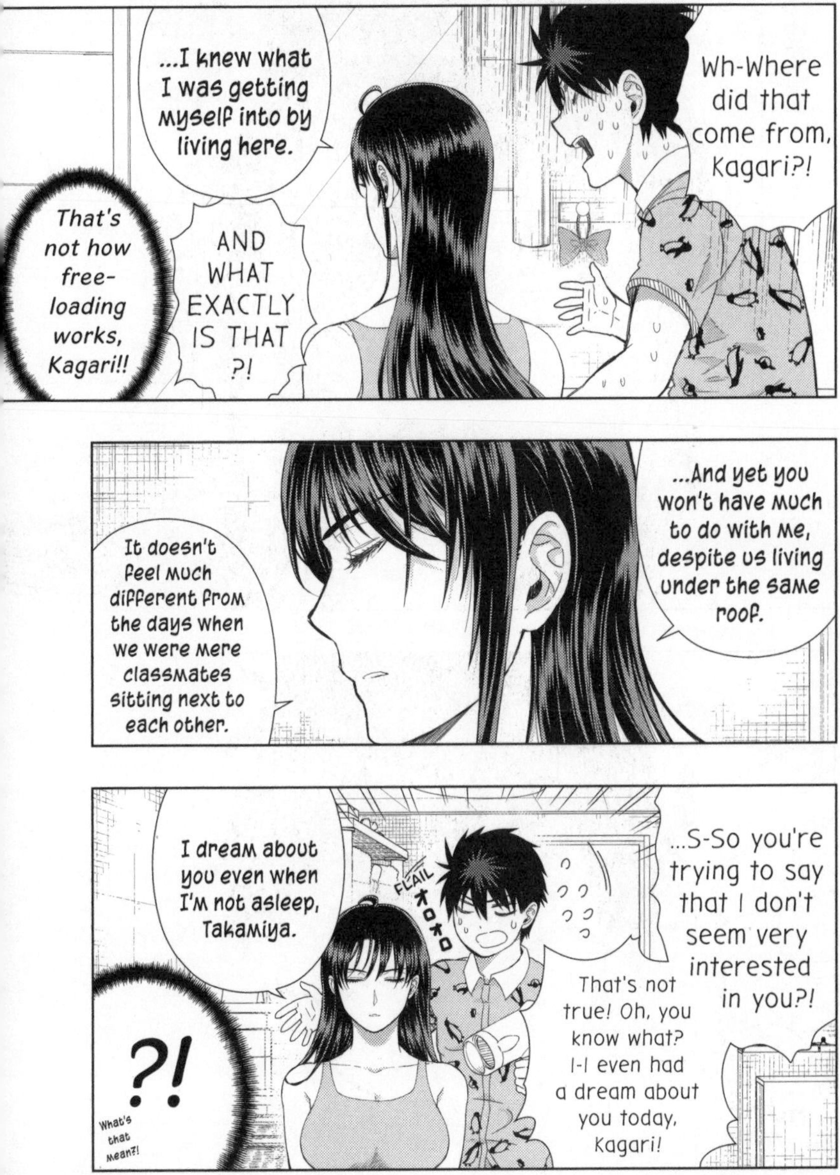
Wh-Where did that come from, Kagari?!
...I knew what I was getting myself into by living here.
AND WHAT EXACTLY IS THAT ?!
That's not how free-loading works, Kagari!!
...And yet you won't have much to do with me, despite us living under the same roof.
It doesn't feel much different from the days when we were mere classmates sitting next to each other.
...S-So you're trying to say that I don't seem very interested in you?!
That's not true! Oh, you know what? I-I even had a dream about you today, Kagari!
FLAIL
I dream about you even when I'm not asleep, Takamiya.
?!
What's that mean?!

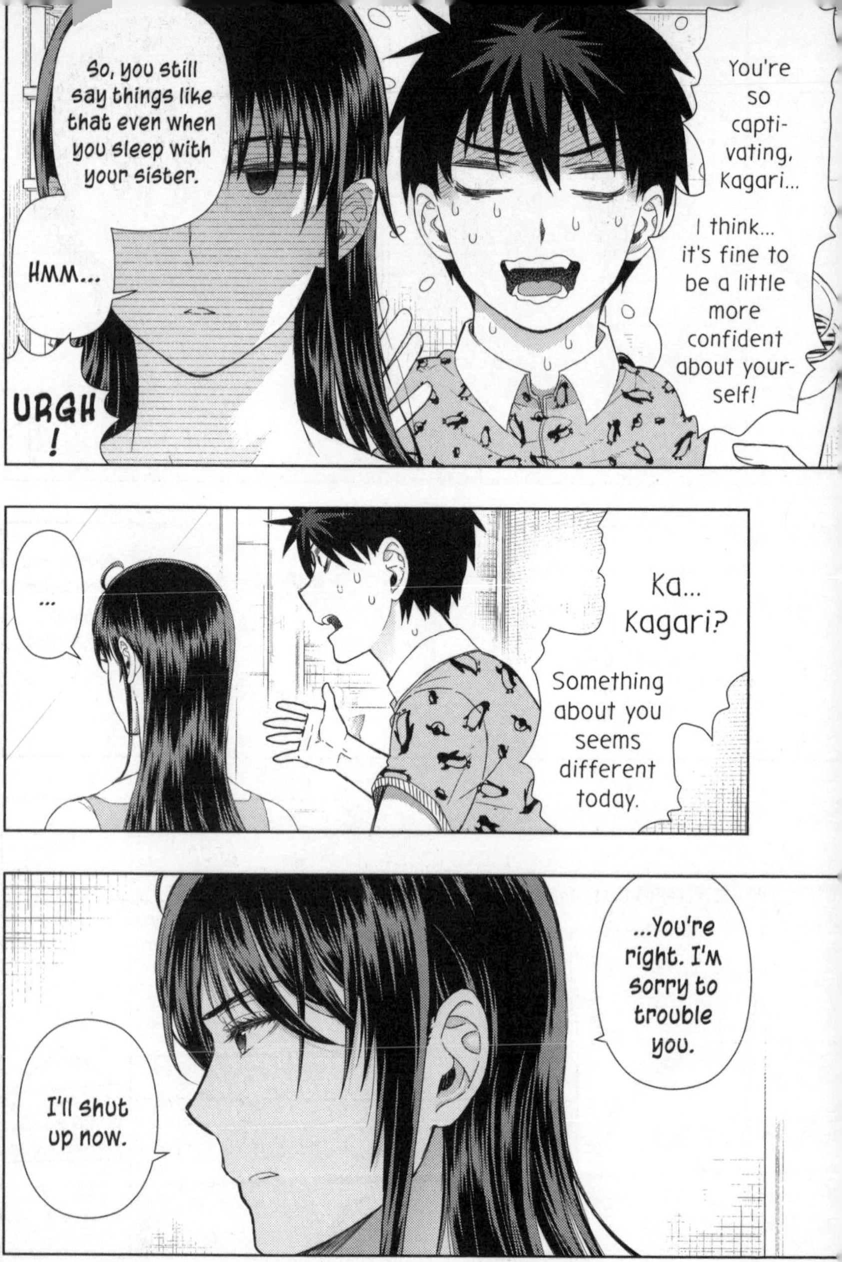
You're so capti-vating, Kagari...
I think... it's fine to be a little more confident about your-self!
So, you still say things like that even when you sleep with your sister.
HMM...
URGH!
Ka... Kagari?
Something about you seems different today.
...
...You're right. I'm sorry to trouble you.
I'll shut up now.

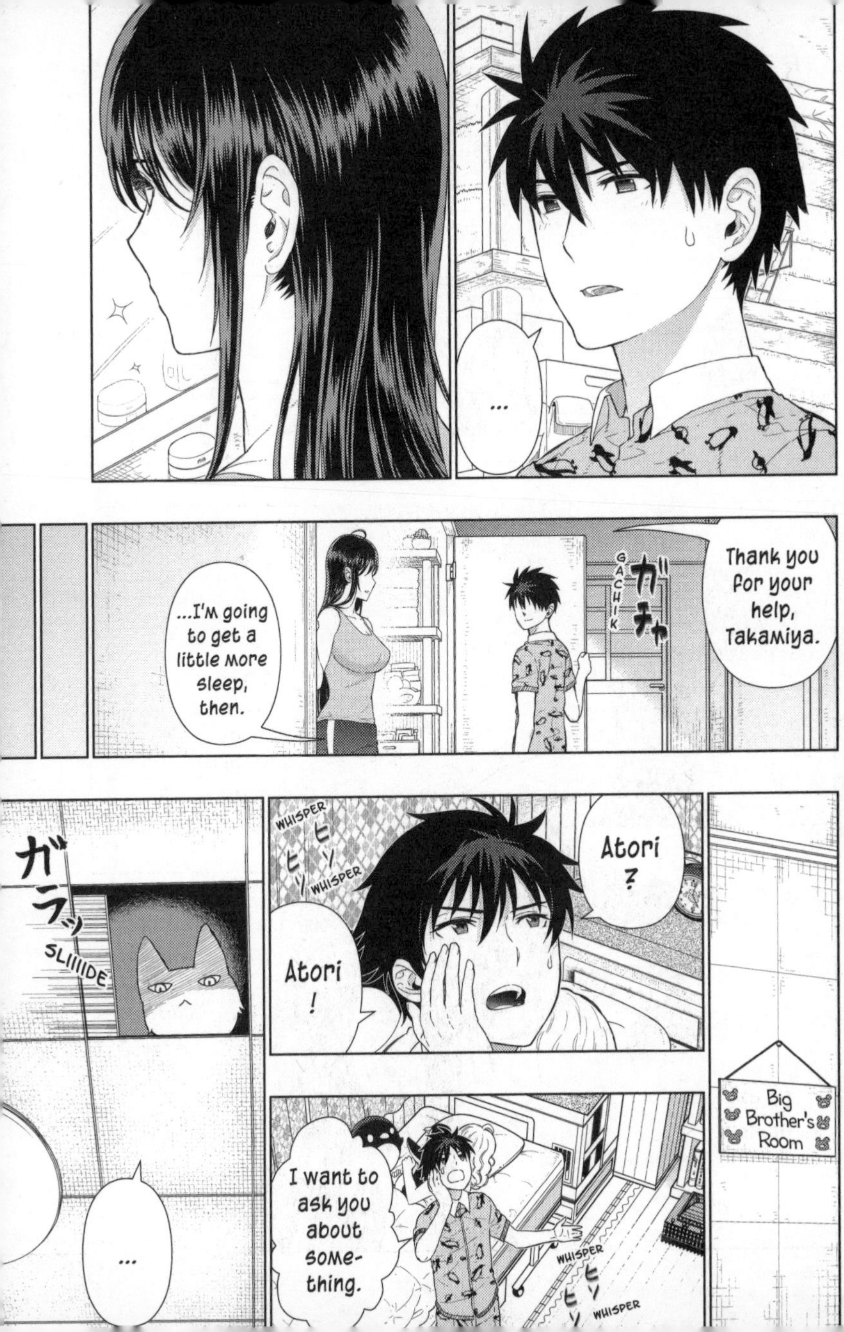
...
Thank you for your help, Takamiya.
ガチャ
GACHIK
...I'm going to get a little more sleep, then.
Big Brother's Room
Atori?
ヒソ ヒソ
WHISPER WHISPER
Atori!
I want to ask you about some-thing.
ヒソ ヒソ
WHISPER WHISPER
ガラッ
SLIIIIDE
...

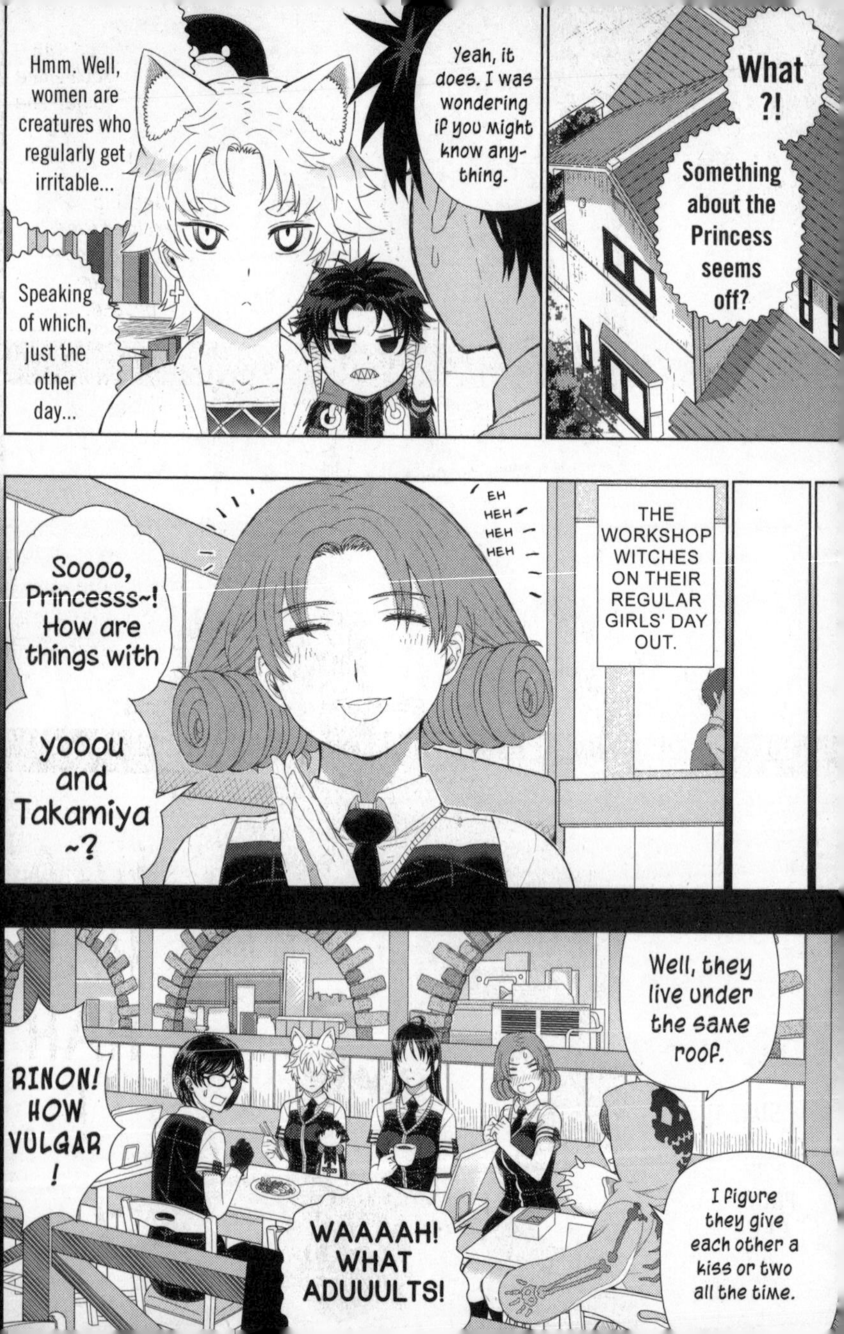

What?!
Something about the Princess seems off?
Yeah, it does. I was wondering if you might know any-thing.
Hmm. Well, women are creatures who regularly get irritable...
Speaking of which, just the other day...
THE WORKSHOP WITCHES ON THEIR REGULAR GIRLS' DAY OUT.
EH HEH HEH HEH
Soooo, Princesss~! How are things with yooou and Takamiya~?
Well, they live under the same roof.
I figure they give each other a kiss or two all the time.
WAAAAH! WHAT ADUUULTS!
RINON! HOW VULGAR!

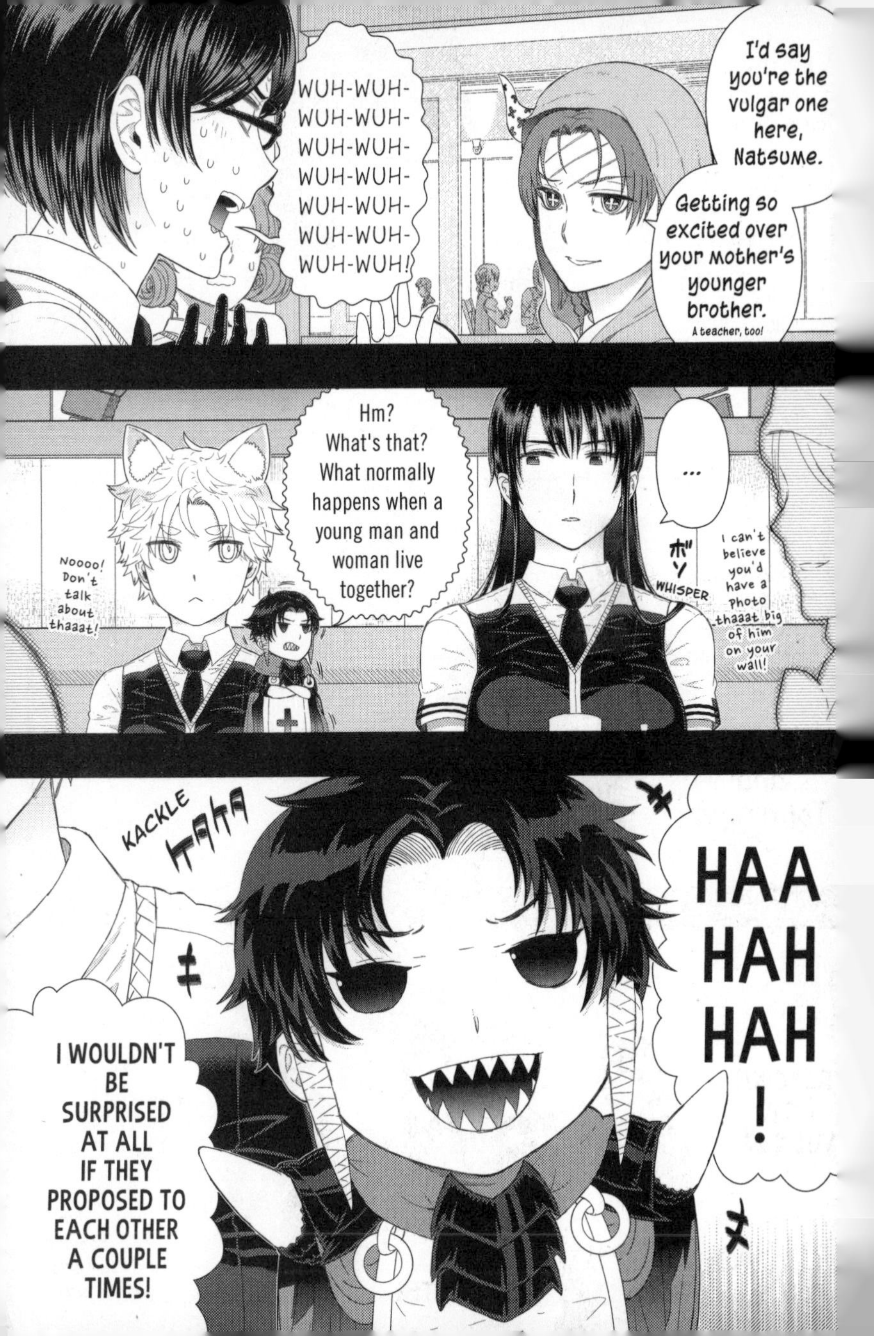
I'd say you're the vulgar one here, Natsume.
Getting so excited over your mother's younger brother.
A teacher, too!
WUH-WUH-WUH-WUH-WUH-WUH-WUH-WUH-WUH-WUH-WUH-WUH-WUH-WUH!
...
ボソ
WHISPER
I can't believe you'd have a photo thaaat big of him on your wall!
Hm? What's that? What normally happens when a young man and woman live together?
Noooo! Don't talk about thaaat!
HAA HAH HAH!
KACKLE
I WOULDN'T BE SURPRISED AT ALL IF THEY PROPOSED TO EACH OTHER A COUPLE TIMES!

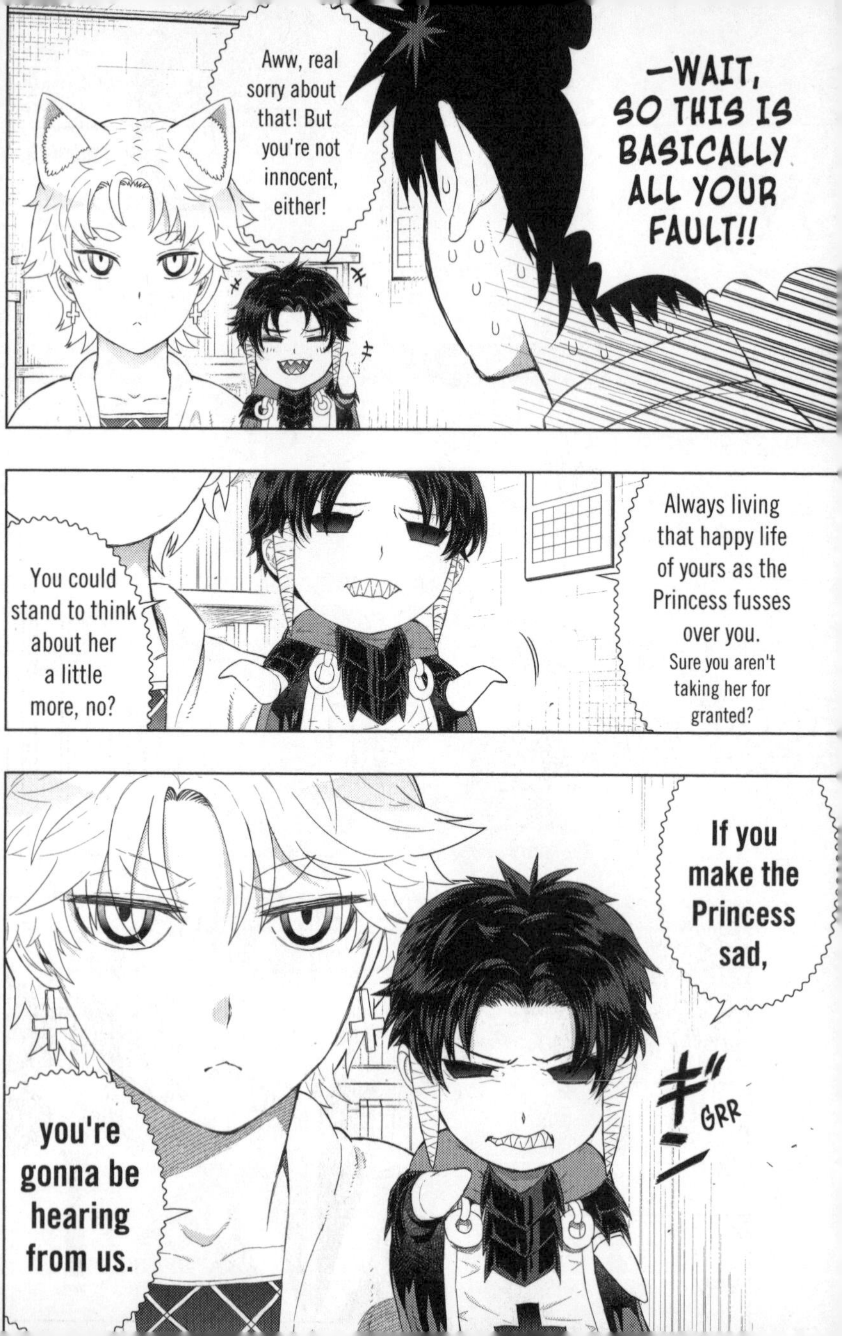
—WAIT, SO THIS IS BASICALLY ALL YOUR FAULT!!
Aww, real sorry about that! But you're not innocent, either!
Always living that happy life of yours as the Princess fusses over you.
Sure you aren't taking her for granted?
You could stand to think about her a little more, no?
If you make the Princess sad,
GRR
you're gonna be hearing from us.

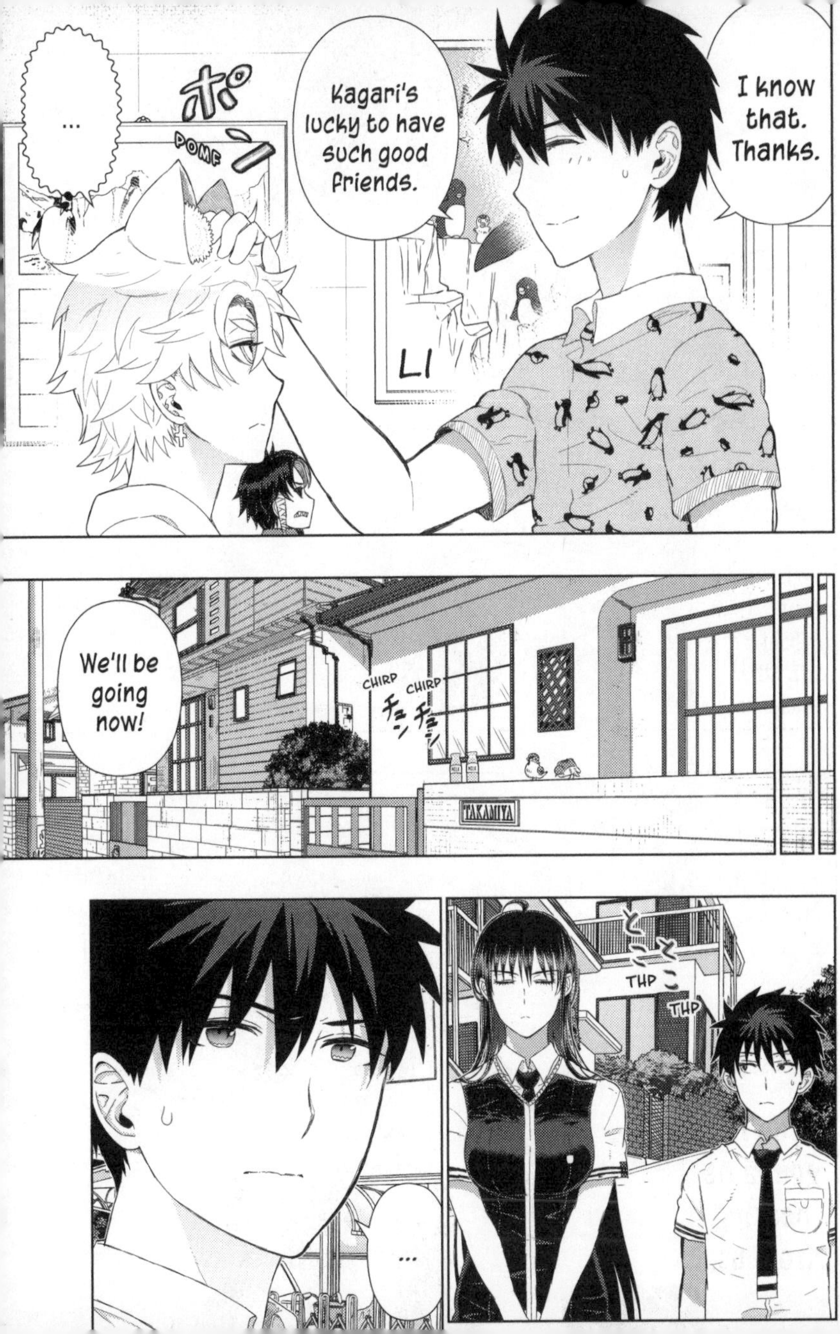
I know that. Thanks.
Kagari's lucky to have such good friends.
ポン
POMF
...
LI
We'll be going now!
チュン
CHIRP
チュン
CHIRP
とことこ
THP
THP
...

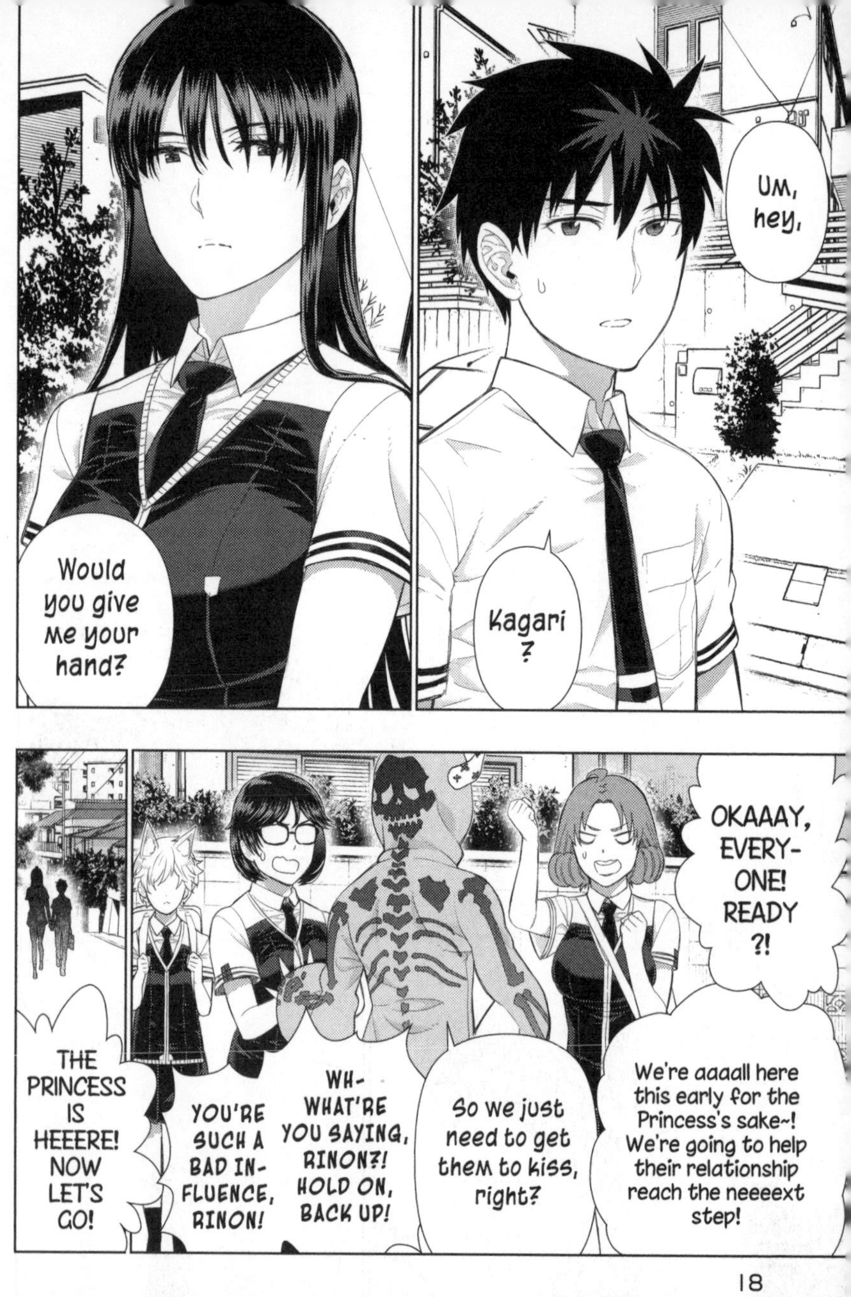
Um, hey,
Kagari?
Would you give me your hand?
OKAAAY, EVERY-ONE! READY?!
We're aaaall here this early for the Princess's sake~! We're going to help their relationship reach the neeeext step!
So we just need to get them to kiss, right?
WH- WHAT'RE YOU SAYING, RINON?! HOLD ON, BACK UP!
YOU'RE SUCH A BAD IN-FLUENCE, RINON!
THE PRINCESS IS HEEERE! NOW LET'S GO!

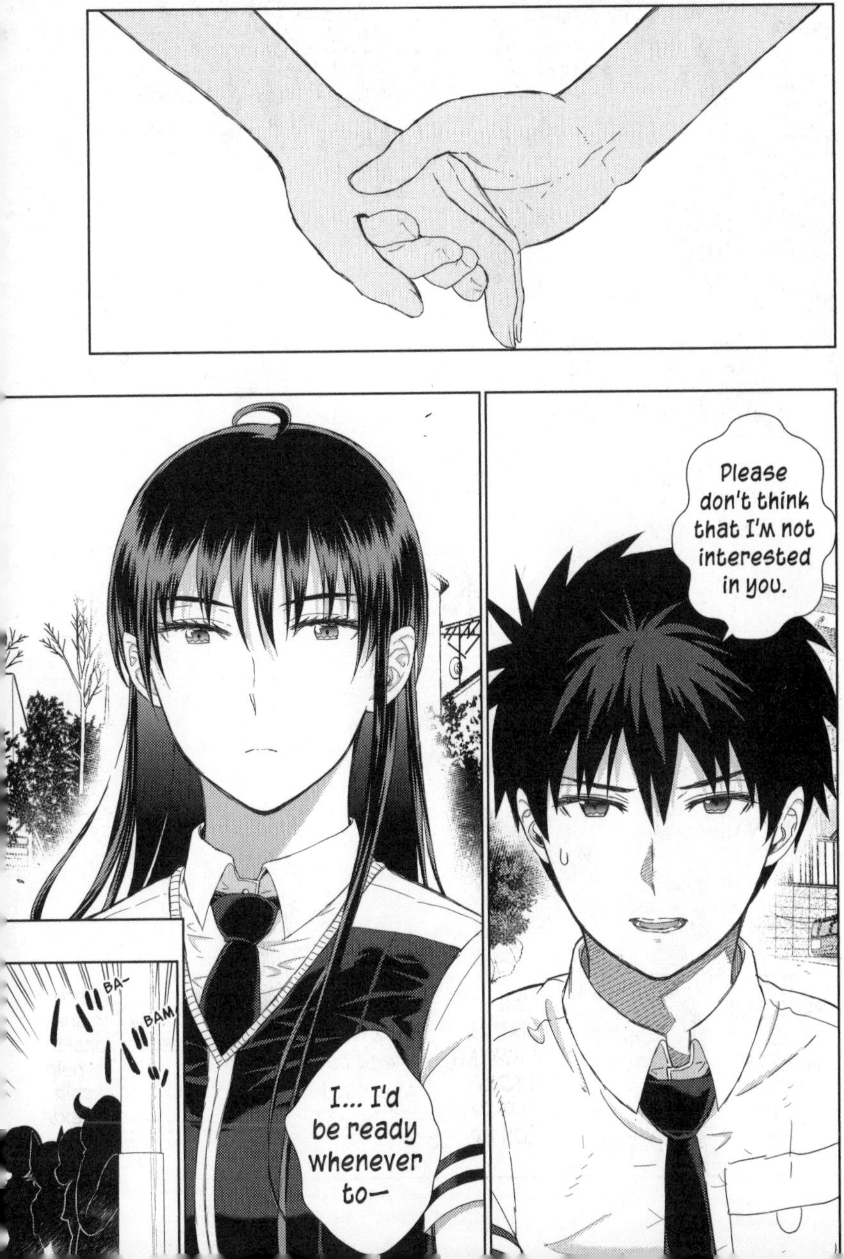
Please don't think that I'm not interested in you.
I... I'd be ready whenever to—
BA-
BAM

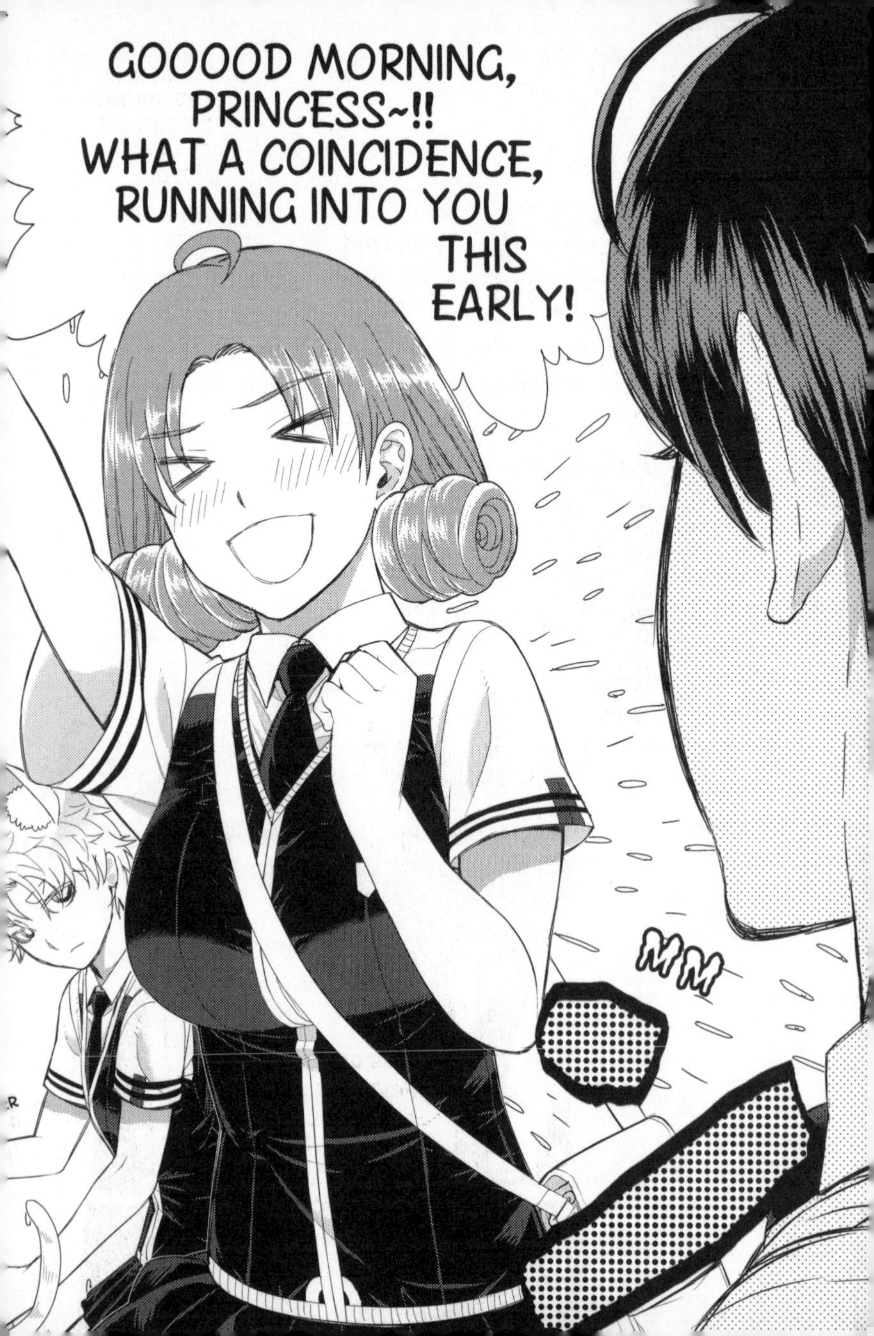
GOOOOD MORNING, PRINCESS~!! WHAT A COINCIDENCE, RUNNING INTO YOU THIS EARLY!
MM

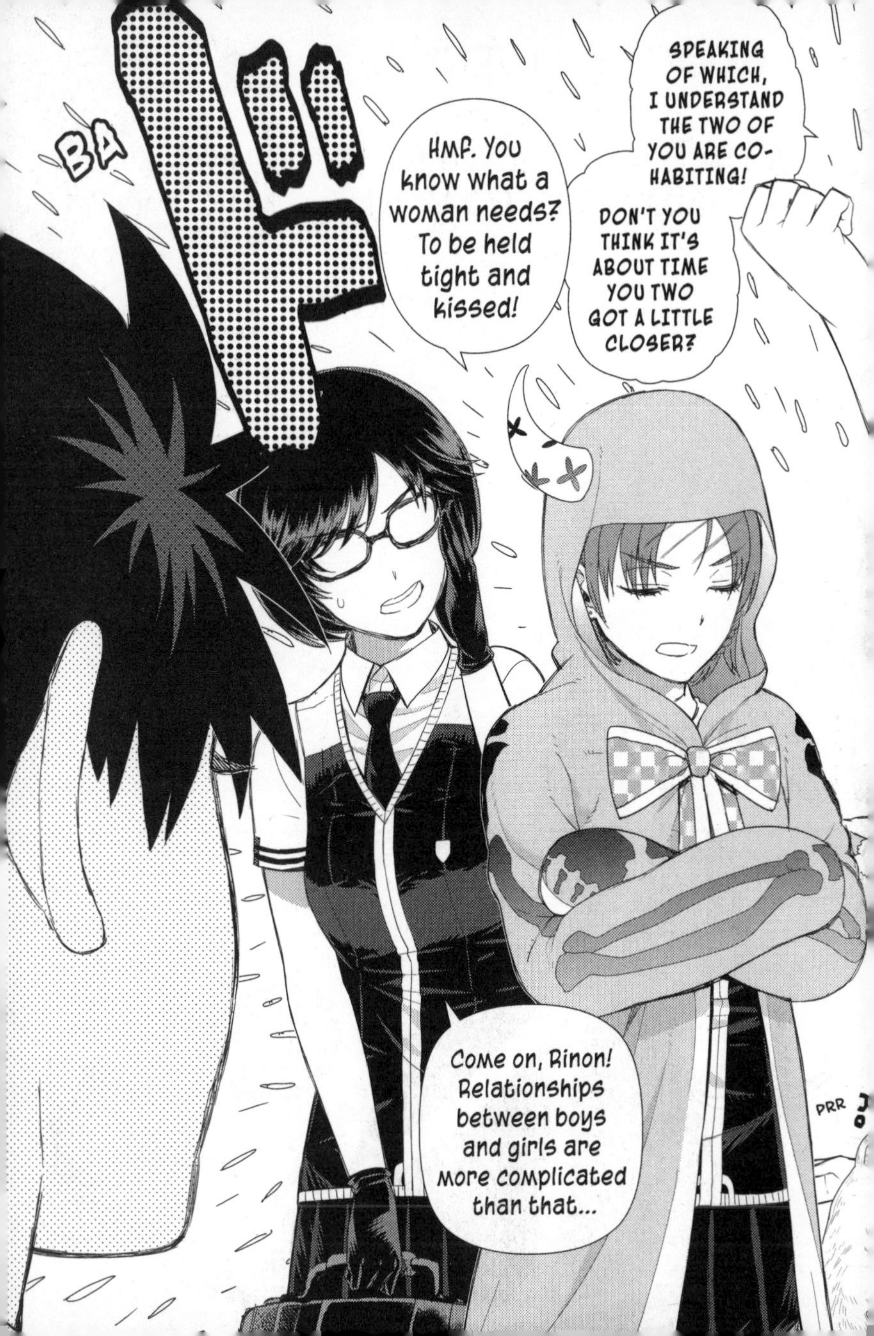

SPEAKING OF WHICH, I UNDERSTAND THE TWO OF YOU ARE CO-HABITING!
DON'T YOU THINK IT'S ABOUT TIME YOU TWO GOT A LITTLE CLOSER?
Hmf. You know what a woman needs? To be held tight and kissed!
BA
PRR
Come on, Rinon! Relationships between boys and girls are more complicated than that...

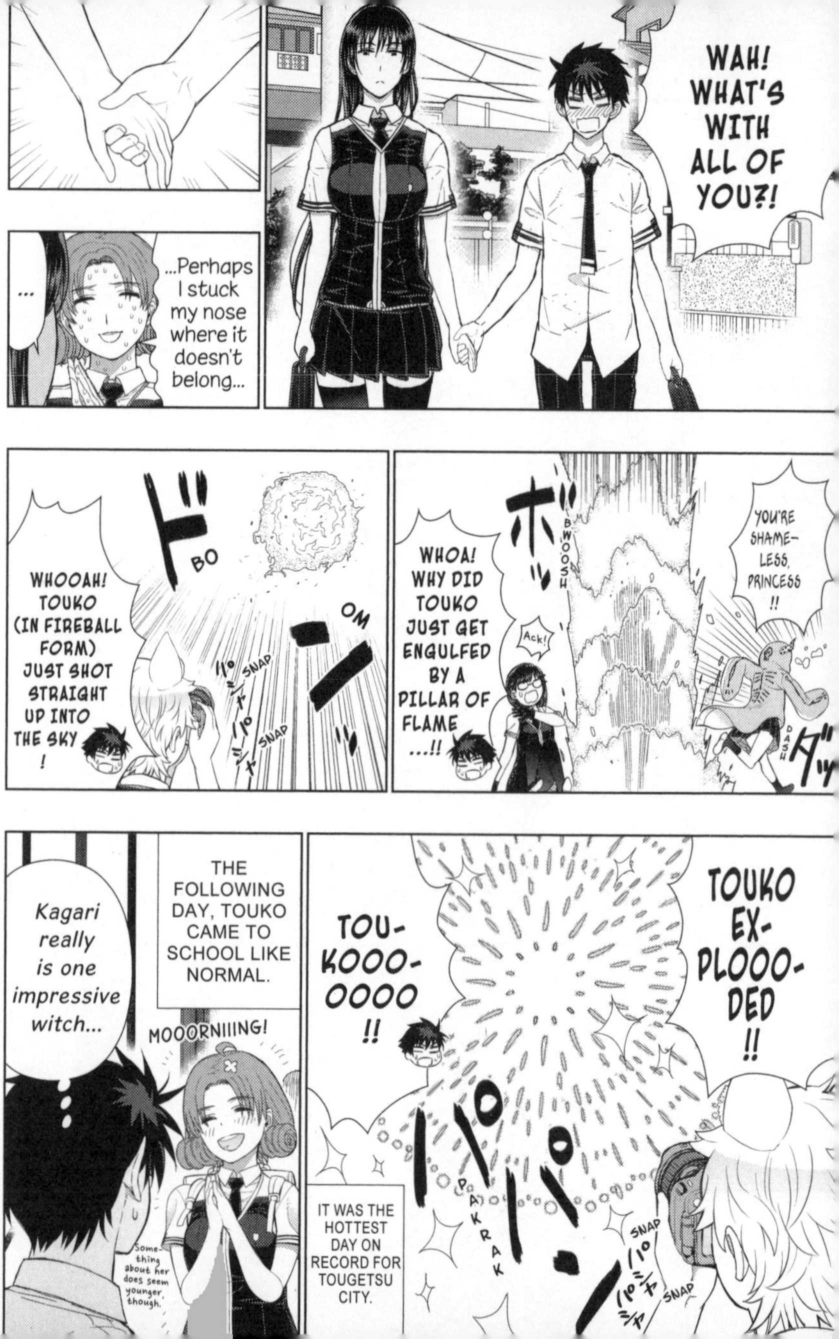
WAH! WHAT'S WITH ALL OF YOU?!
...
...Perhaps I stuck my nose where it doesn't belong...
YOU'RE SHAME-LESS, PRINCESS !!
BWOOSH
WHOA! WHY DID TOUKO JUST GET ENGULFED BY A PILLAR OF FLAME ...!!
Ack!
DASH
BO
OM
WHOOAH! TOUKO (IN FIREBALL FORM) JUST SHOT STRAIGHT UP INTO THE SKY !
SNAP
SNAP
TOUKO EX-PLOOO-DED !!
TOU-KOOO-OOOO !!
PAKRAK
SNAP
SNAP
IT WAS THE HOTTEST DAY ON RECORD FOR TOUGETSU CITY.
THE FOLLOWING DAY, TOUKO CAME TO SCHOOL LIKE NORMAL.
Kagari really is one impressive witch...
MOOORNIIING!
Some-thing about her does seem younger, though.

CHAPTER 71 END

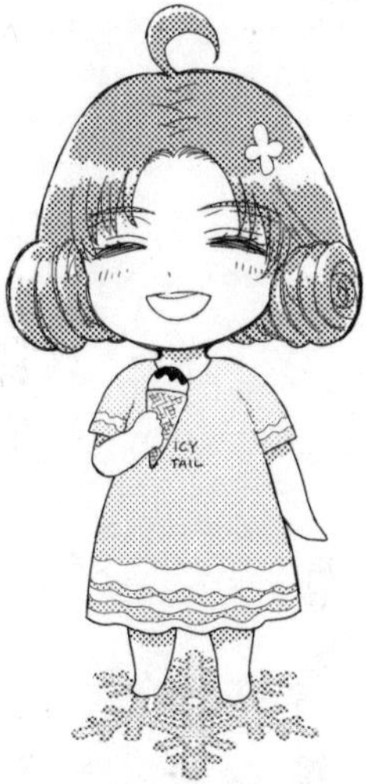
ICY
TAIL

Witchcraft Works

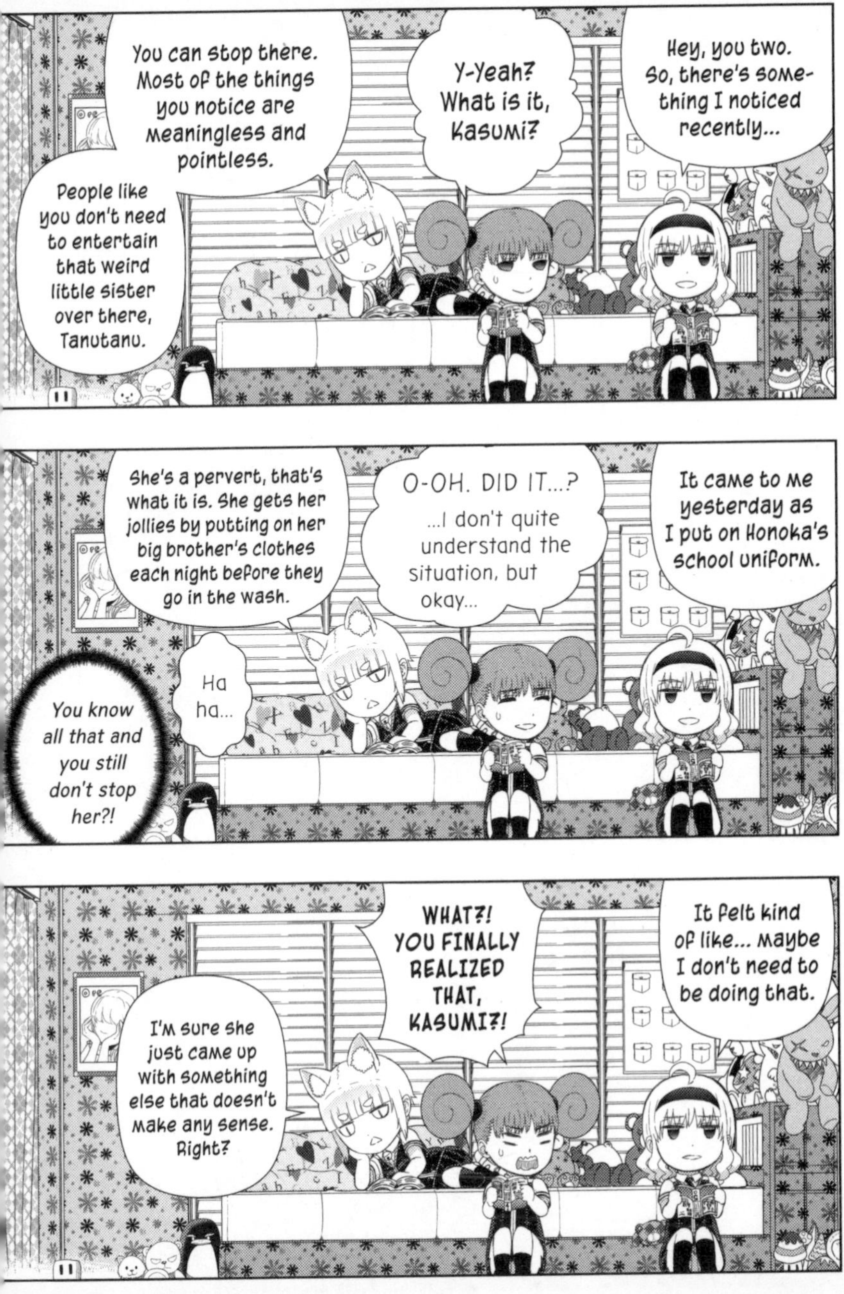
Hey, you two. So, there's something I noticed recently...
Y-Yeah? What is it, Kasumi?
You can stop there. Most of the things you notice are meaningless and pointless.
People like you don't need to entertain that weird little sister over there, Tanutanu.
It came to me yesterday as I put on Honoka's school uniform.
O-OH. DID IT...?
...I don't quite understand the situation, but okay...
She's a pervert, that's what it is. She gets her jollies by putting on her big brother's clothes each night before they go in the wash.
Ha ha...
You know all that and you still don't stop her?!
It felt kind of like... maybe I don't need to be doing that.
WHAT?! YOU FINALLY REALIZED THAT, KASUMI?!
I'm sure she just came up with something else that doesn't make any sense. Right?

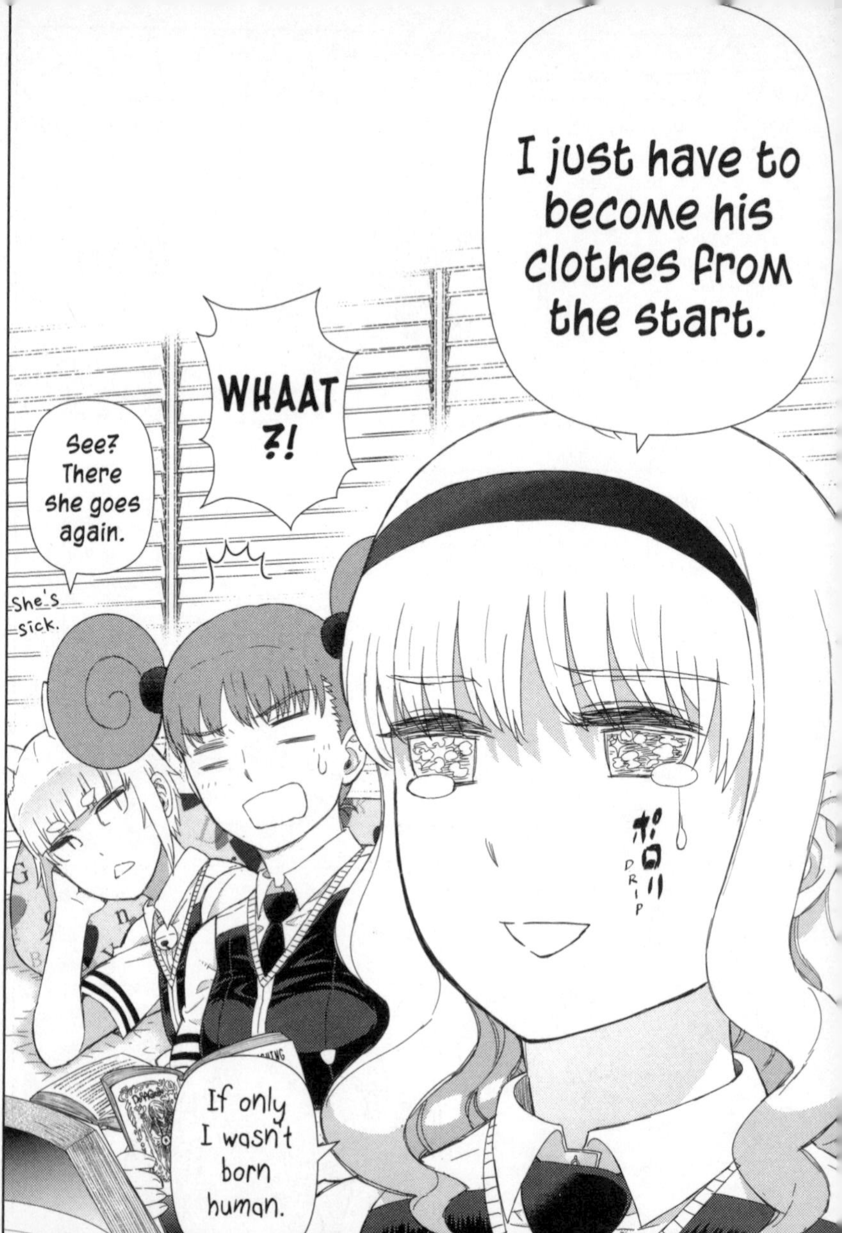
I just have to become his clothes from the start.
ポロリ
DRIP
WHAAT ?!
See? There she goes again.
She's sick.
If only I wasn't born human.

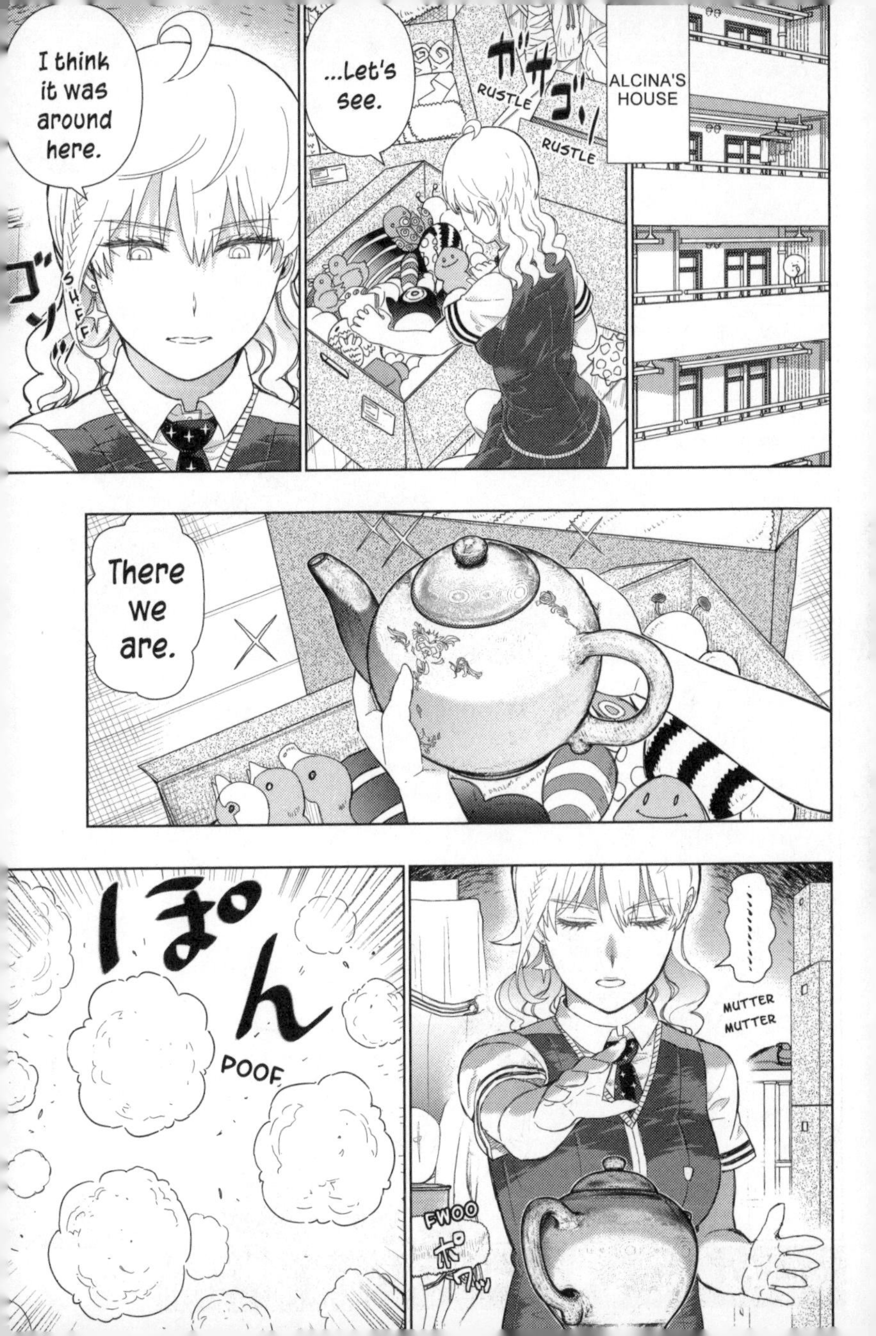
ALCINA'S HOUSE
ガサゴソ
RUSTLE
RUSTLE
...Let's see.
I think it was around here.
ゴソ
SHUFF
There we are.
......
MUTTER MUTTER
FWOO
ポワッ
ぽん
POOF

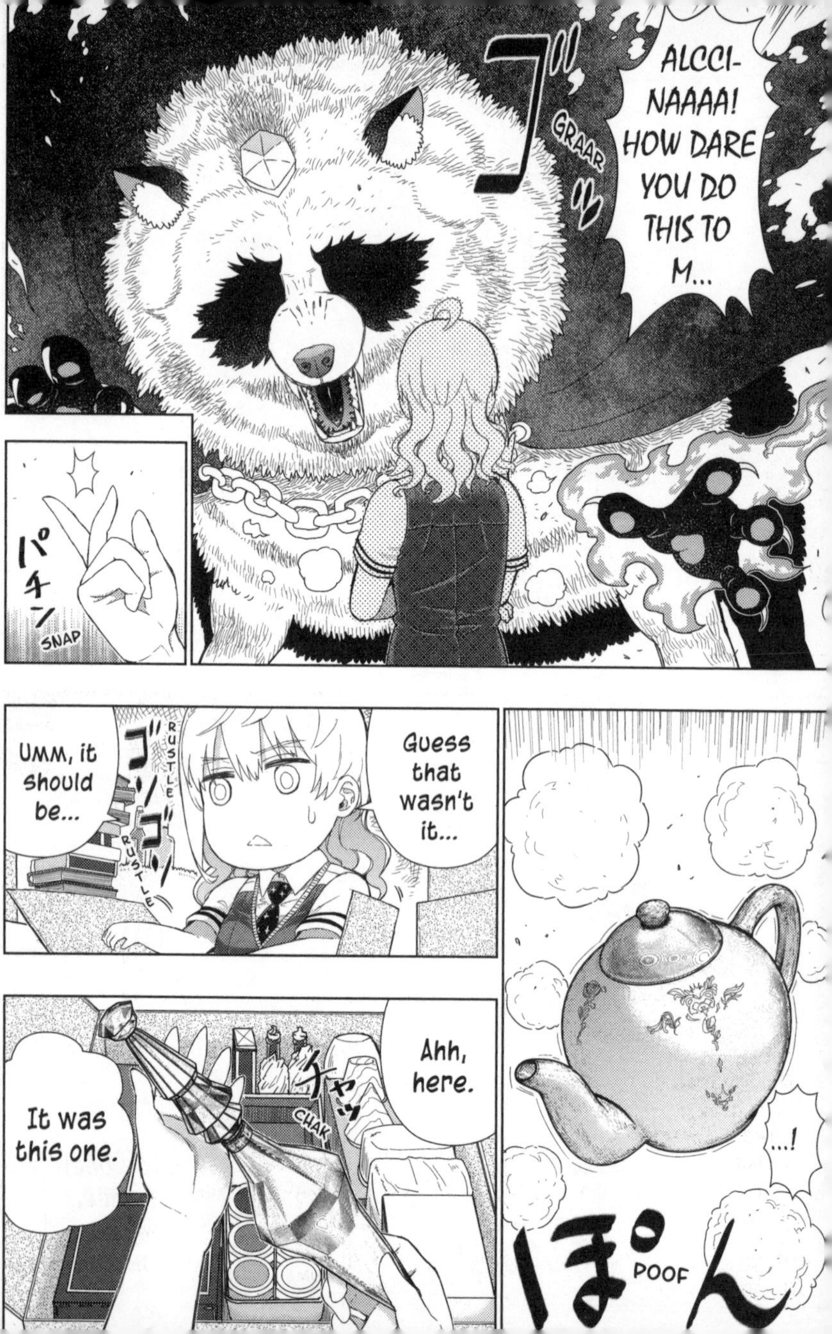ゴッ
GRAAR
ALCCI-NAAAA! HOW DARE YOU DO THIS TO M...
パチン
SNAP
ぽん
POOF
...!
Guess that wasn't it...
UMM, it should be...
ゴソゴソ
RUSTLE
RUSTLE
Ahh, here.
チャッ
CHAK
It was this one.

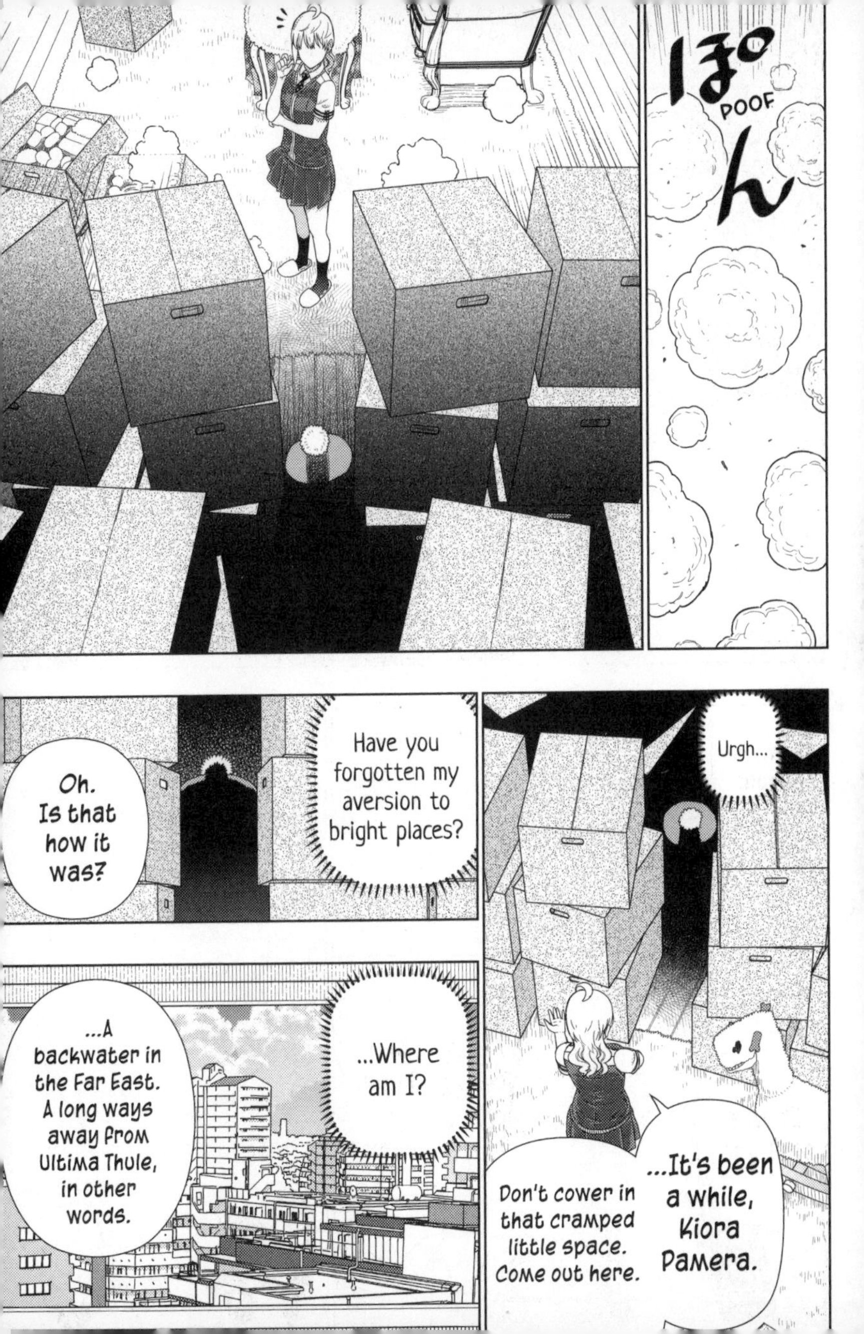
ぽん
POOF
Urgh...
...It's been a while, Kiora Pamera.
Don't cower in that cramped little space. Come out here.
Have you forgotten my aversion to bright places?
Oh. Is that how it was?
...Where am I?
...A backwater in the Far East. A long ways away from Ultima Thule, in other words.

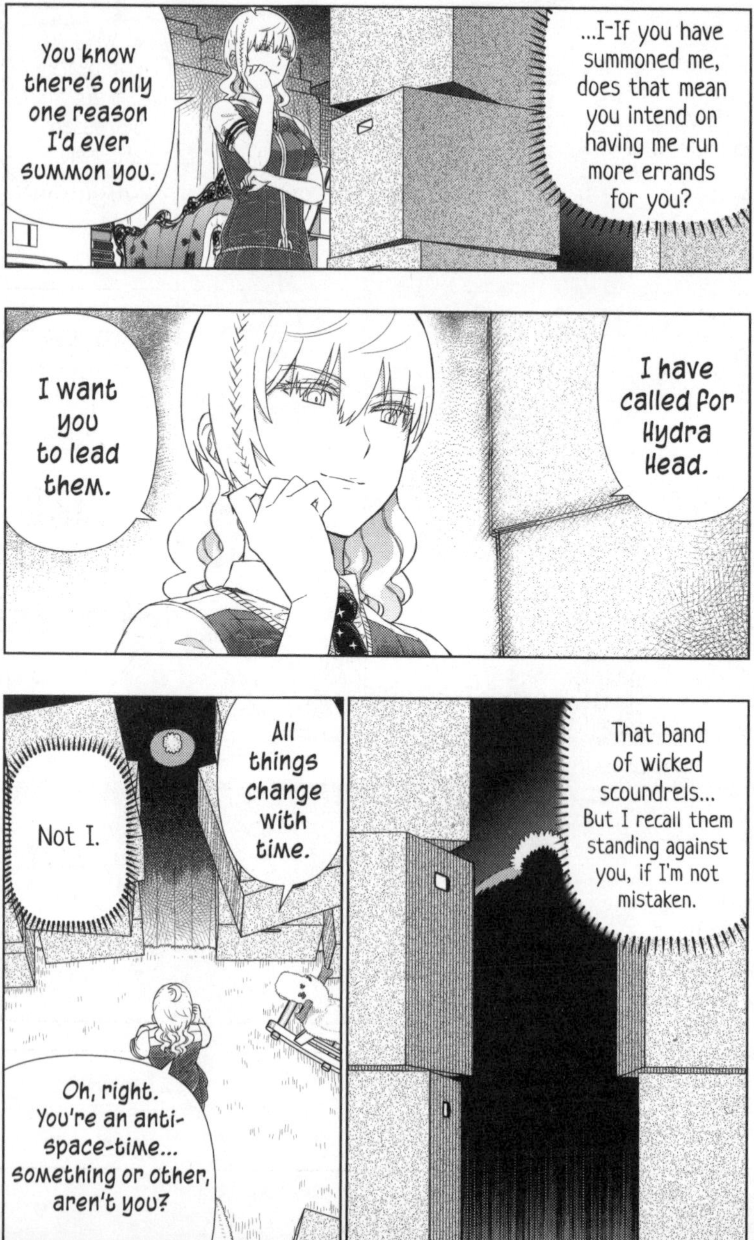
...I-If you have summoned me, does that mean you intend on having me run more errands for you?
You know there's only one reason I'd ever summon you.
I have called for Hydra Head.
I want you to lead them.
That band of wicked scoundrels... But I recall them standing against you, if I'm not mistaken.
All things change with time.
Not I.
Oh, right. You're an anti-space-time... something or other, aren't you?

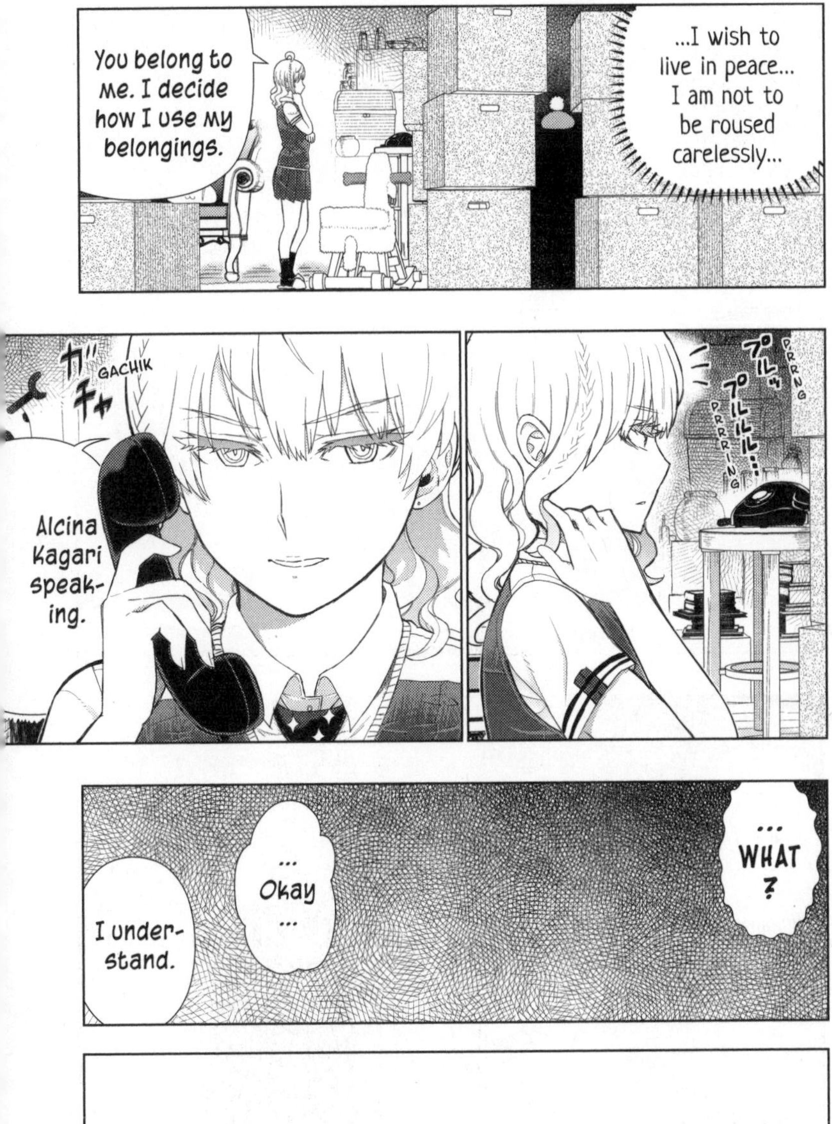
...I wish to live in peace... I am not to be roused carelessly...
You belong to me. I decide how I use my belongings.
プルル
PRRRNG
プルルル…
PRRRING
ガチャ
GACHIK
Alcina Kagari speak-ing.
...WHAT?
...Okay...
I under-stand.

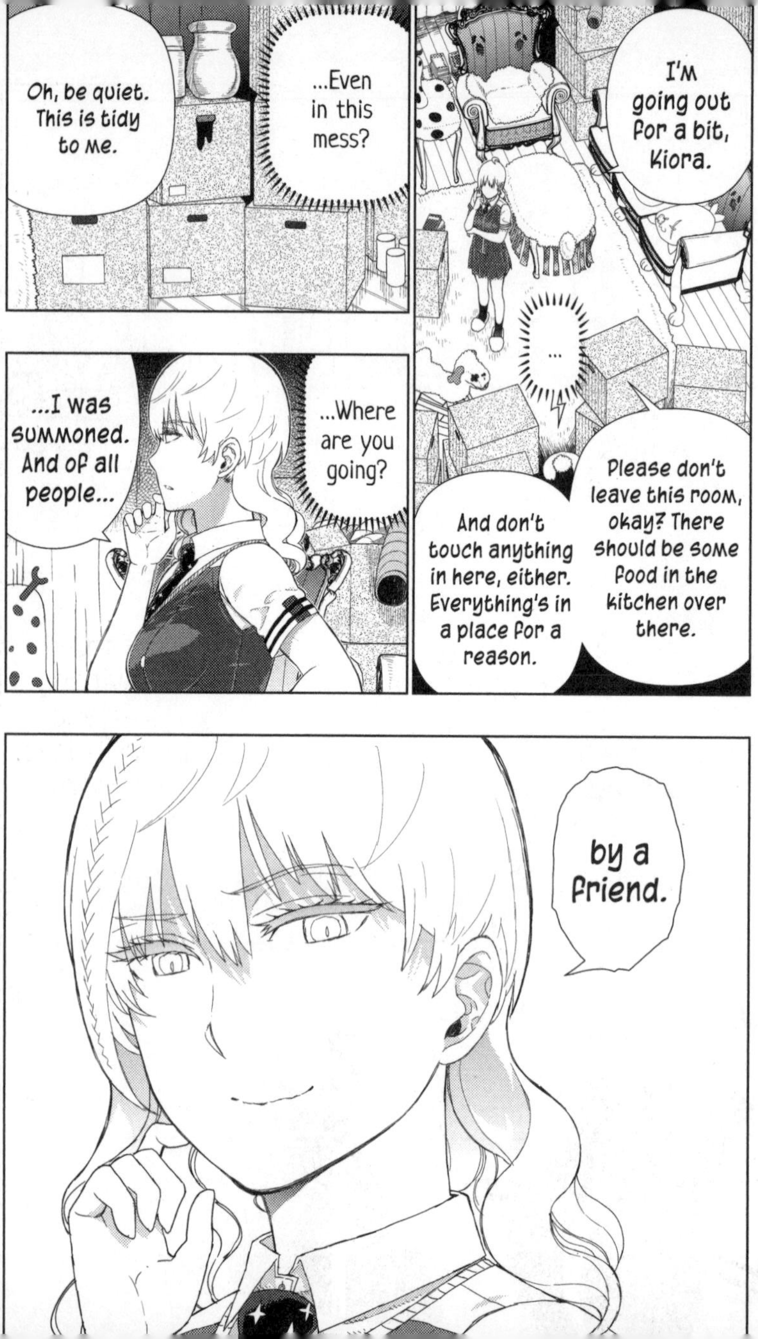
I'm going out for a bit, Kiora.
...
Please don't leave this room, okay? There should be some food in the kitchen over there.
And don't touch anything in here, either. Everything's in a place for a reason.
...Even in this mess?
Oh, be quiet. This is tidy to me.
...Where are you going?
...I was summoned. And of all people...
by a friend.

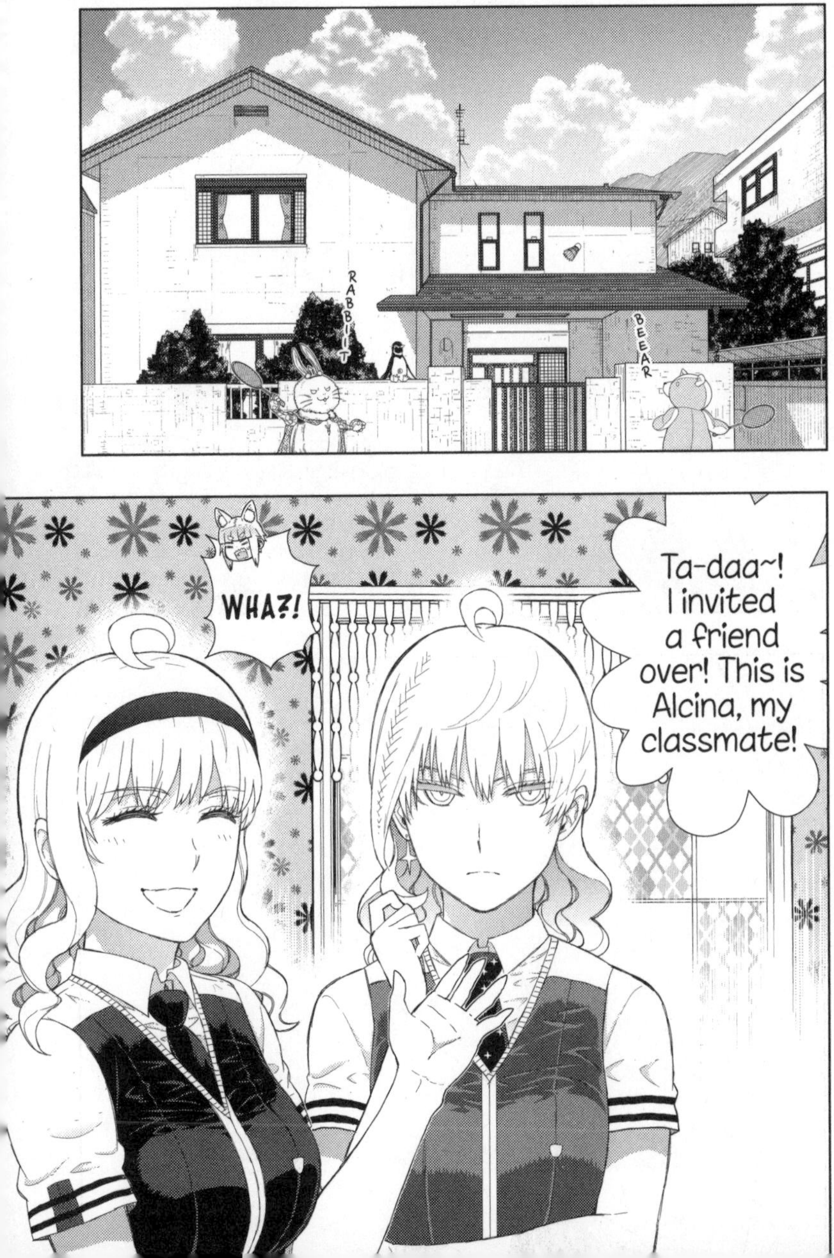
RABBIT
BEEAR
Ta-daa~! I invited a friend over! This is Alcina, my classmate!
WHA?!

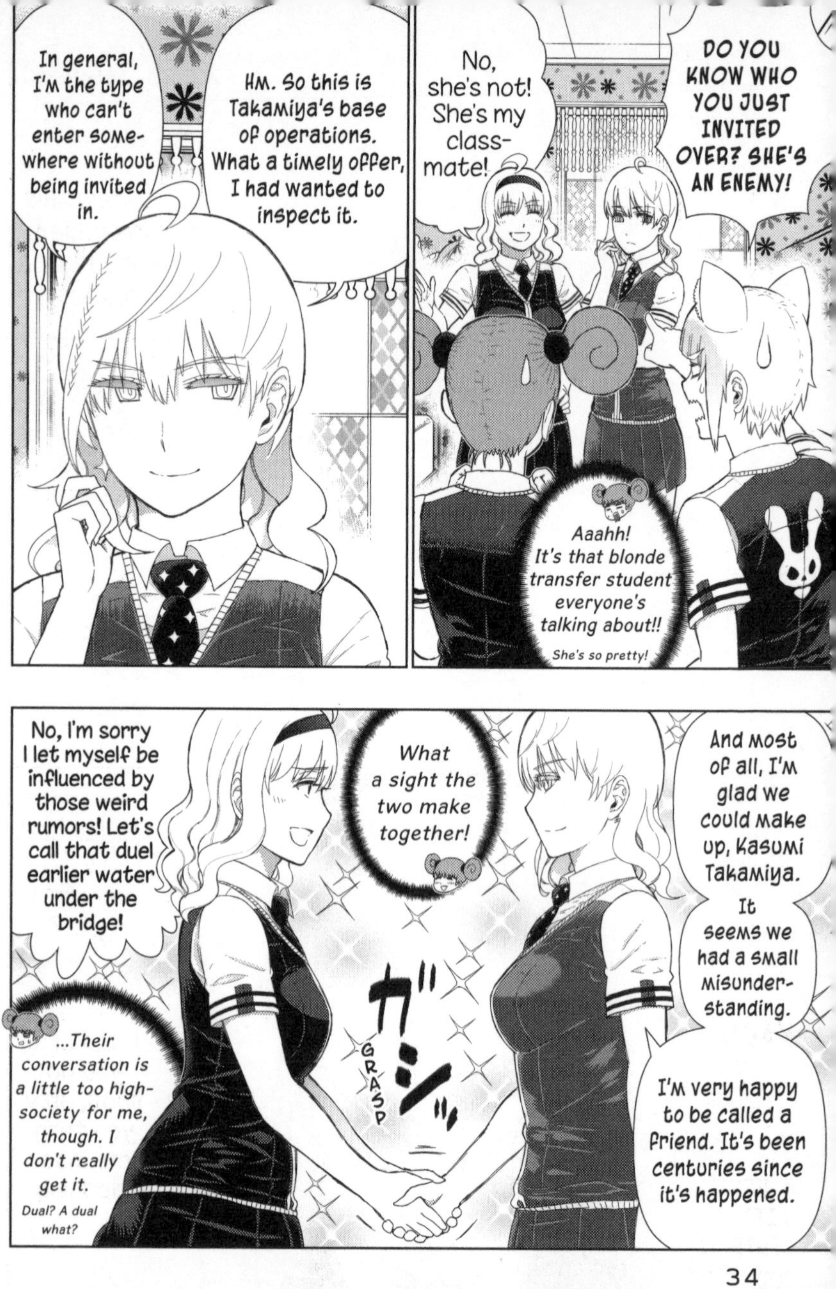
DO YOU KNOW WHO YOU JUST INVITED OVER? SHE'S AN ENEMY!
No, she's not! She's my class-mate!
Aaahh! It's that blonde transfer student everyone's talking about!!
She's so pretty!
Hm. So this is Takamiya's base of operations. What a timely offer, I had wanted to inspect it.
In general, I'm the type who can't enter some-where without being invited in.
And most of all, I'm glad we could make up, Kasumi Takamiya.
It seems we had a small misunder-standing.
I'm very happy to be called a friend. It's been centuries since it's happened.
What a sight the two make together!
No, I'm sorry I let myself be influenced by those weird rumors! Let's call that duel earlier water under the bridge!
GRASP
...Their conversation is a little too high-society for me, though. I don't really get it.
Dual? A dual what?

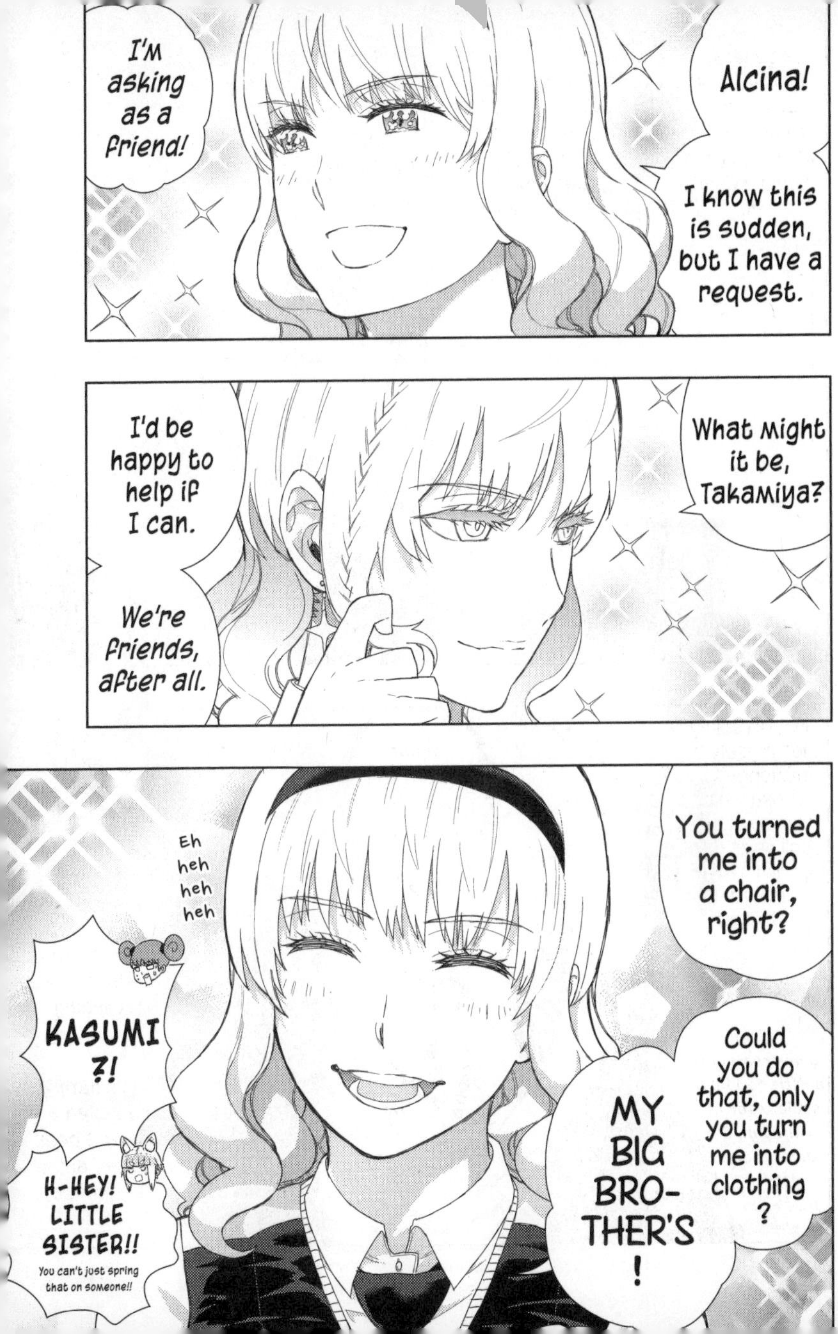
Alcina!
I know this is sudden, but I have a request.
I'm asking as a friend!
What might it be, Takamiya?
I'd be happy to help if I can.
We're friends, after all.
You turned me into a chair, right?
Could you do that, only you turn me into clothing?
MY BIG BRO-THER'S!
Eh heh heh heh
KASUMI?!
H-HEY! LITTLE SISTER!!
You can't just spring that on someone!!

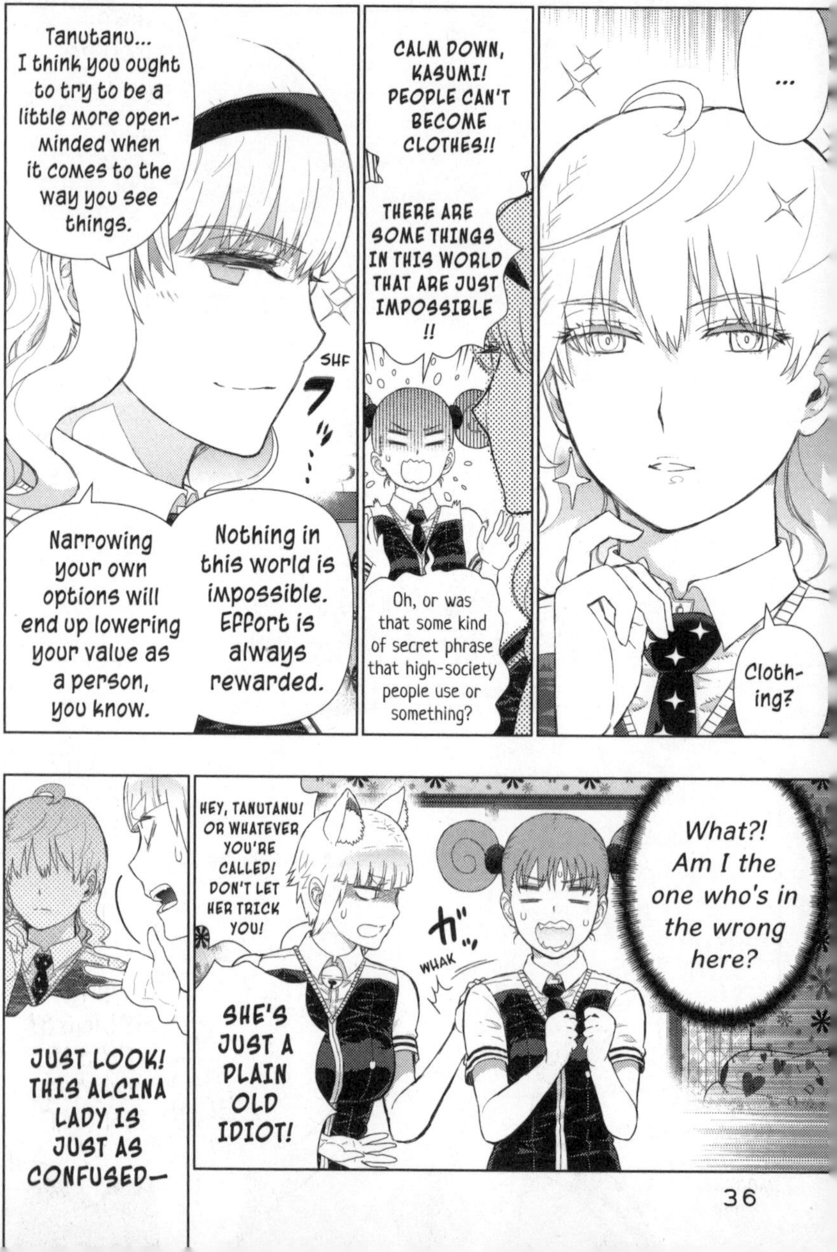
...
Cloth-ing?
CALM DOWN, KASUMI! PEOPLE CAN'T BECOME CLOTHES!!
THERE ARE SOME THINGS IN THIS WORLD THAT ARE JUST IMPOSSIBLE!!
Oh, or was that some kind of secret phrase that high-society people use or something?
Tanutanu... I think you ought to try to be a little more open-minded when it comes to the way you see things.
SHF
Nothing in this world is impossible. Effort is always rewarded.
Narrowing your own options will end up lowering your value as a person, you know.
What?! Am I the one who's in the wrong here?
HEY, TANUTANU! OR WHATEVER YOU'RE CALLED! DON'T LET HER TRICK YOU!
WHAK
SHE'S JUST A PLAIN OLD IDIOT!
JUST LOOK! THIS ALCINA LADY IS JUST AS CONFUSED—

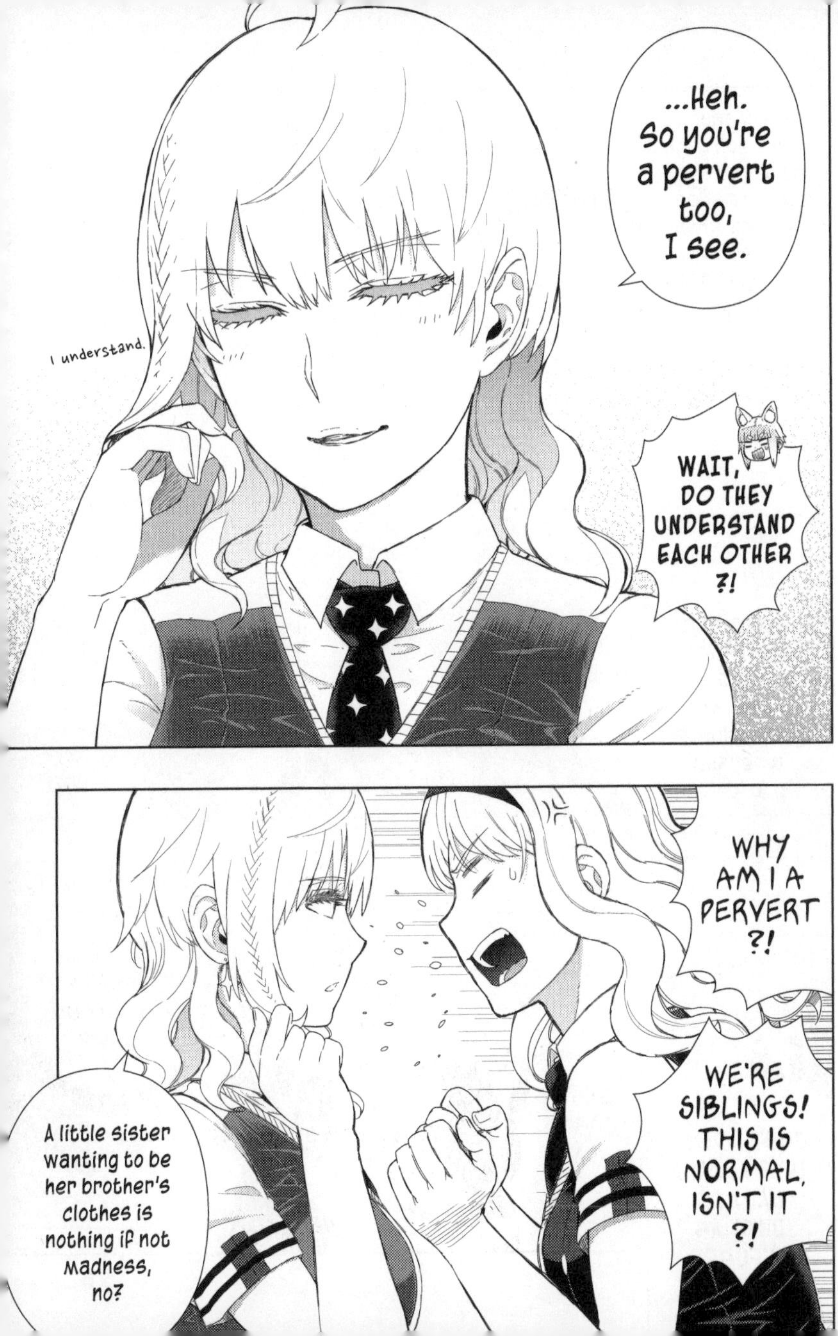
...Heh. So you're a pervert too, I see.
I understand.
WAIT, DO THEY UNDERSTAND EACH OTHER ?!
WHY AM I A PERVERT ?!
WE'RE SIBLINGS! THIS IS NORMAL, ISN'T IT ?!
A little sister wanting to be her brother's clothes is nothing if not madness, no?

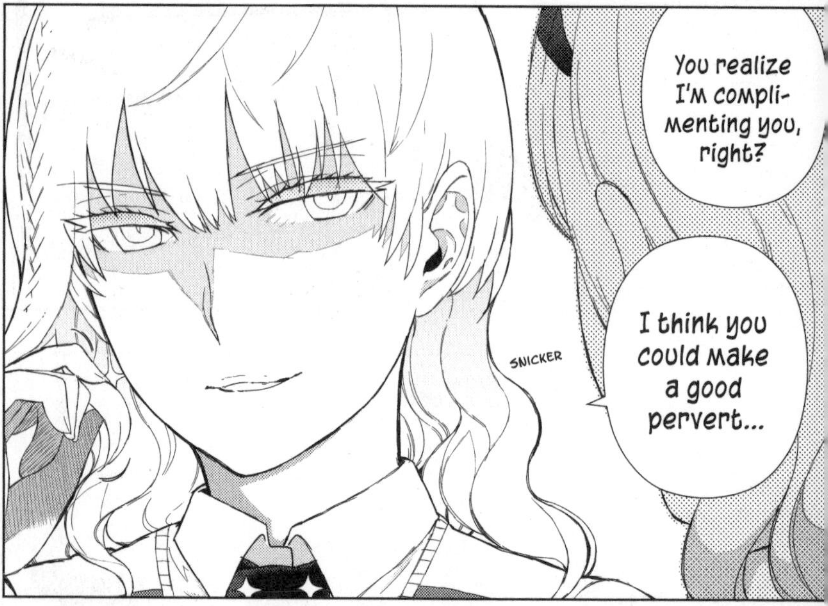
You realize I'M compli-menting you, right?
I think you could make a good pervert...
SNICKER
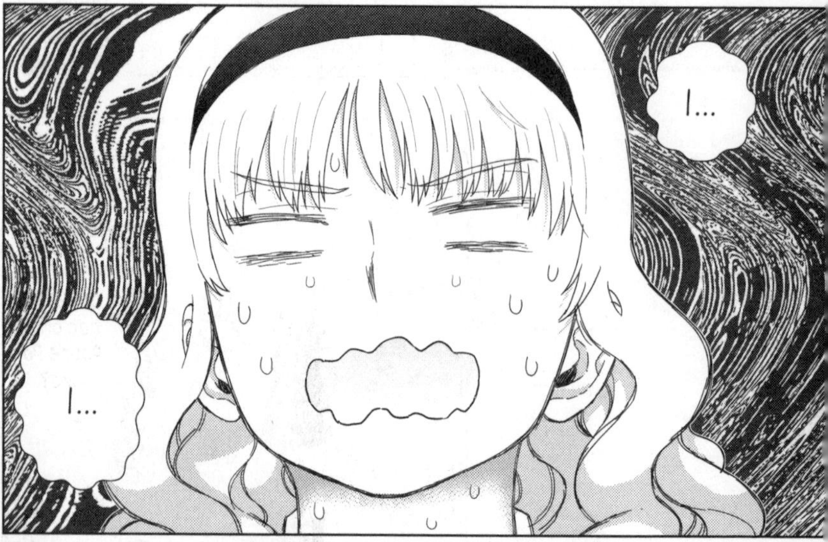
I...
I...

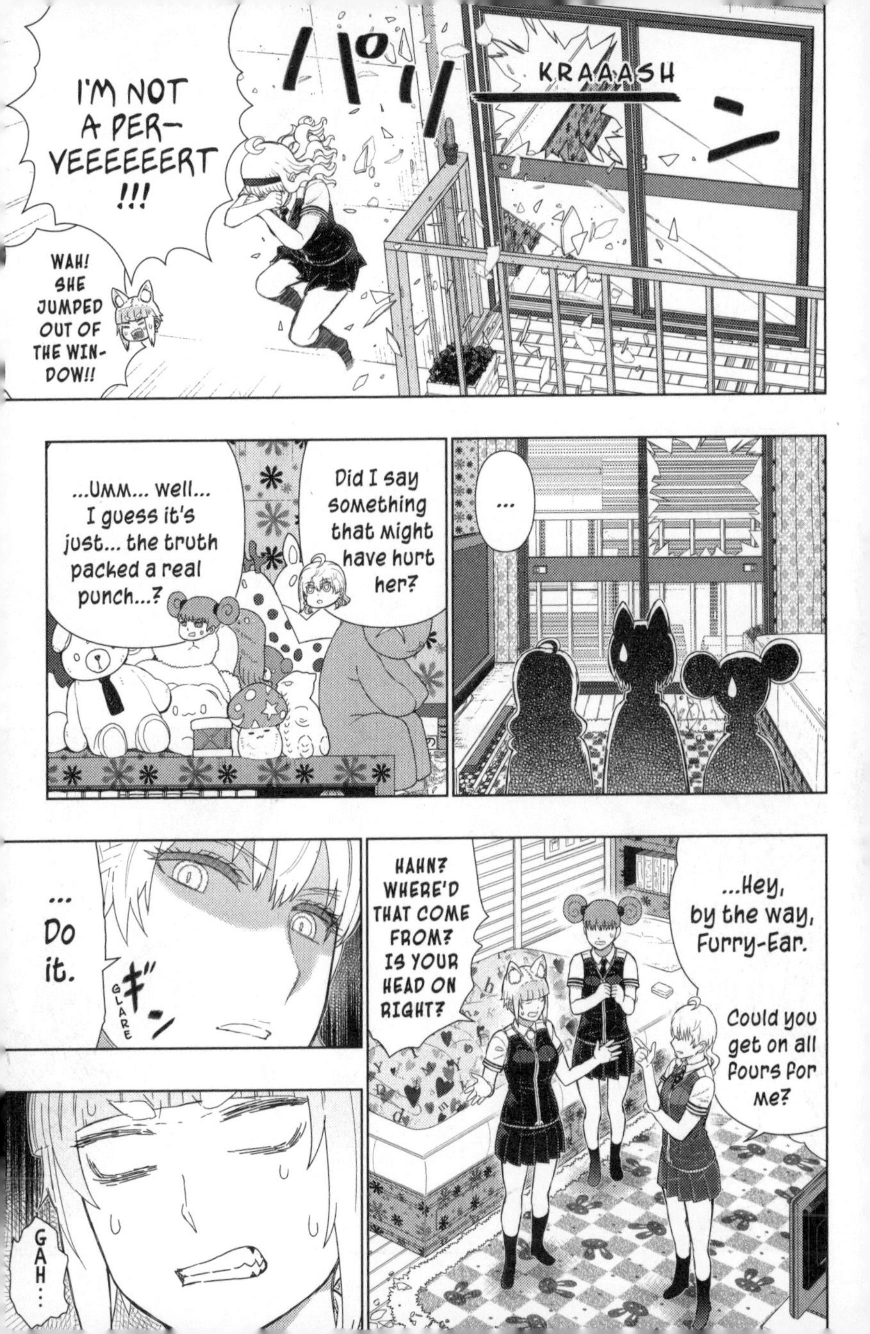
KRAAASH
I'M NOT A PER-VEEEEEERT!!!
WAH! SHE JUMPED OUT OF THE WIN-DOW!!
...
Did I say something that might have hurt her?
...Umm... well... I guess it's just... the truth packed a real punch...?
...Hey, by the way, Furry-Ear.
Could you get on all fours for me?
HAHN? WHERE'D THAT COME FROM? IS YOUR HEAD ON RIGHT?
... Do it.
GLARE
GAH...

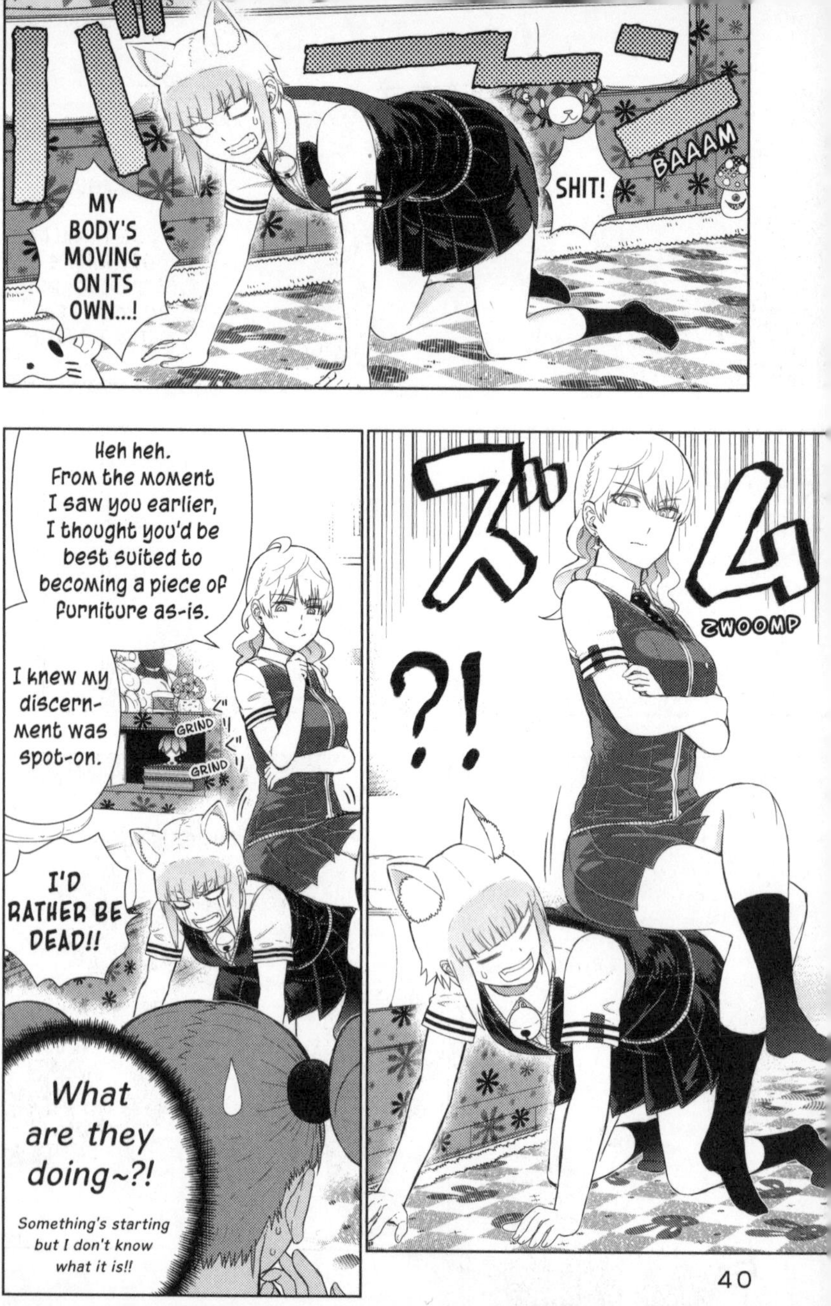
BAAAM
SHIT!
MY BODY'S MOVING ON ITS OWN...!
ズム
ZWOOMP
?!
Heh heh. From the moment I saw you earlier, I thought you'd be best suited to becoming a piece of furniture as-is.
I knew my discern-ment was spot-on.
GRIND
GRIND
I'D RATHER BE DEAD!!
What are they doing~?!
Something's starting but I don't know what it is!!

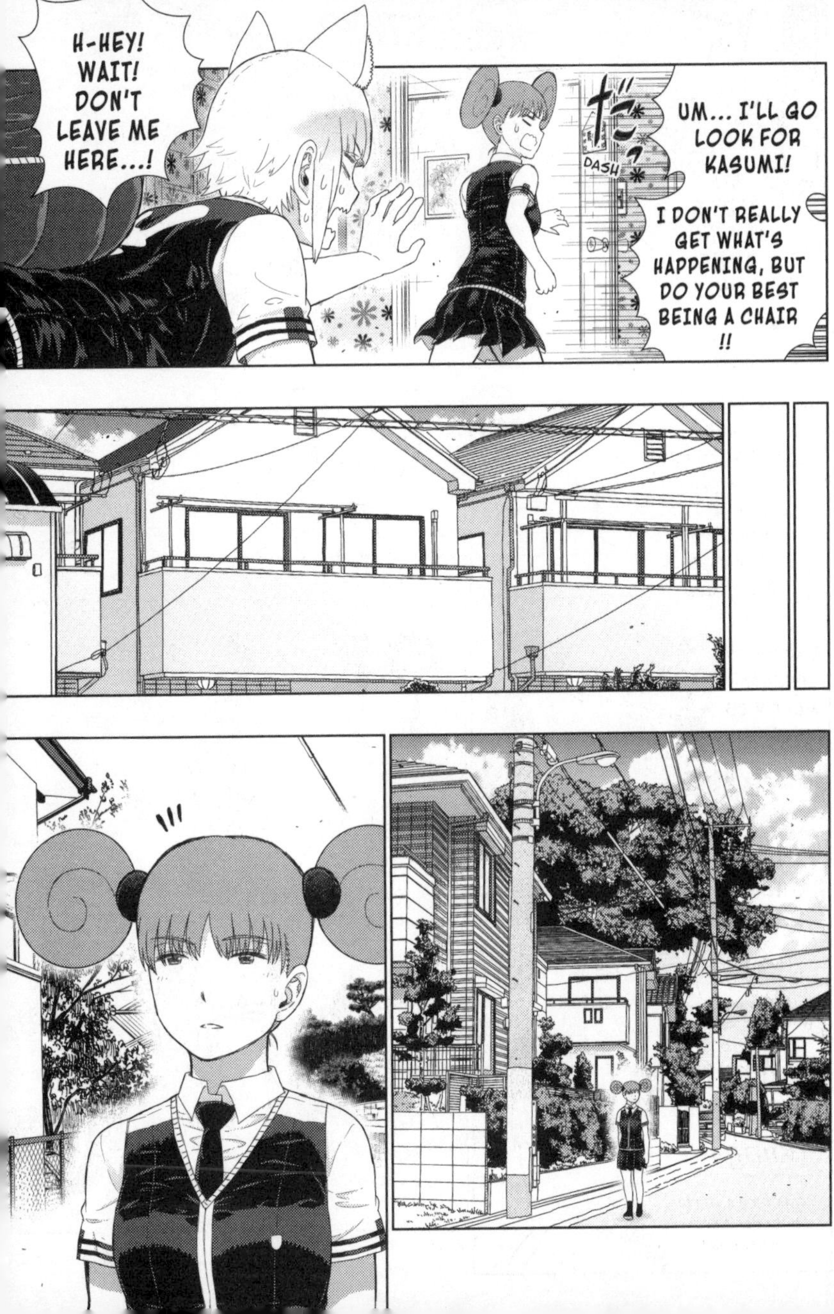
UM... I'LL GO LOOK FOR KASUMI!
I DON'T REALLY GET WHAT'S HAPPENING, BUT DO YOUR BEST BEING A CHAIR !!
DASH
H-HEY! WAIT! DON'T LEAVE ME HERE...!

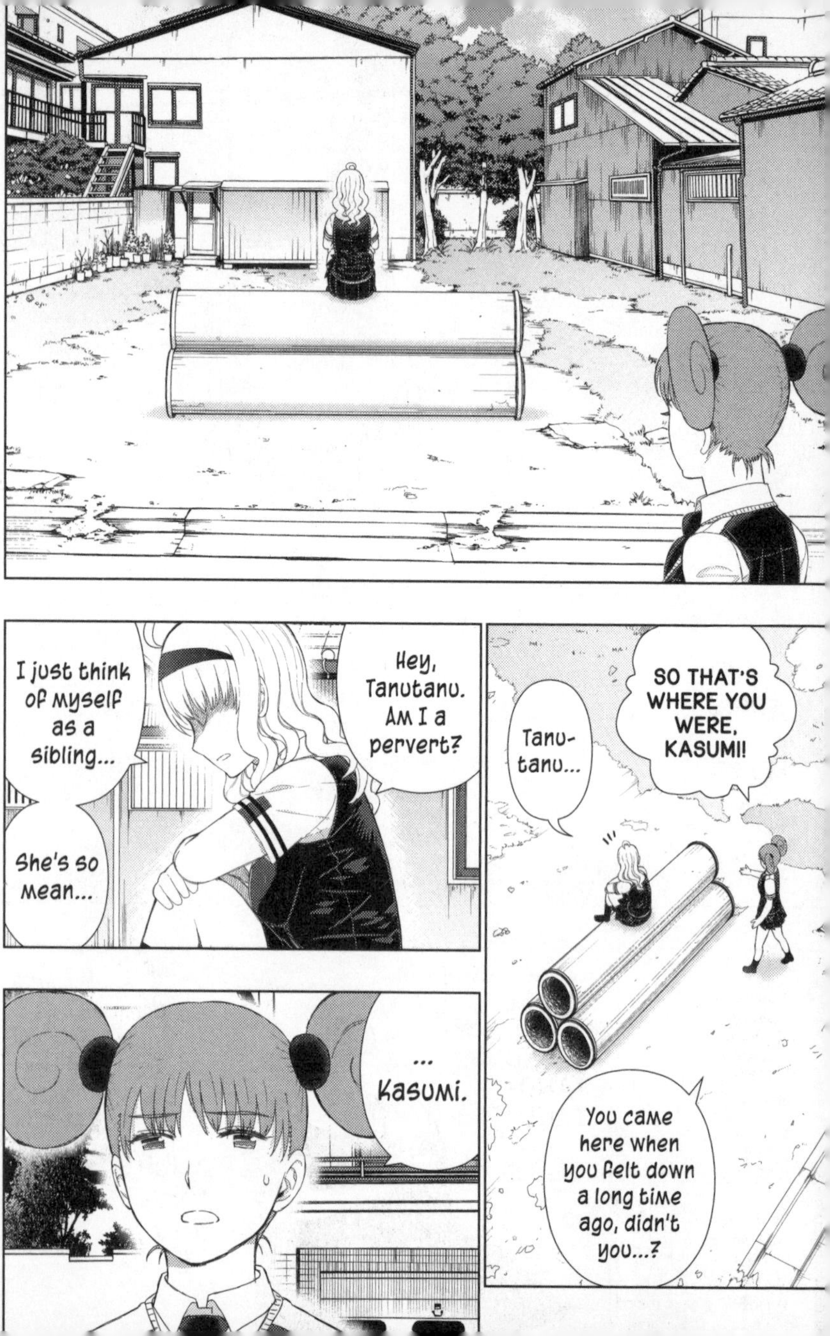
SO THAT'S WHERE YOU WERE, KASUMI!
Tanu-tanu...
You came here when you felt down a long time ago, didn't you...?
Hey, Tanutanu. Am I a pervert?
I just think of myself as a sibling...
She's so mean...
... Kasumi.

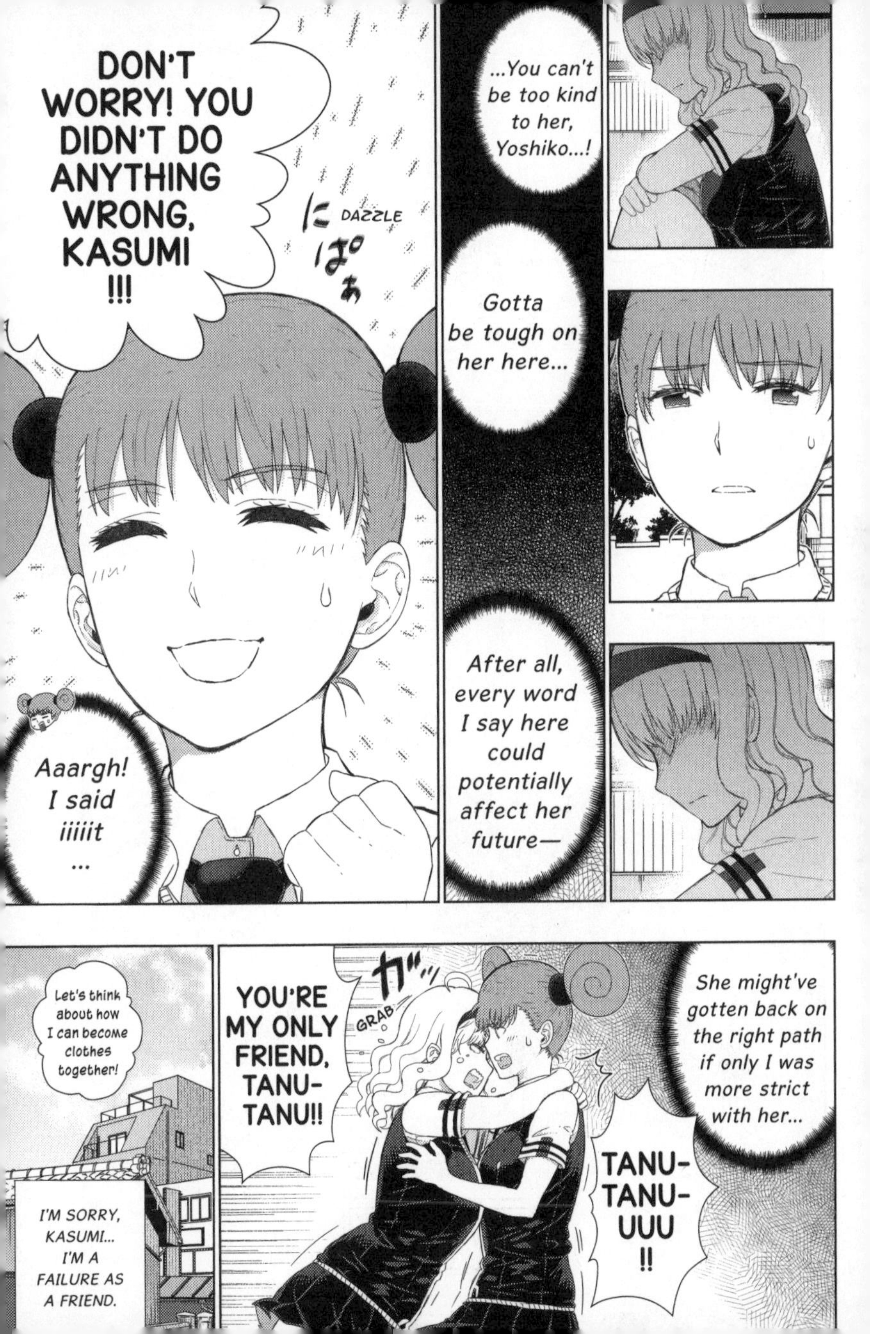
...You can't be too kind to her, Yoshiko...!
Gotta be tough on her here...
After all, every word I say here could potentially affect her future—
DON'T WORRY! YOU DIDN'T DO ANYTHING WRONG, KASUMI !!!
にぱぁ DAZZLE
Aaargh! I said iiiiit ...
She might've gotten back on the right path if only I was more strict with her...
TANU-TANU-UUU !!
ガッ GRAB
YOU'RE MY ONLY FRIEND, TANU-TANU!!
Let's think about how I can become clothes together!
I'M SORRY, KASUMI... I'M A FAILURE AS A FRIEND.

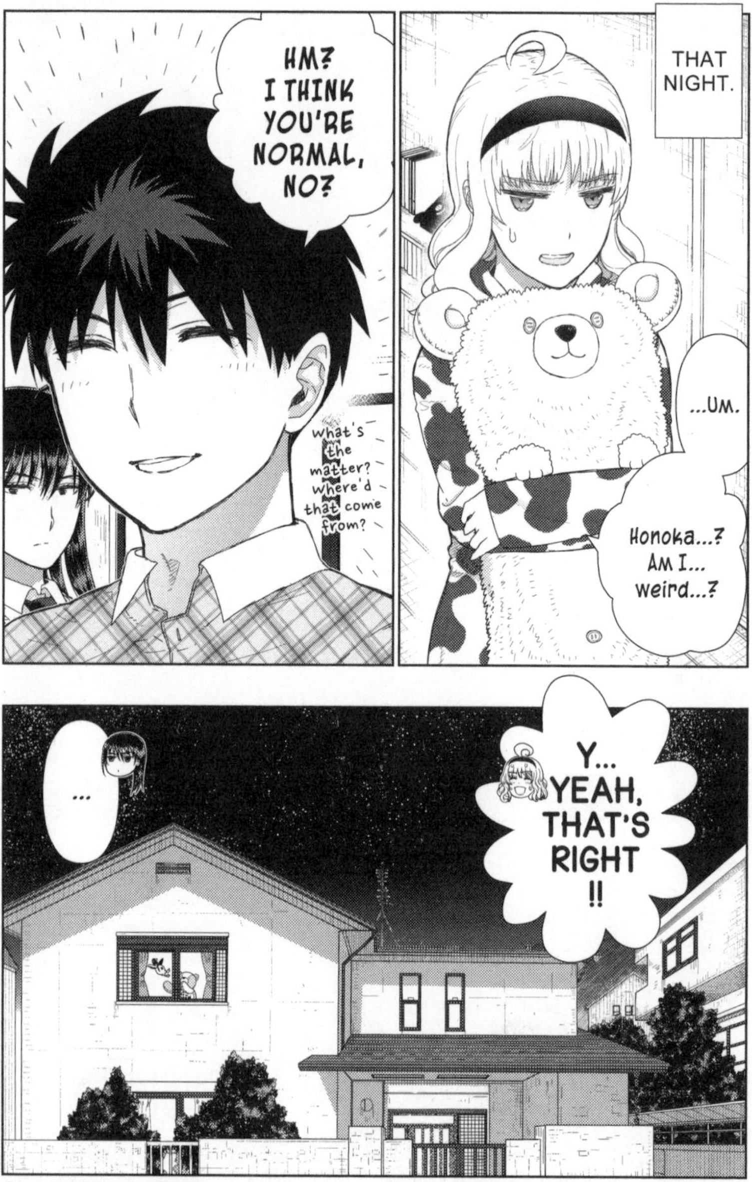
THAT NIGHT.
...UM.
Honoka...? AM I... weird...?
HM? I THINK YOU'RE NORMAL, NO?
what's the matter? where'd that come from?
Y... YEAH, THAT'S RIGHT !!
...

CHAPTER 72: *END*

Witchcraft Works

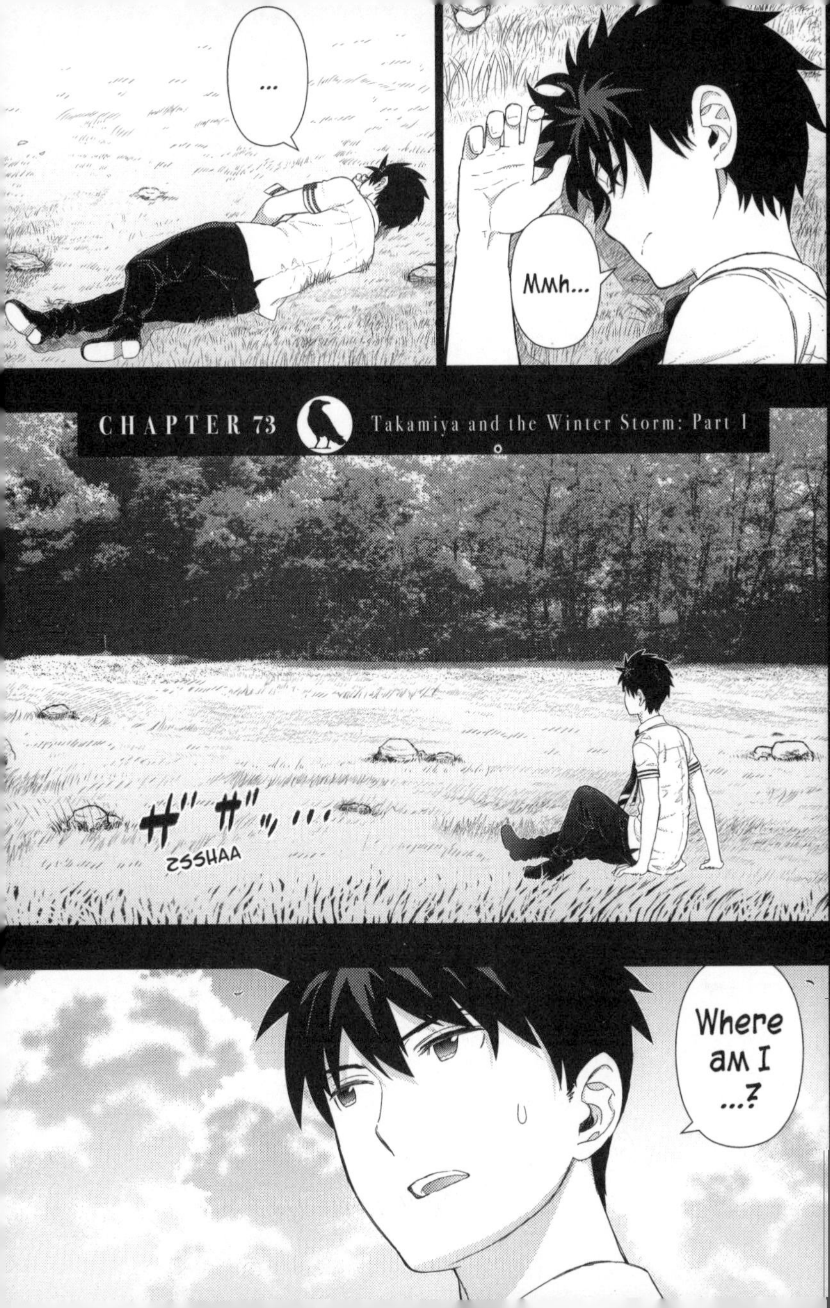
Mmh...
...
CHAPTER 73
Takamiya and the Winter Storm: Part 1
ZSSHAA
Where am I ...?

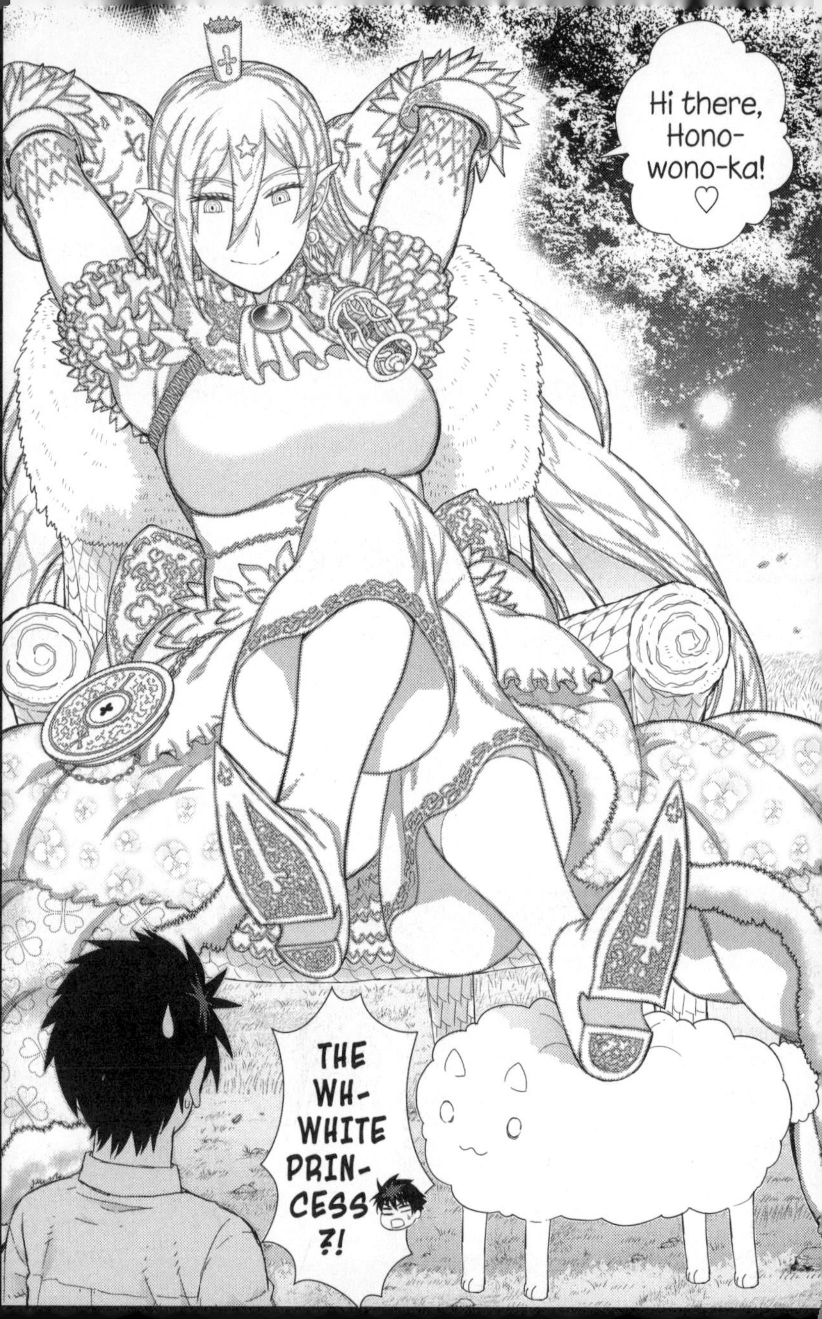
Hi there, Hono-wono-ka! ♡
THE WH-WHITE PRIN-CESS?!

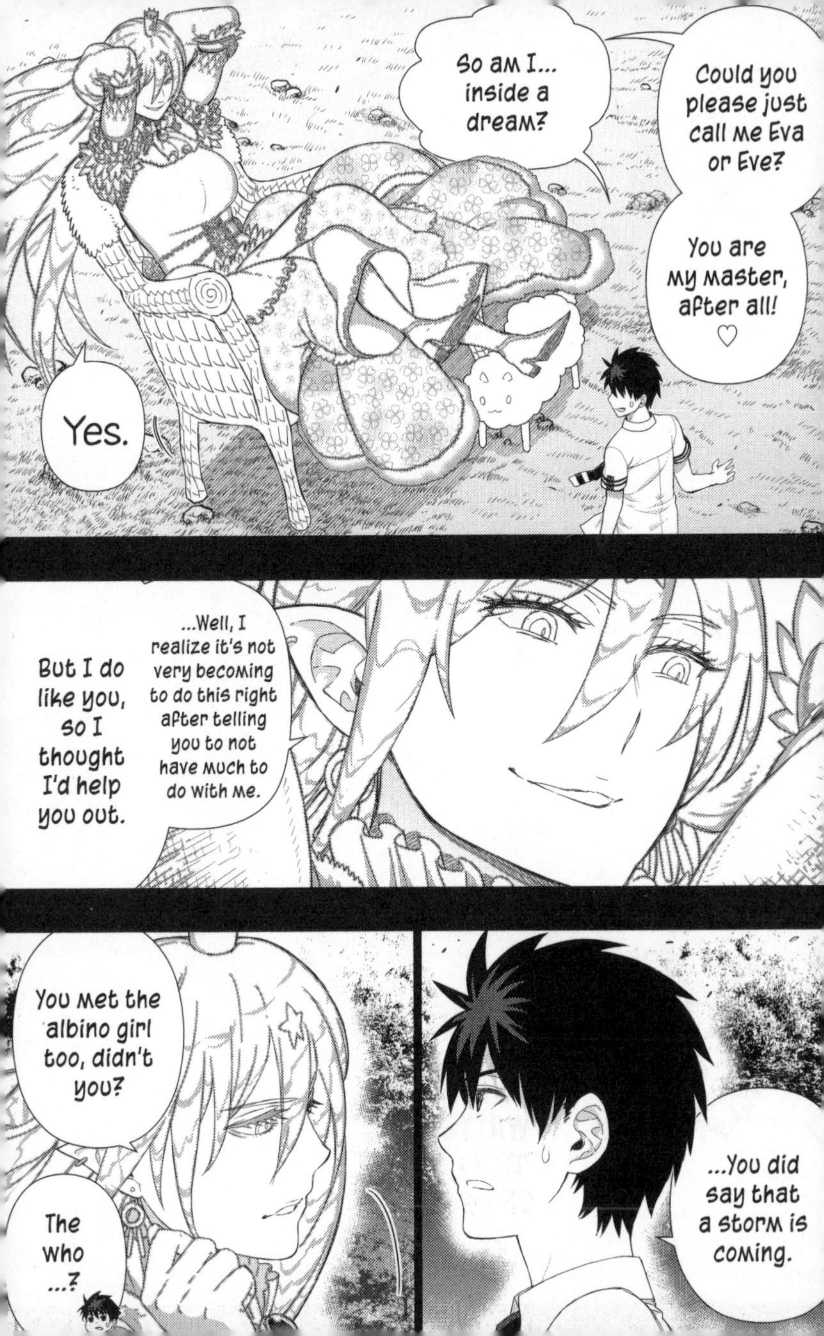
Could you please just call me Eva or Eve?
You are my master, after all! ♡
So am I... inside a dream?
Yes.
...Well, I realize it's not very becoming to do this right after telling you to not have much to do with me.
But I do like you, so I thought I'd help you out.
...You did say that a storm is coming.
You met the albino girl too, didn't you?
The who ...?

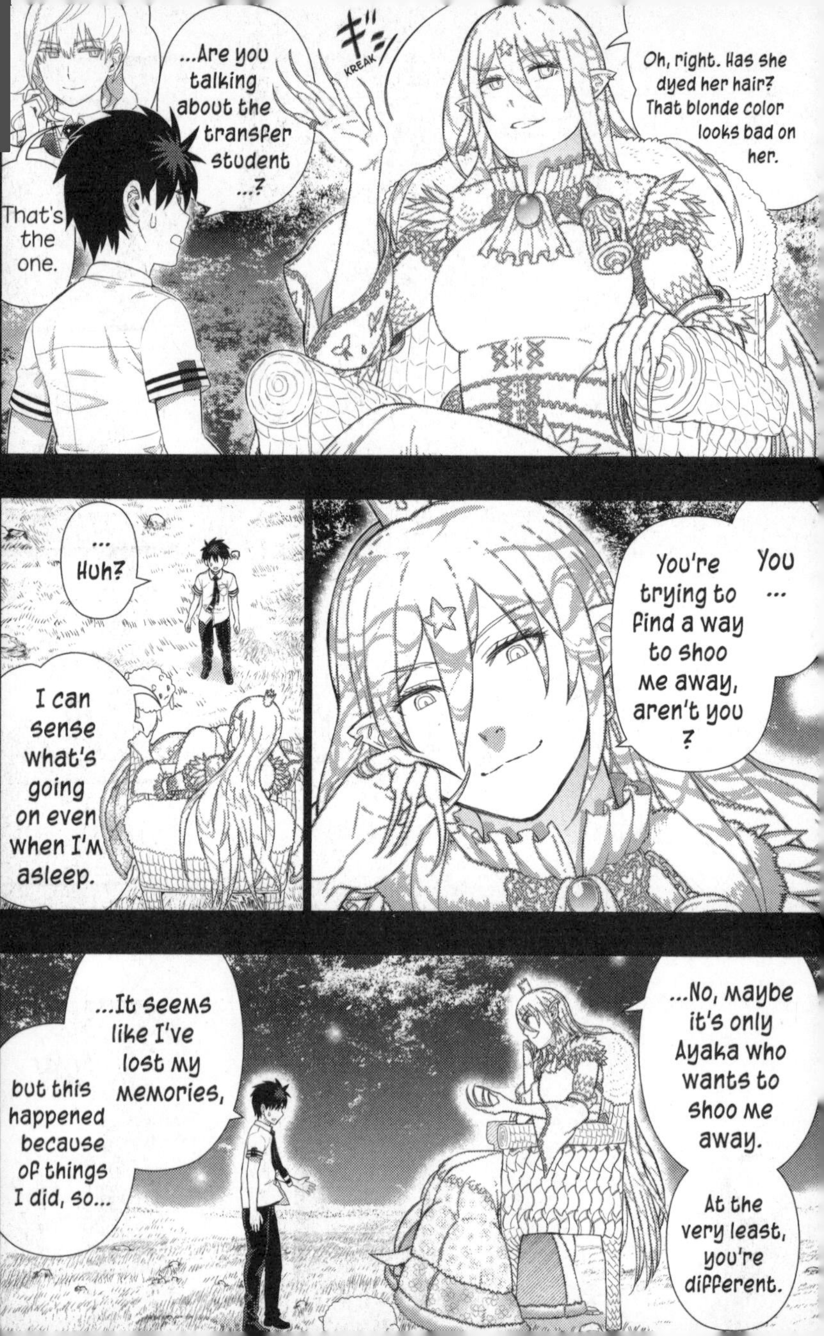

Oh, right. Has she dyed her hair? That blonde color looks bad on her.
ギッ
KREAK
...Are you talking about the transfer student ...?
That's the one.
You ...
You're trying to find a way to shoo me away, aren't you ?
... Huh?
I can sense what's going on even when I'm asleep.
...No, maybe it's only Ayaka who wants to shoo me away.
At the very least, you're different.
...It seems like I've lost my memories,
but this happened because of things I did, so...

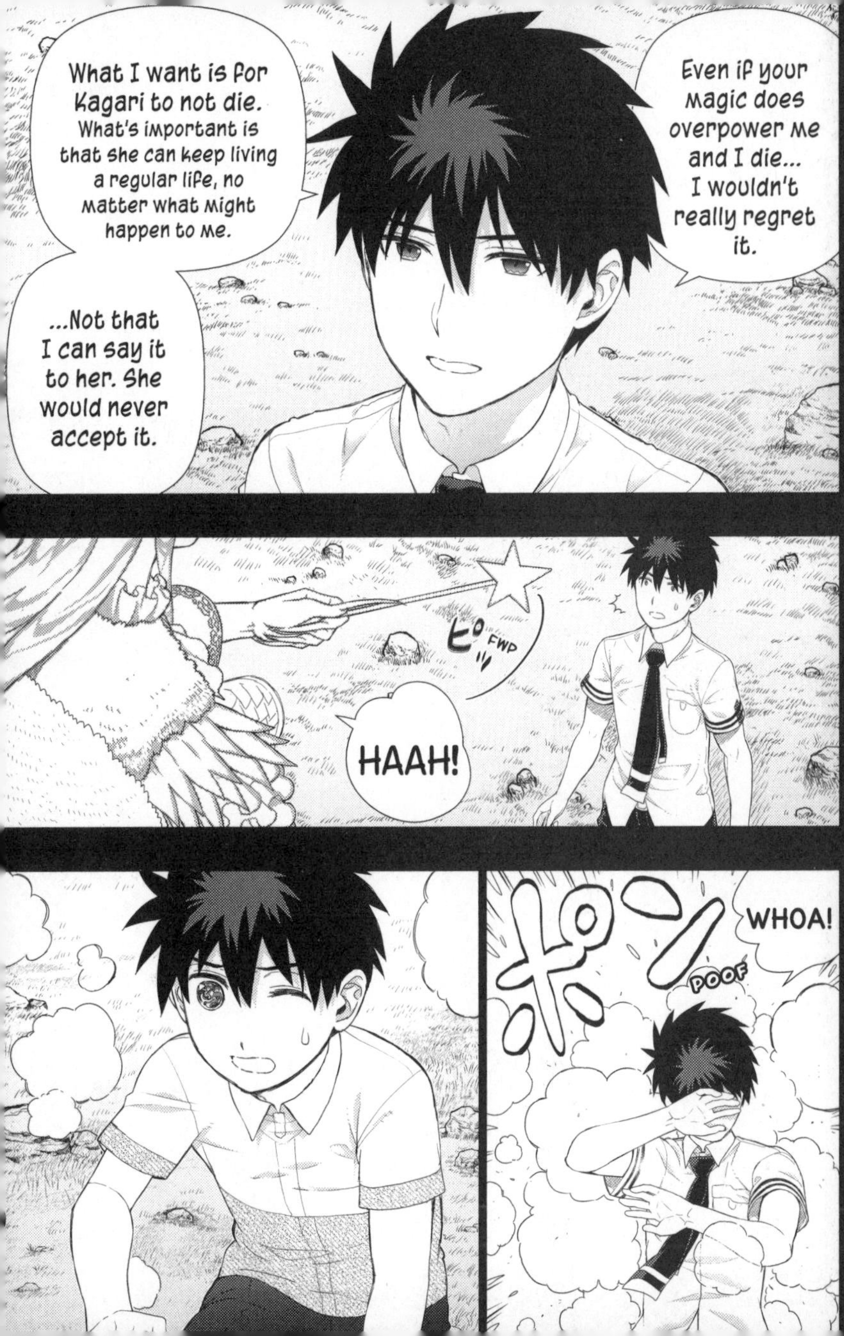
Even if your magic does overpower me and I die... I wouldn't really regret it.
What I want is for Kagari to not die. What's important is that she can keep living a regular life, no matter what might happen to me.
...Not that I can say it to her. She would never accept it.
ピッ
FWP
HAAH!
WHOA!
ポン
POOF

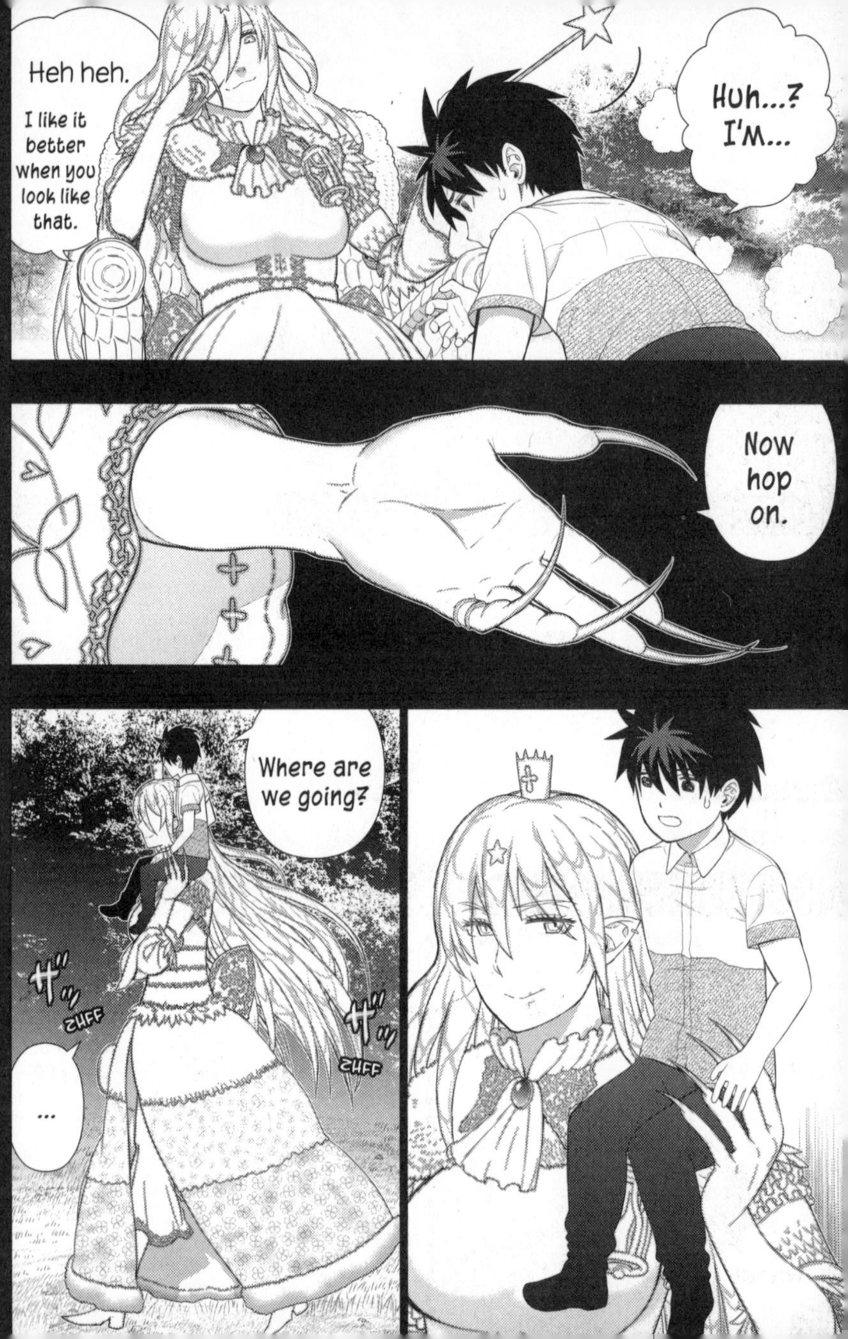

HUH...? I'M...
Heh heh.
I like it better when you look like that.
Now hop on.
Where are we going?
ZHFF
ZHFF
...

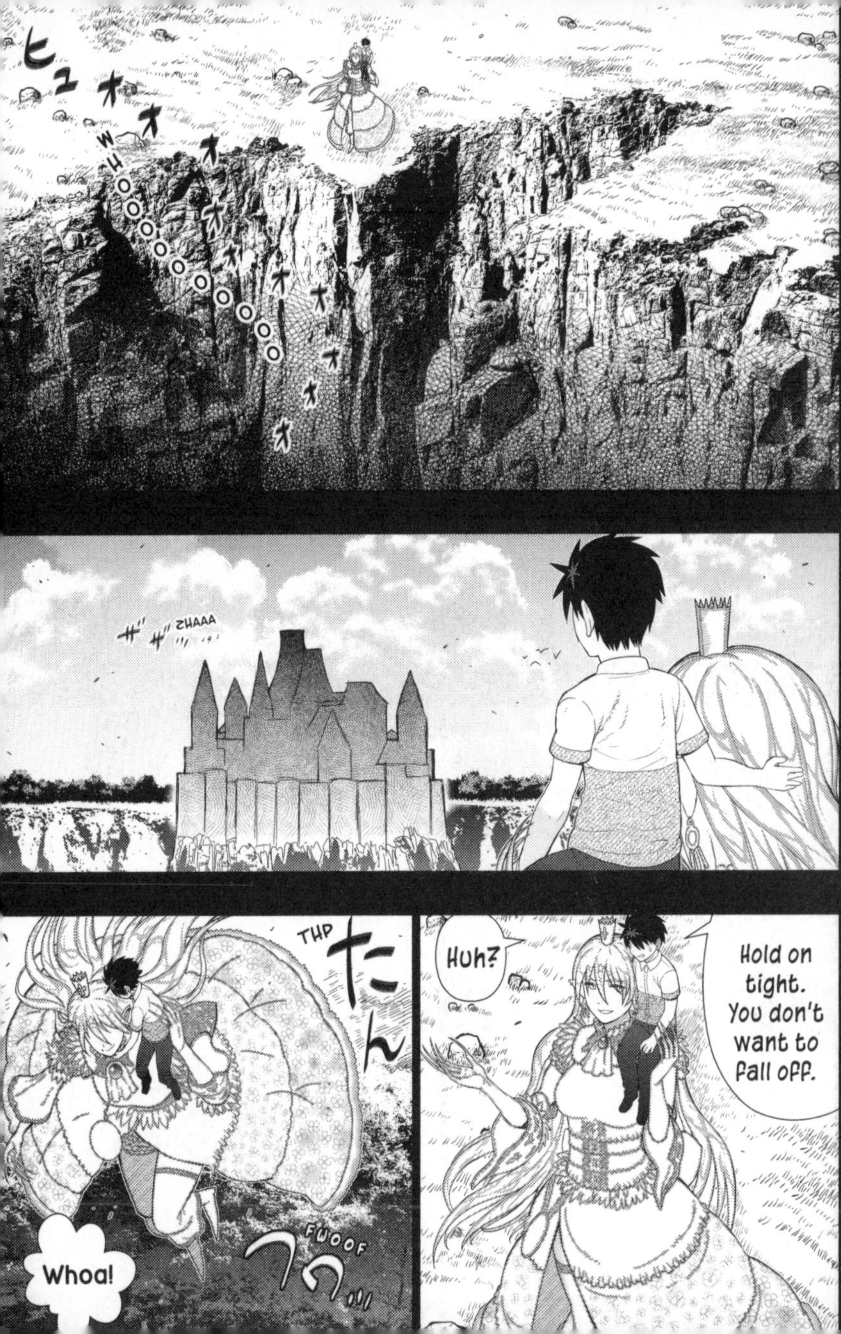

ヒュオオオオオオオオオオ
WHOOOOOOOOOOOO
ザザ
ZHAAA
Huh?
Hold on tight. You don't want to fall off.
たん
THP
Whoa!
つ
FWOOF

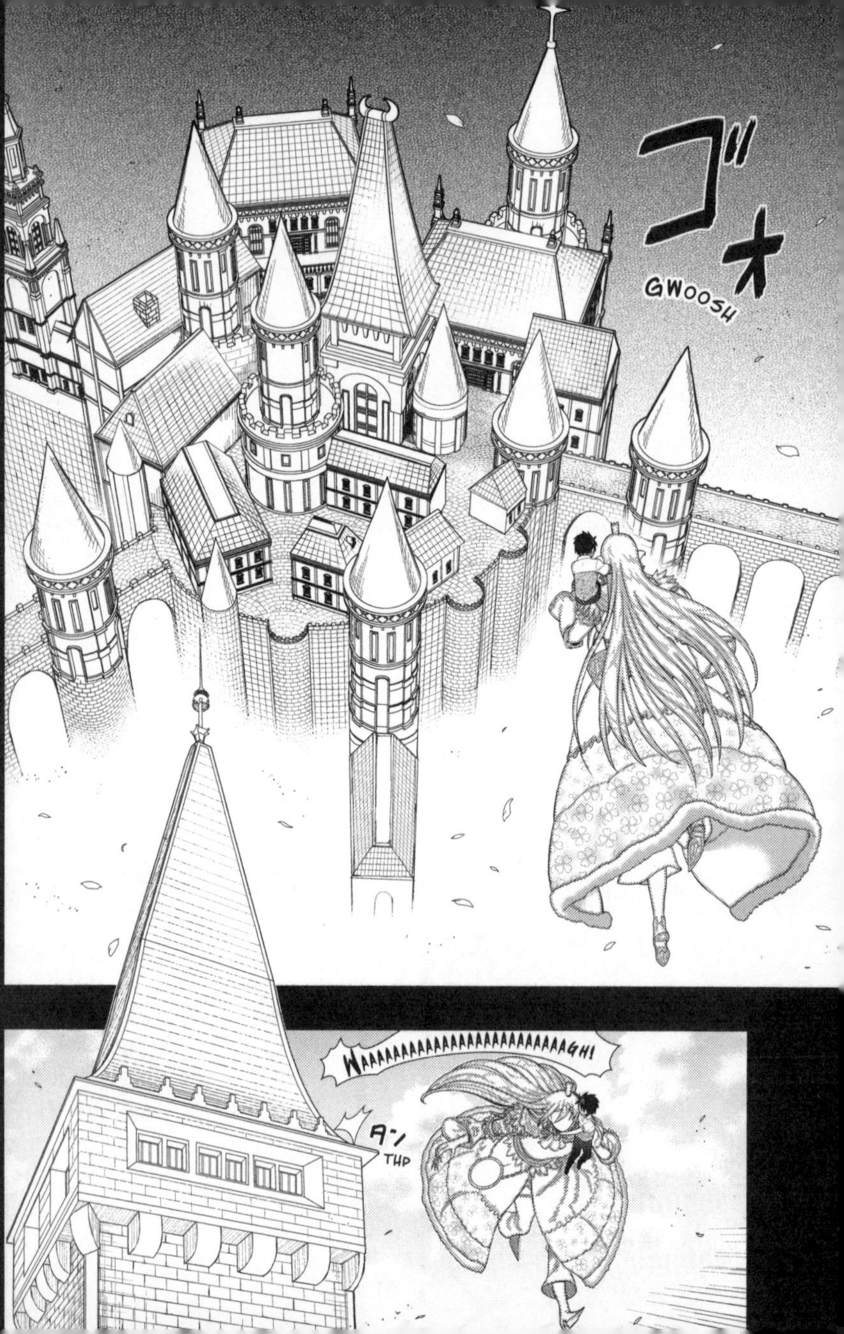
ゴオ
GWOOSH
WAAAAAAAAAAAAAAAAAAAAAAAAAAGH!
ダッ
THP

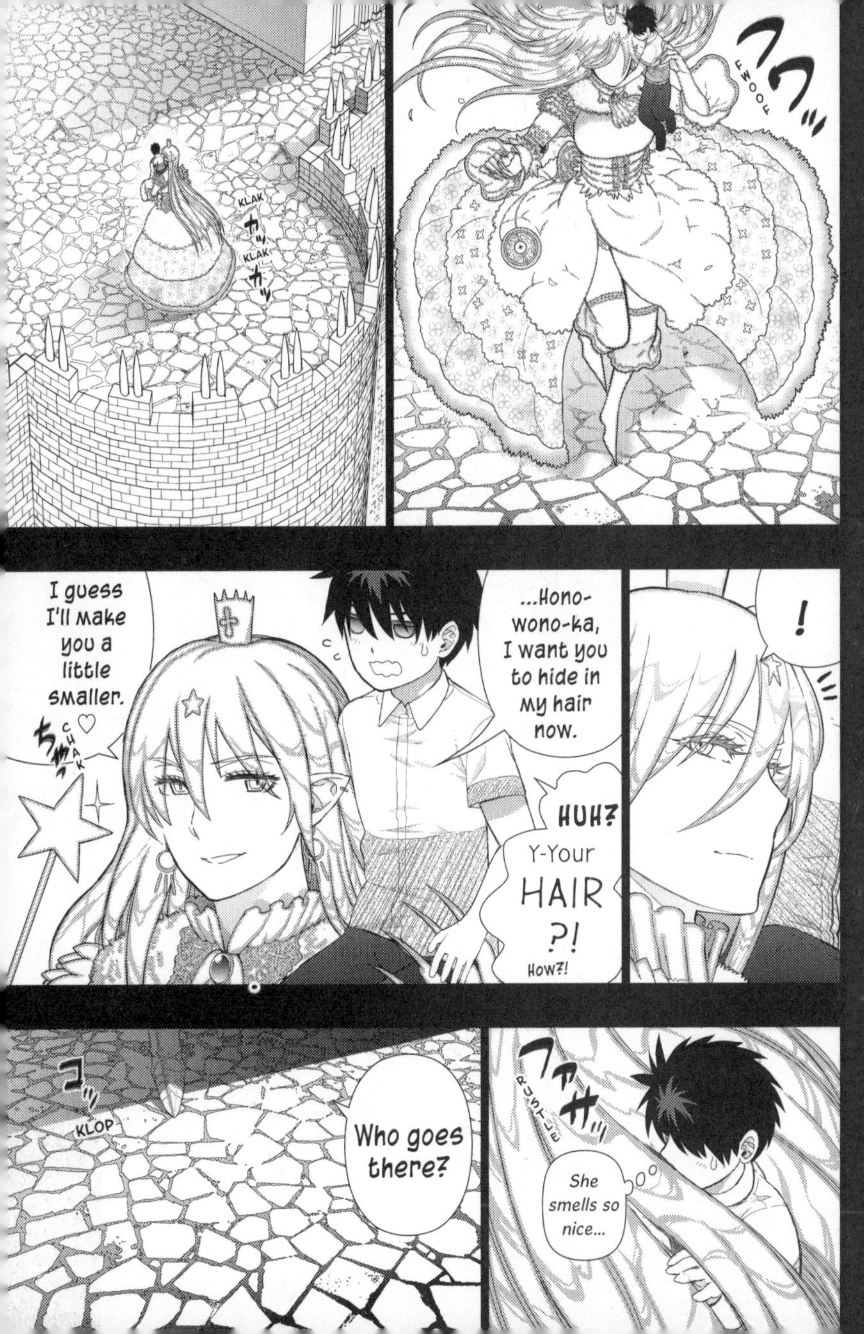
FWOOF
KLAK
KLAK
!
...Hono-wono-ka, I want you to hide in my hair now.
HUH?
Y-Your HAIR?!
HOW?!
I guess I'll make you a little smaller.
CHAK
RUSTLE
She smells so nice...
KLOP
Who goes there?

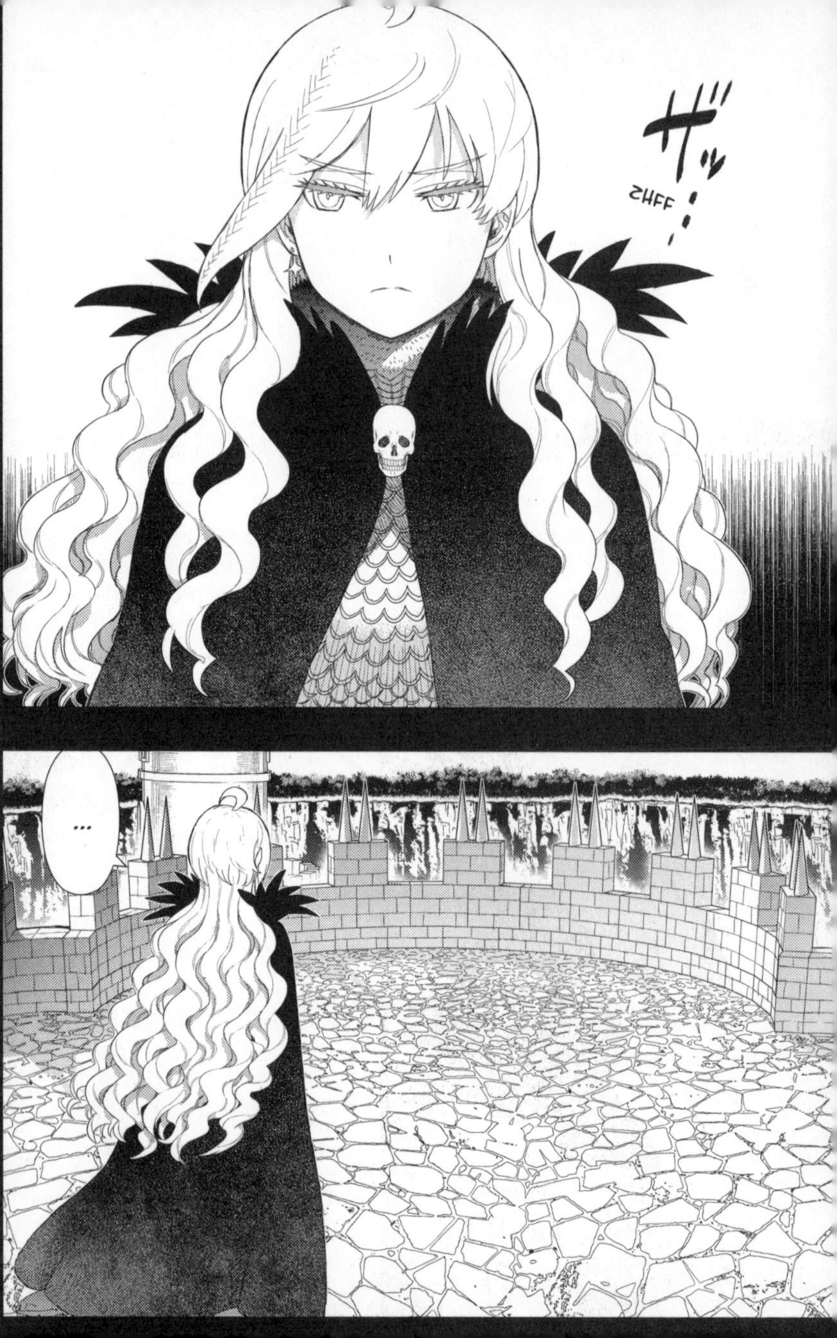
ザッ
ZHFF
...

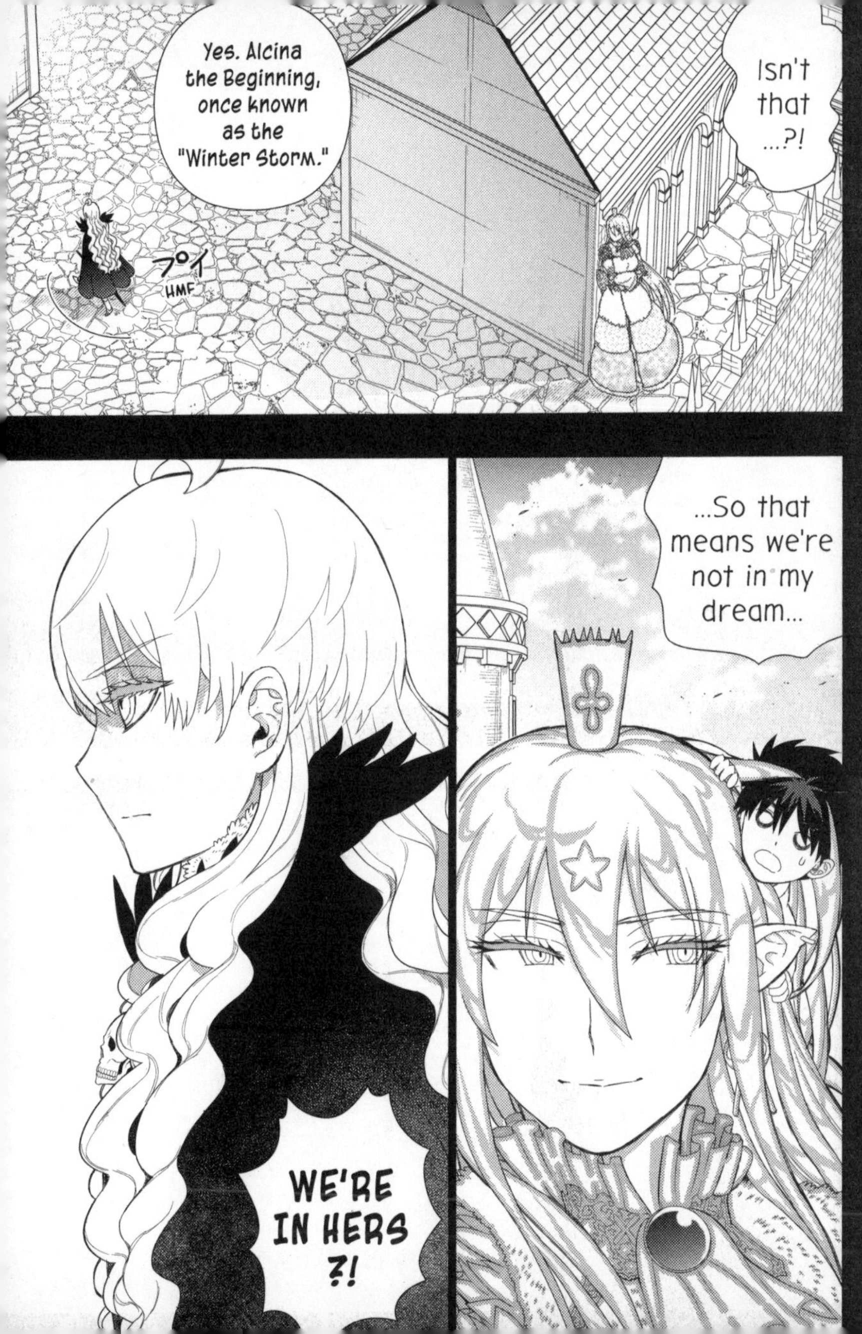
Isn't that ...?!
Yes. Alcina the Beginning, once known as the "Winter Storm."
プイ
HMF
...So that means we're not in my dream...
WE'RE IN HERS ?!

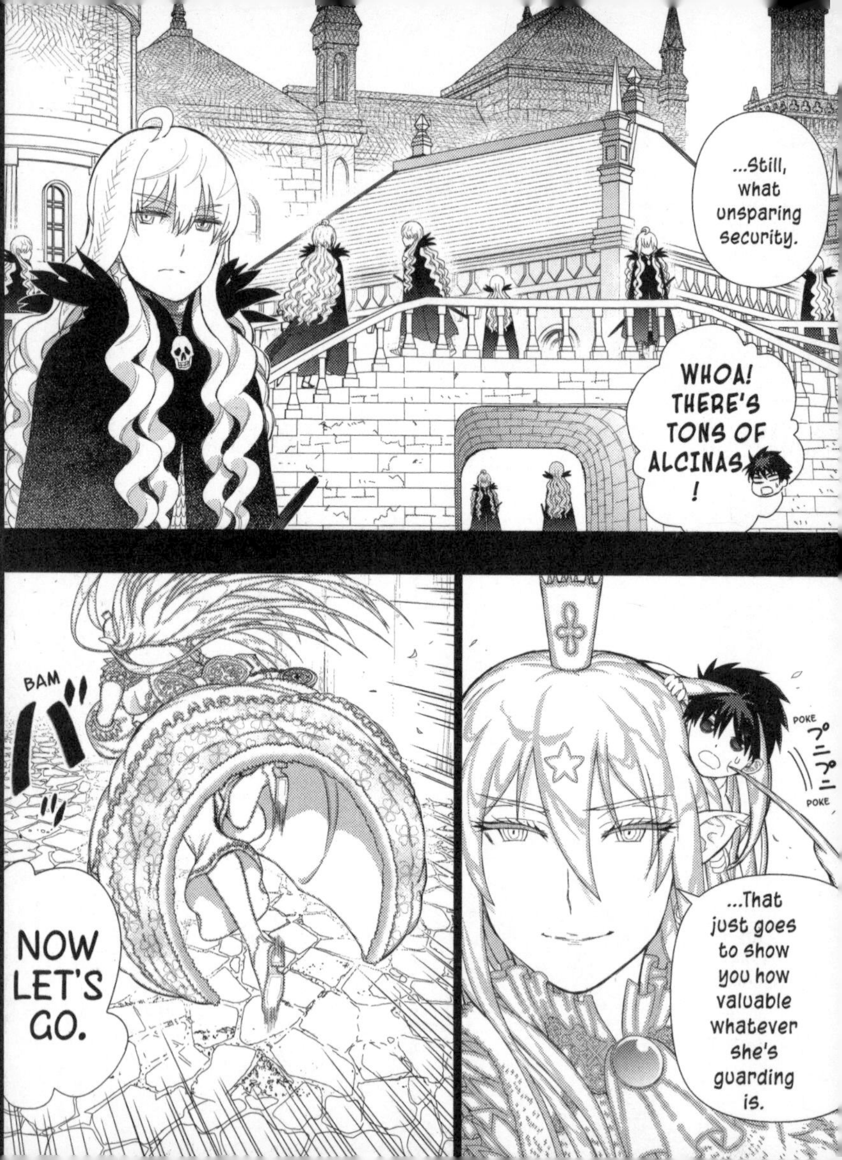
...Still, what unsparing security.
WHOA! THERE'S TONS OF ALCINAS!
POKE
プニプニ
POKE
...That just goes to show you how valuable whatever she's guarding is.
BAM
バ
NOW LET'S GO.

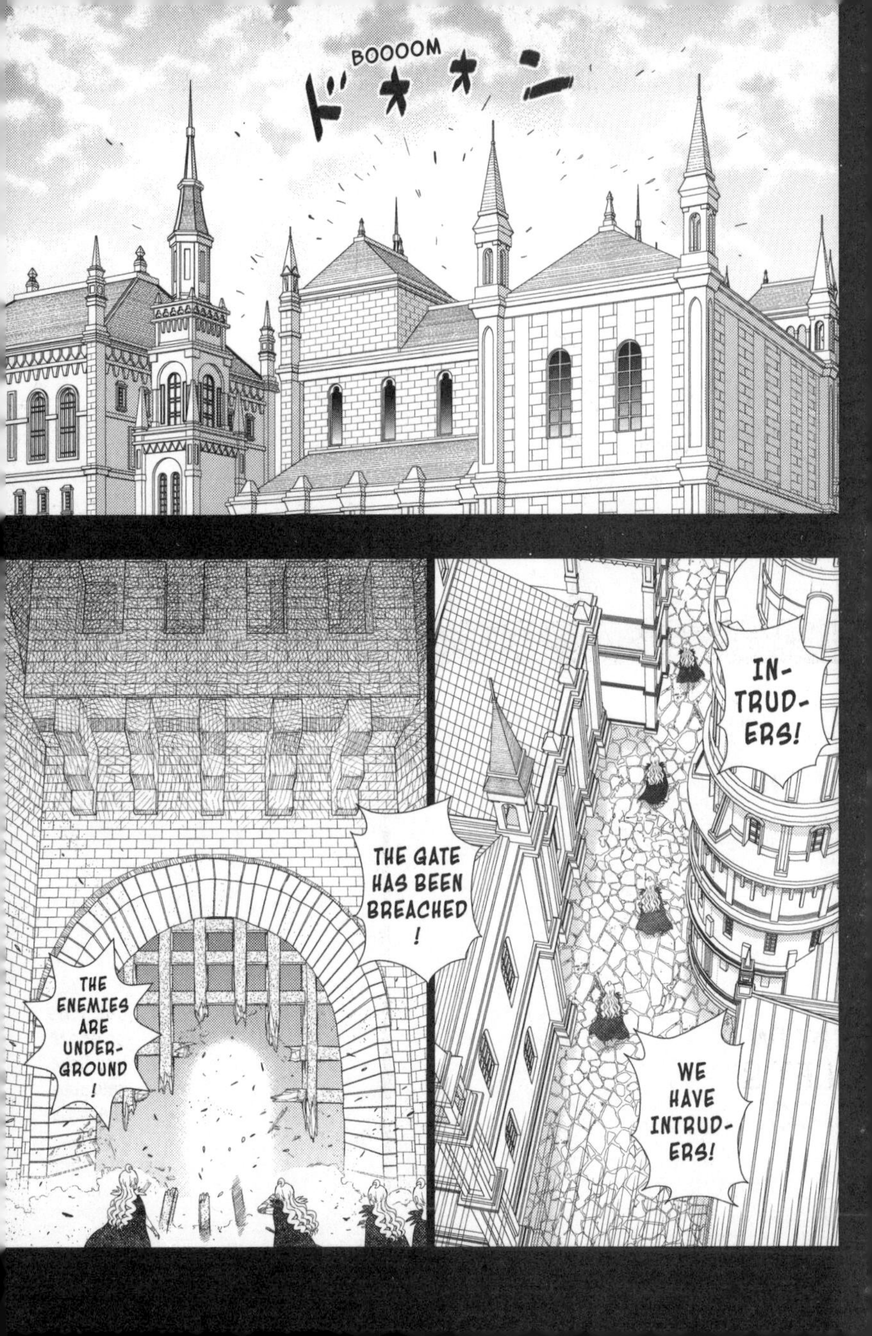
BOOOOM
ドォオー
IN-TRUD-ERS!
WE HAVE INTRUD-ERS!
THE GATE HAS BEEN BREACHED!
THE ENEMIES ARE UNDER-GROUND!

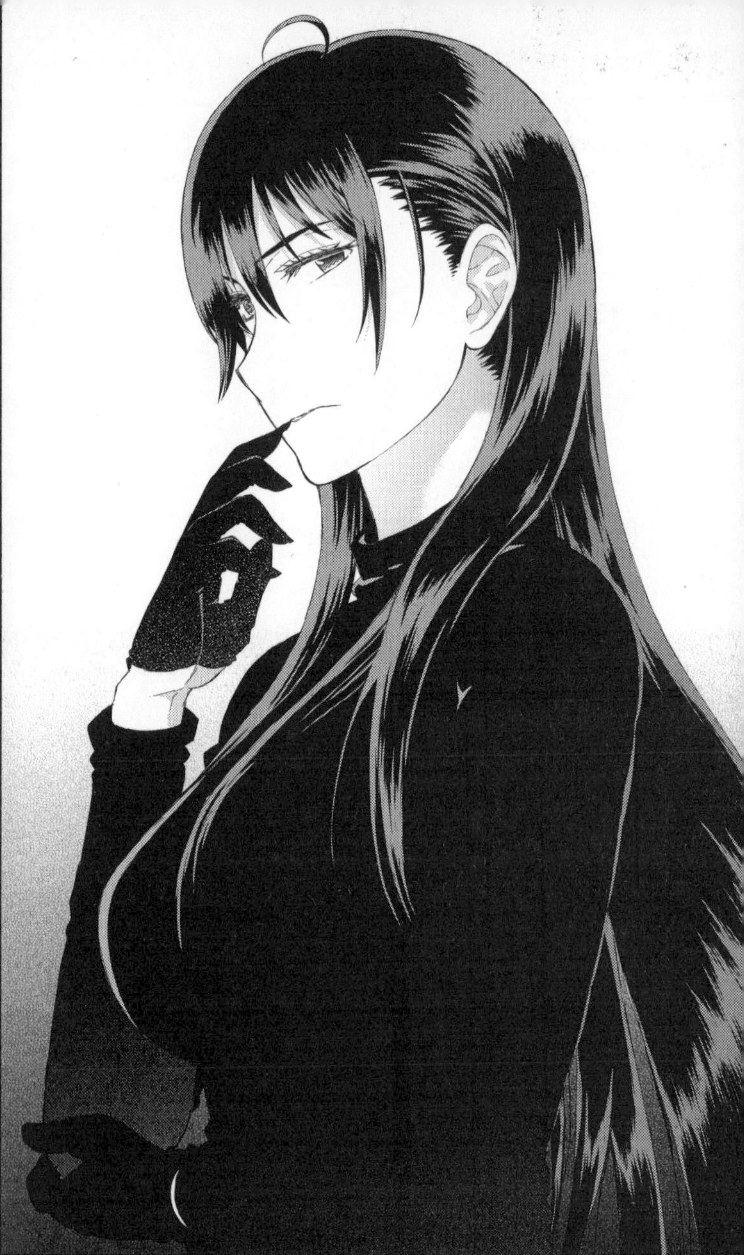

CHAPTER 74 Takamiya and the Winter Storm: Part 2

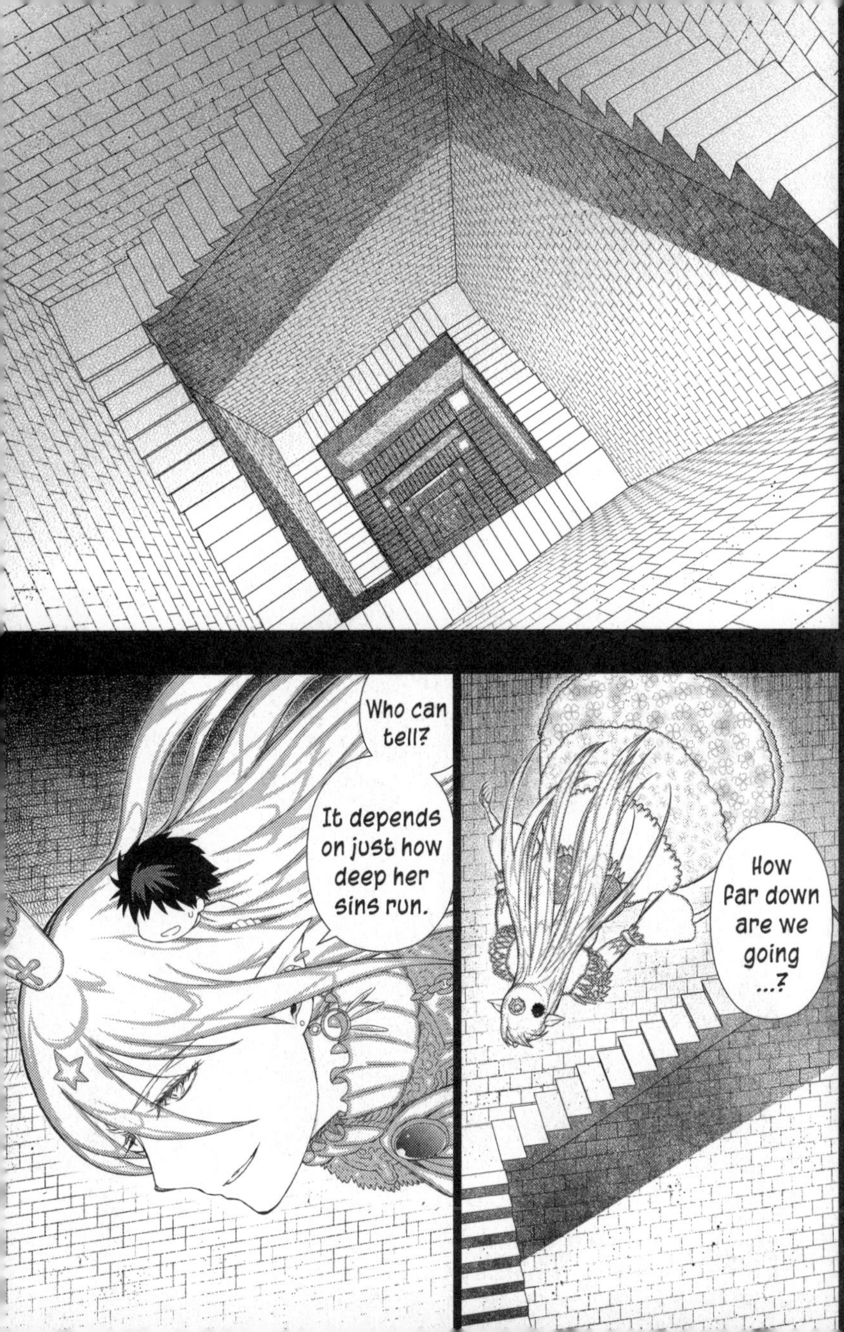
How far down are we going ...?
Who can tell?
It depends on just how deep her sins run.

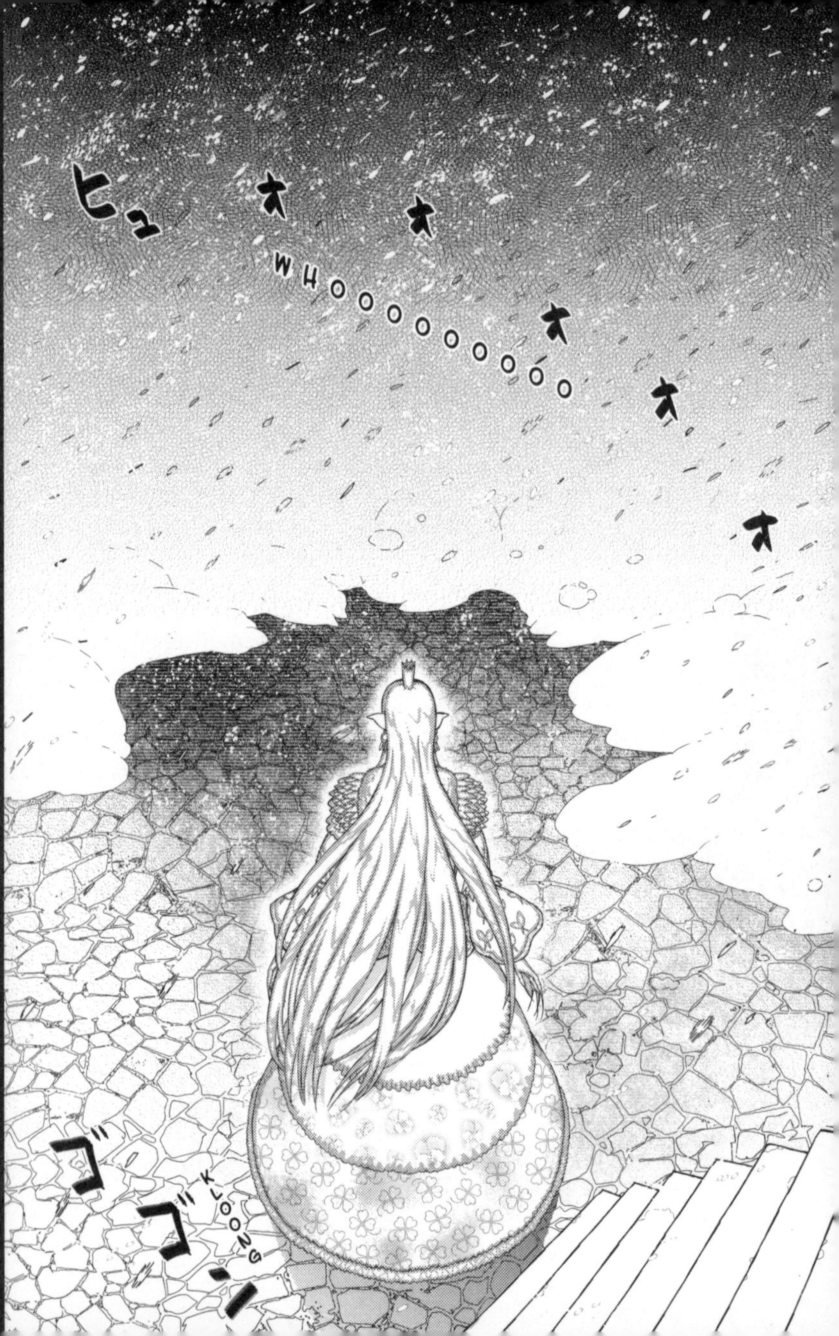
ヒュオオオオオ
WHOOOOOOOOO
ゴゴーン
KLOONG

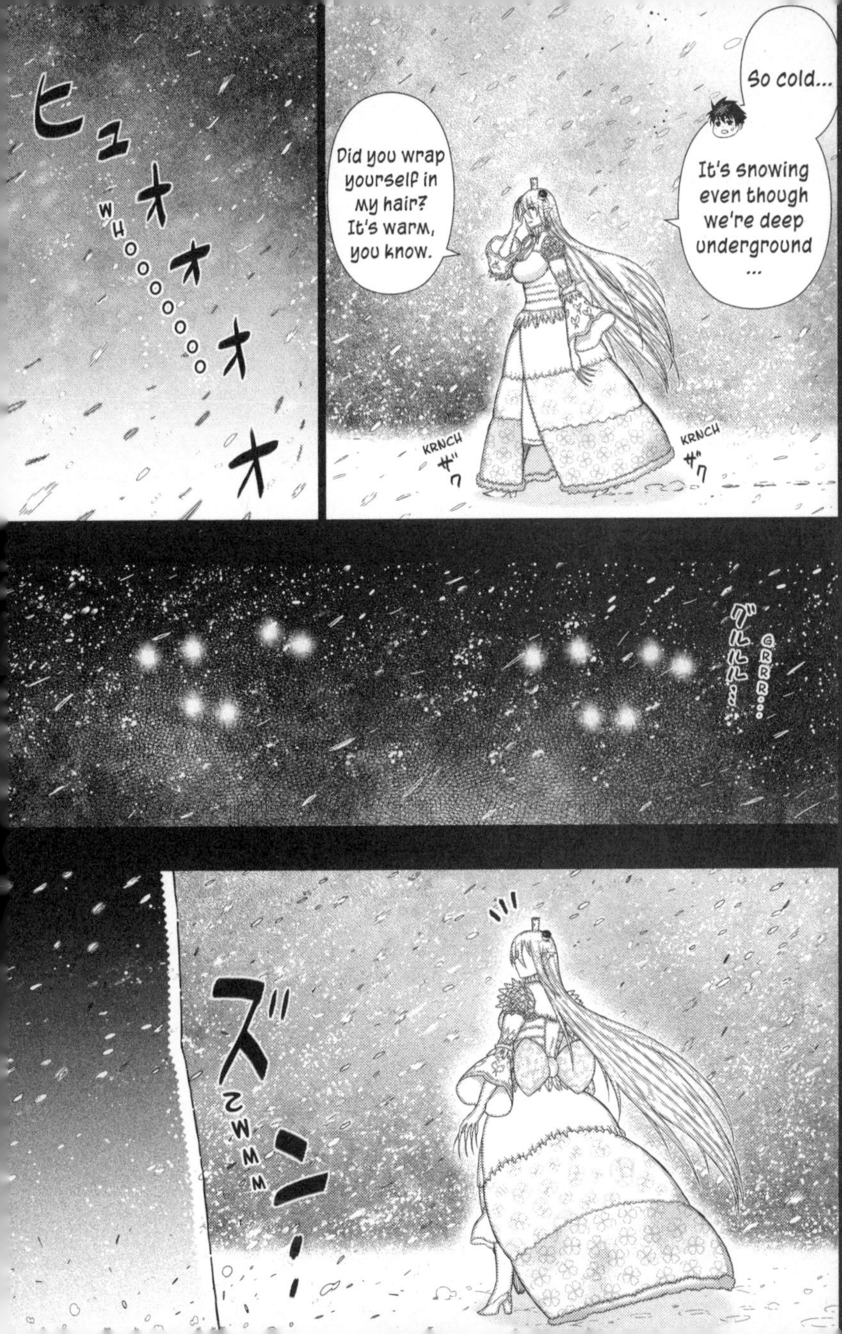
So cold...
It's snowing even though we're deep underground ...
Did you wrap yourself in my hair? It's warm, you know.
KRNCH ザク
KRNCH ザク
ヒュオオオオ
WHOOOOOOOO
グルル...
GRRR...
ズゥン
ZWMM

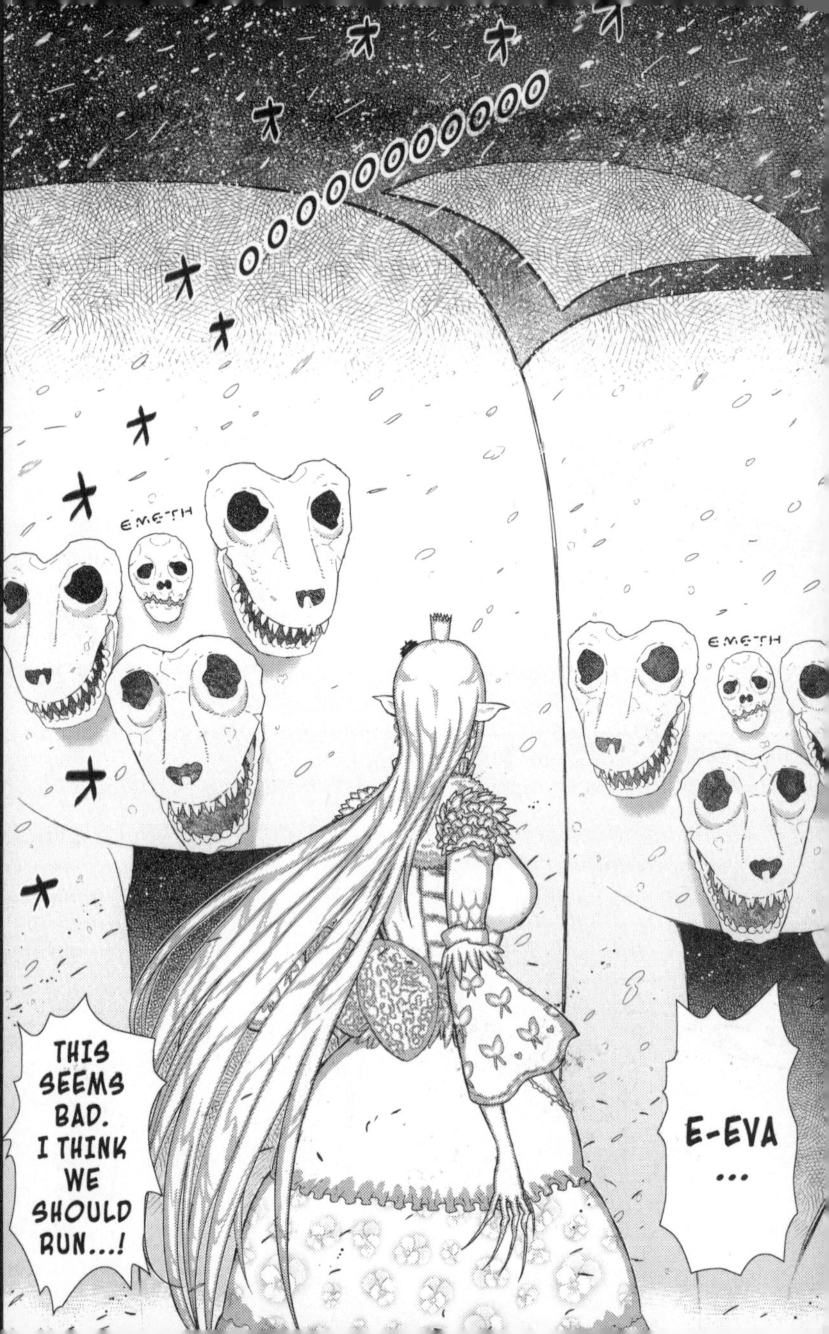
オオオオオオオオオオ
OOOOOOOOOOOOO
E-ME-TH
E-ME-TH
E-EVA ...
THIS SEEMS BAD. I THINK WE SHOULD RUN...!

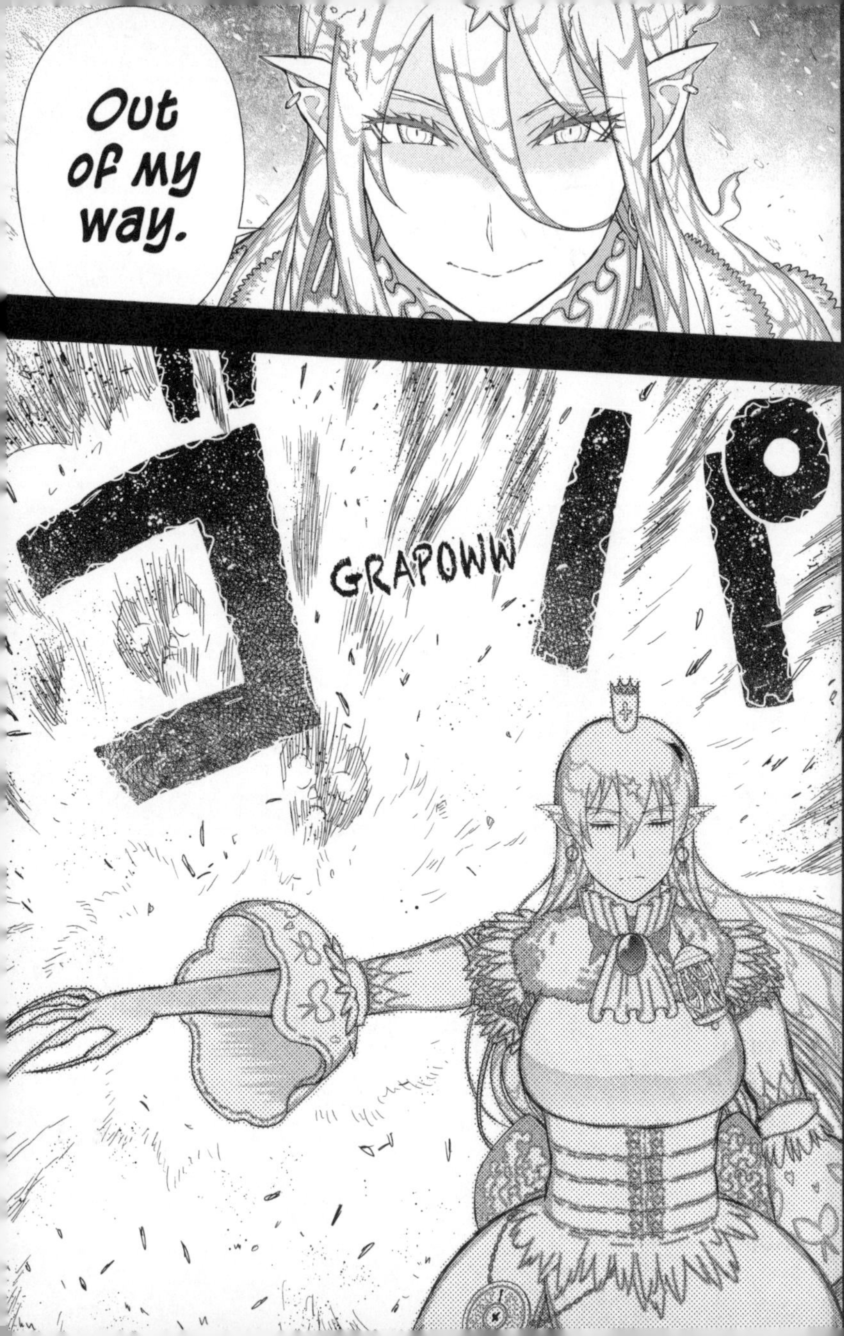
Out of my way.
GRAPOWW

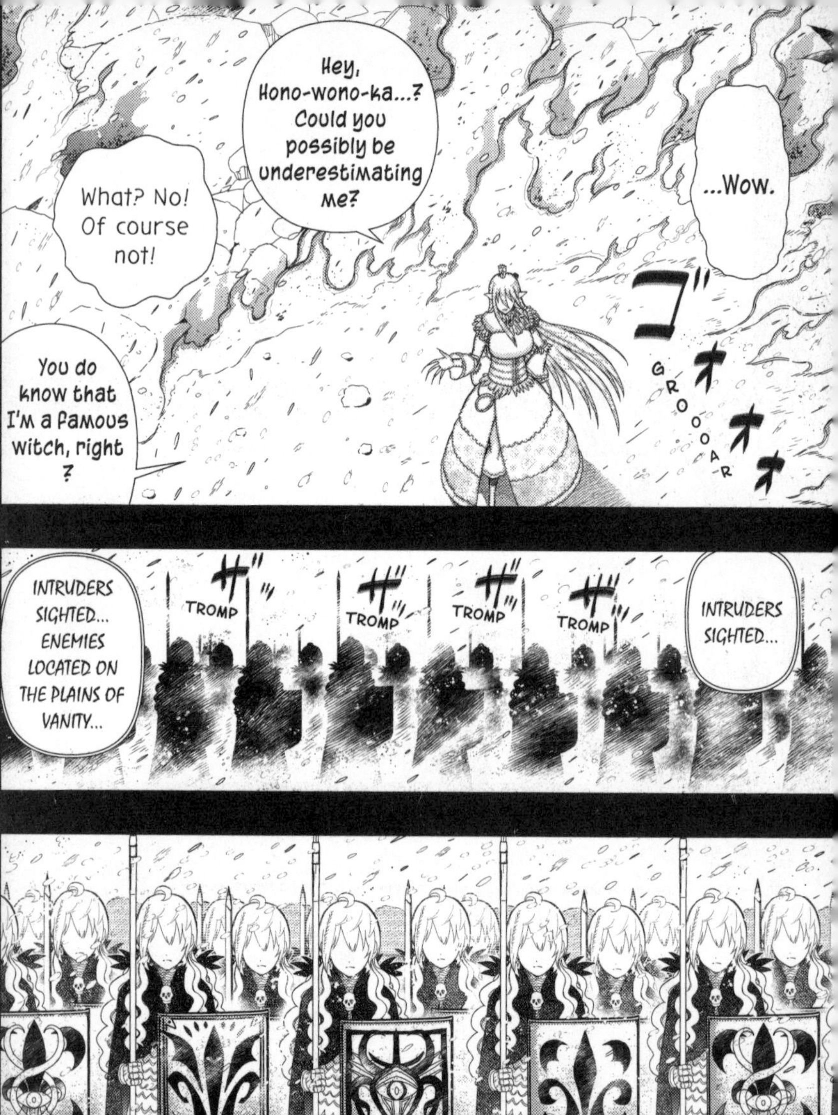
...Wow.
ゴオオオ
GROOOOAR
Hey, Hono-wono-ka...? Could you possibly be underestimating me?
What? No! Of course not!
You do know that I'm a famous witch, right?
INTRUDERS SIGHTED...
ザ
TROMP
ザ
TROMP
ザ
TROMP
ザ
TROMP
INTRUDERS SIGHTED... ENEMIES LOCATED ON THE PLAINS OF VANITY...
ザ
TROMP
ザ
TROMP
ザ
TROMP
ザ
TROMP

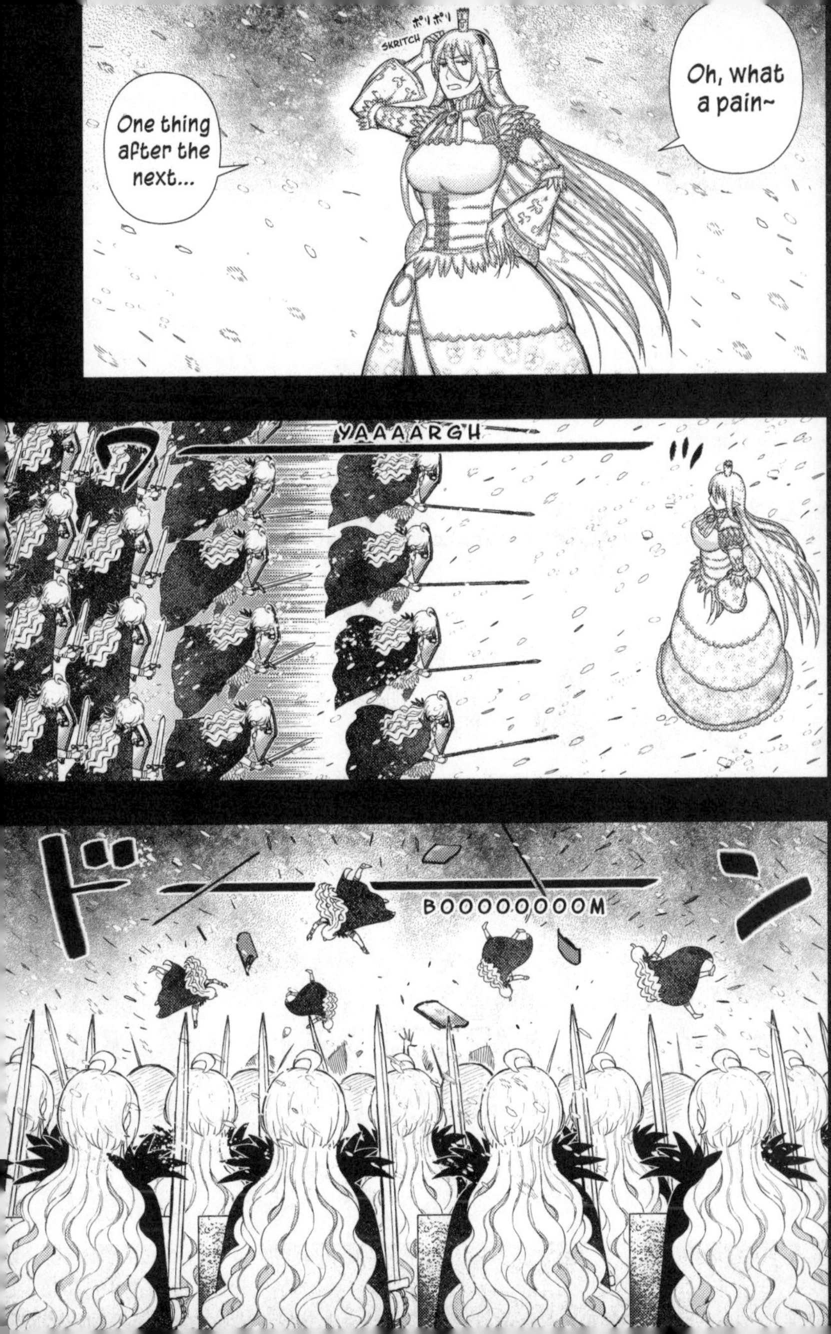
Oh, what a pain~
ポリポリ
SKRITCH
One thing after the next...
YAAAARGH
ドーン
BOOOOOOOOM

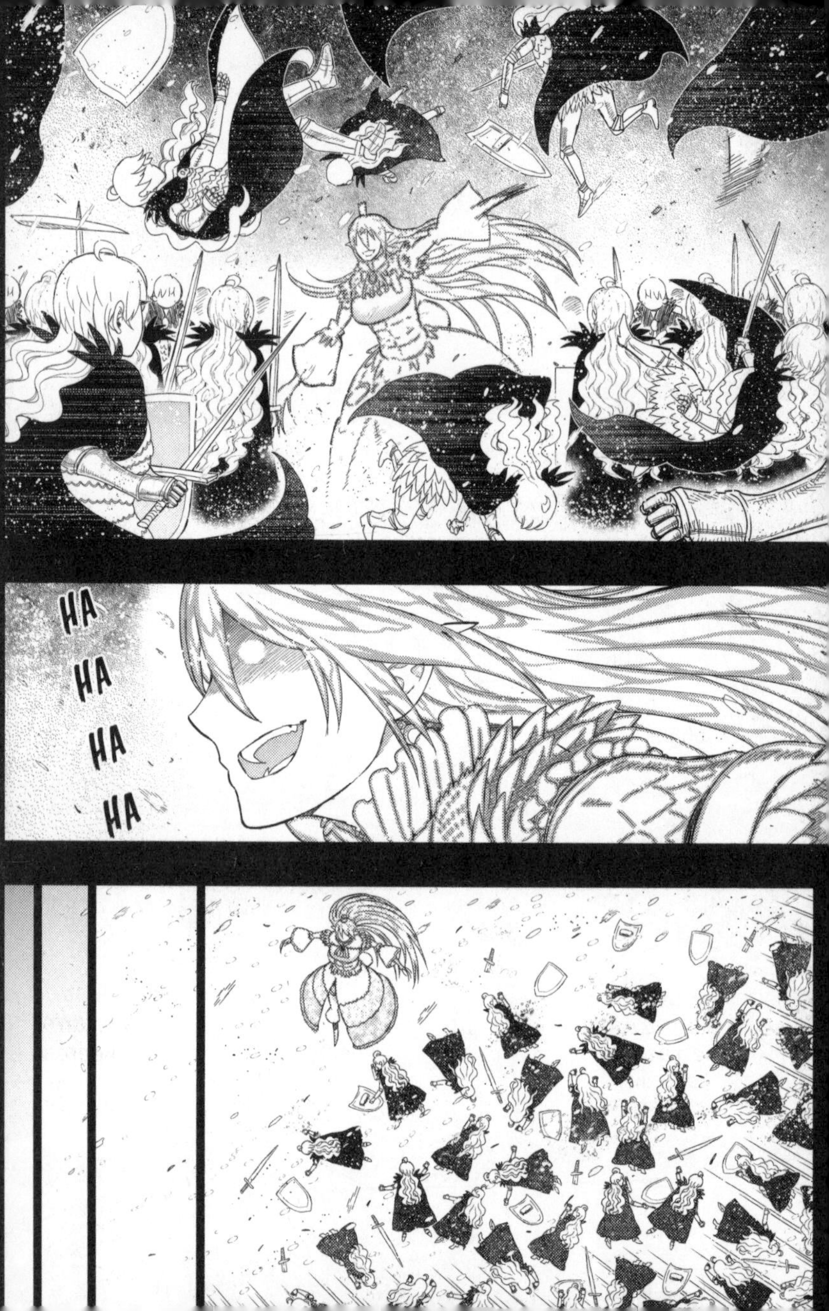
HA
HA
HA
HA

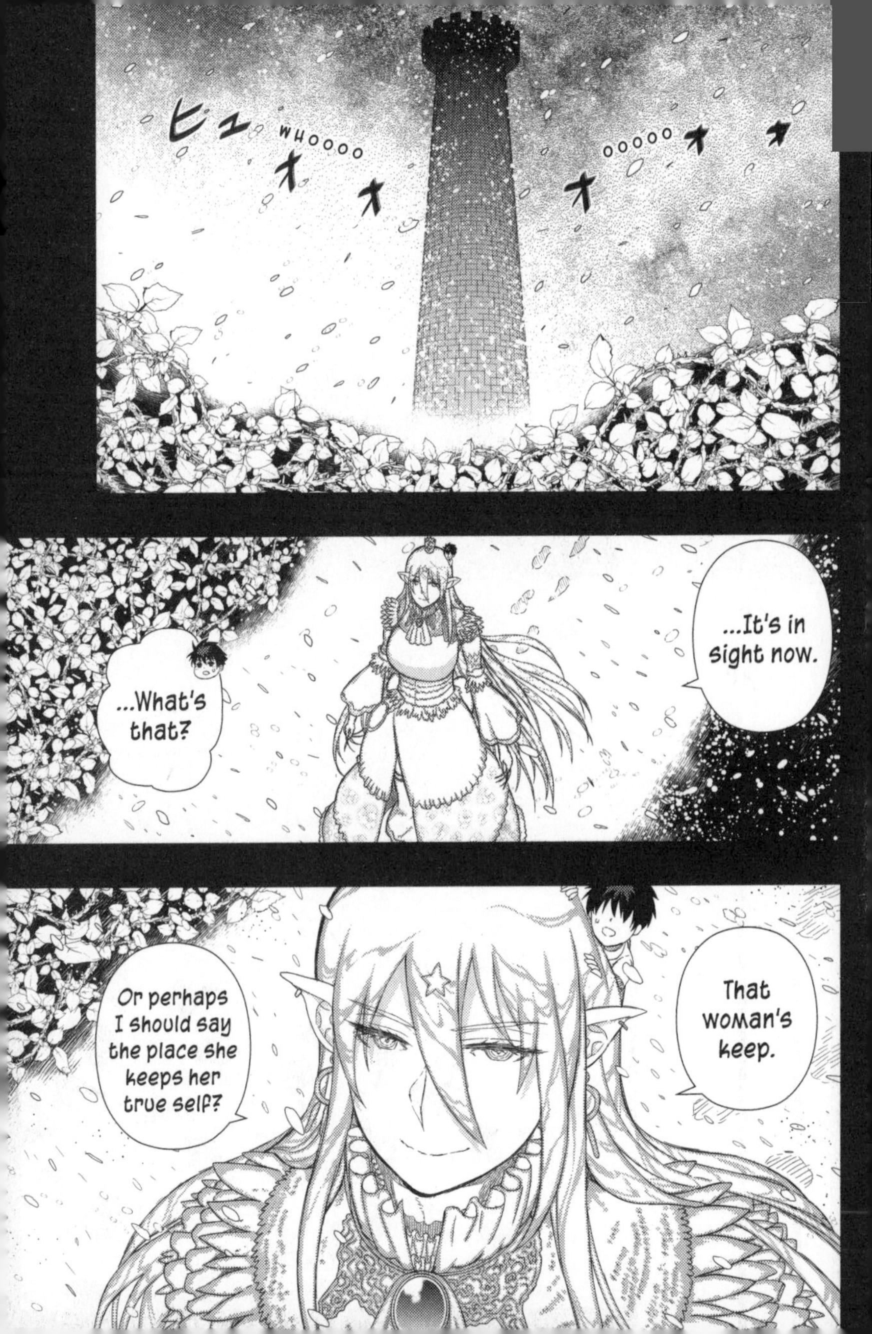
ヒュ WHOOOO オオ
OOOOO オオオ
...It's in sight now.
...What's that?
That woman's keep.
Or perhaps I should say the place she keeps her true self?

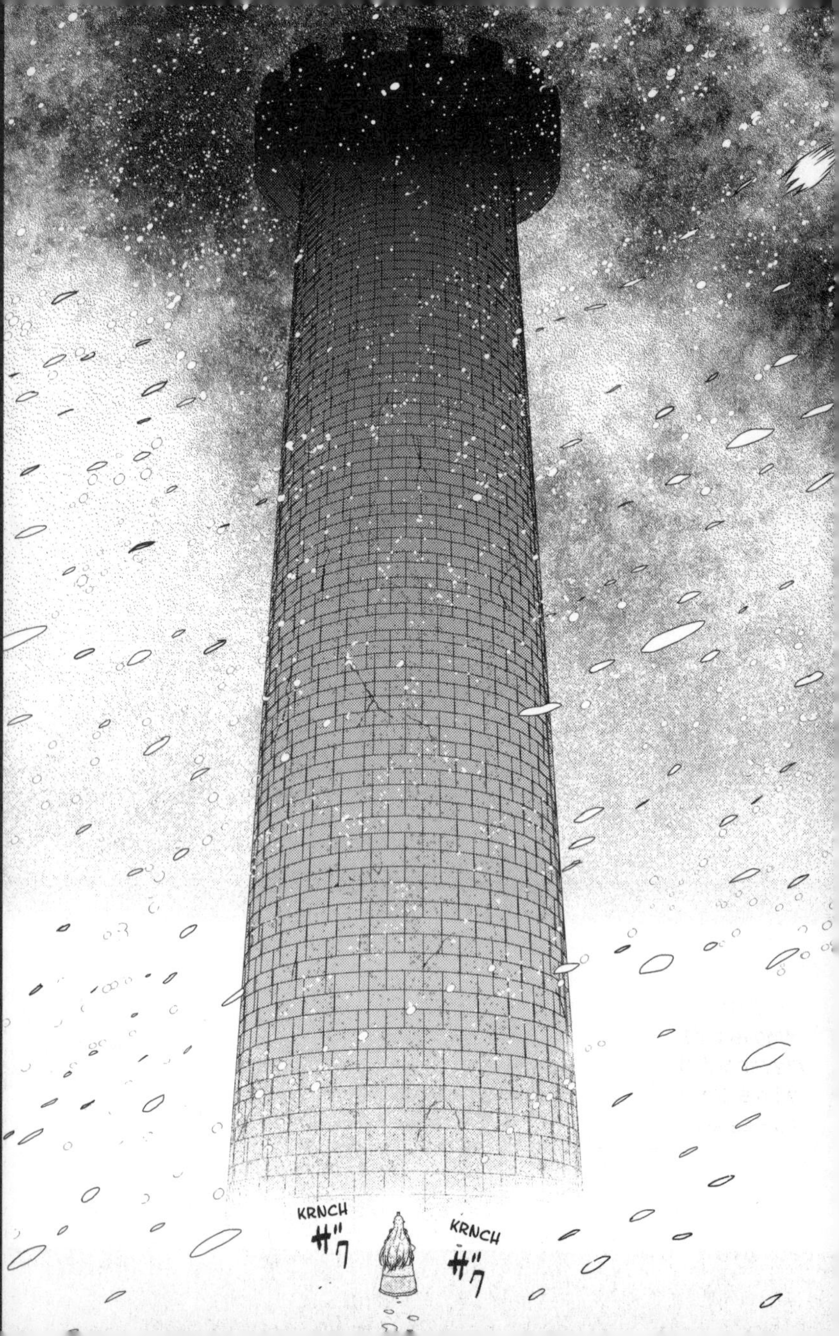
KRNCH
ザク
KRNCH
ザク

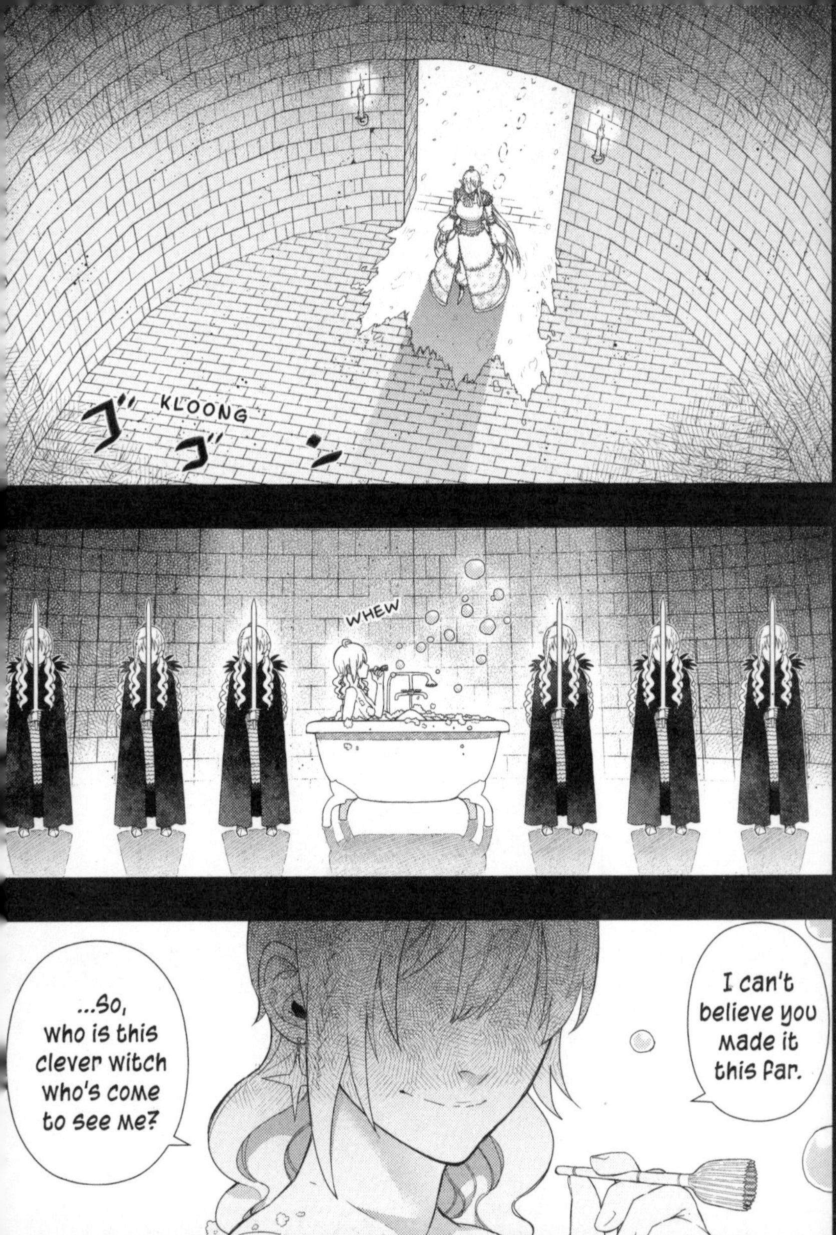
ゴゴン
KLOONG
WHEW
I can't believe you made it this far.
...So, who is this clever witch who's come to see me?

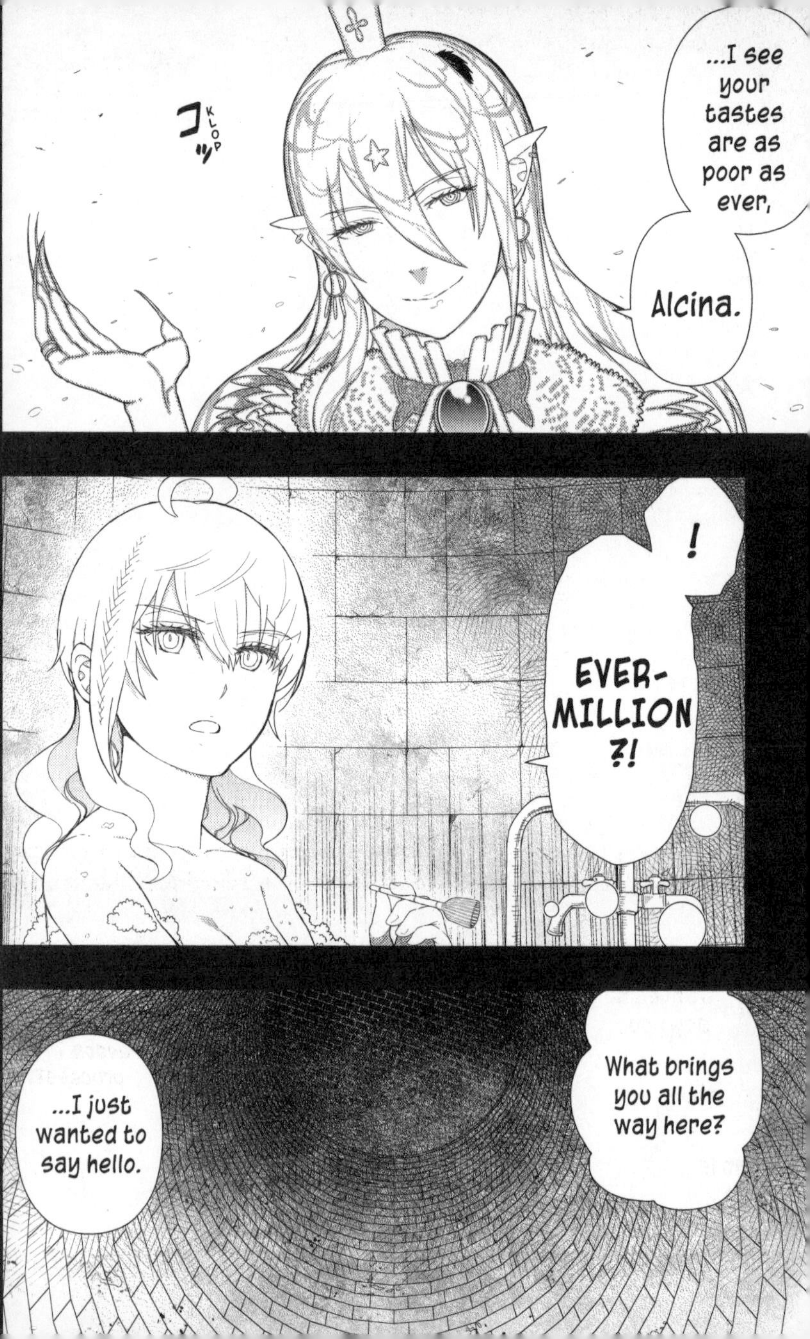
コッ
KLOP
...I see your tastes are as poor as ever,
Alcina.
!
EVER-MILLION ?!
What brings you all the way here?
...I just wanted to say hello.

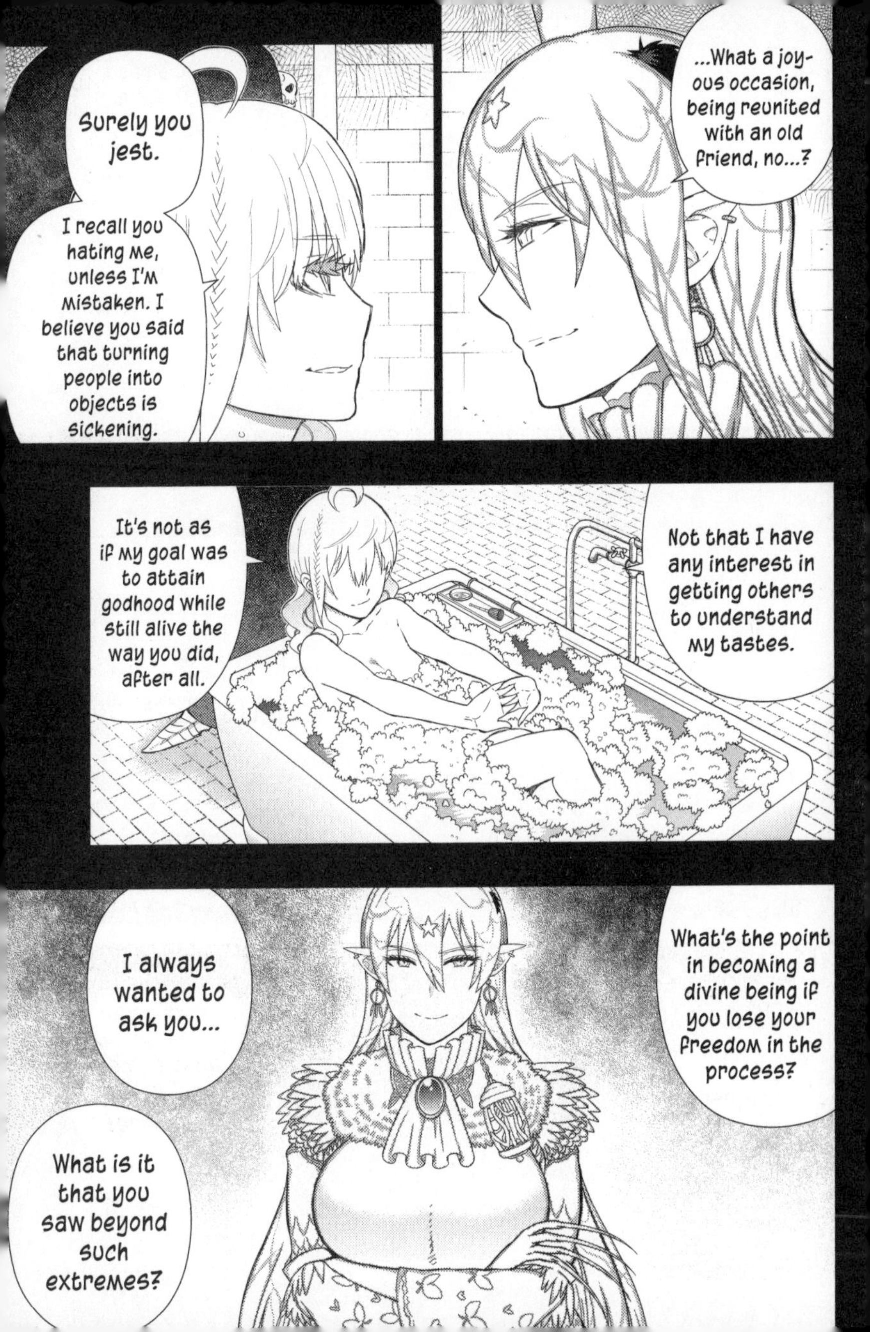
...What a joy-ous occasion, being reunited with an old friend, no...?
Surely you jest.
I recall you hating me, unless I'm mistaken. I believe you said that turning people into objects is sickening.
Not that I have any interest in getting others to understand my tastes.
It's not as if my goal was to attain godhood while still alive the way you did, after all.
I always wanted to ask you...
What's the point in becoming a divine being if you lose your freedom in the process?
What is it that you saw beyond such extremes?

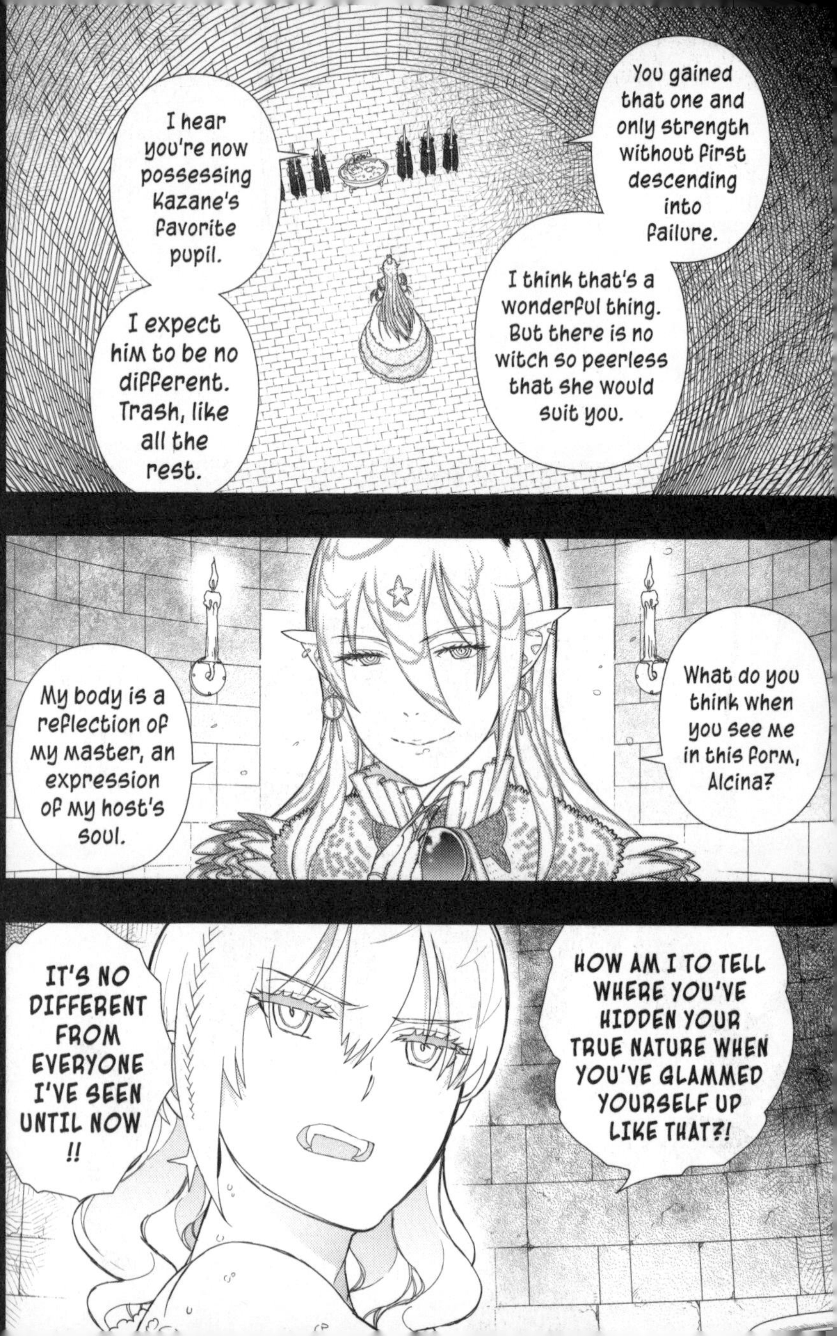
You gained that one and only strength without first descending into failure.
I think that's a wonderful thing. But there is no witch so peerless that she would suit you.
I hear you're now possessing Kazane's favorite pupil.
I expect him to be no different. Trash, like all the rest.
What do you think when you see me in this form, Alcina?
My body is a reflection of my master, an expression of my host's soul.
HOW AM I TO TELL WHERE YOU'VE HIDDEN YOUR TRUE NATURE WHEN YOU'VE GLAMMED YOURSELF UP LIKE THAT?!
IT'S NO DIFFERENT FROM EVERYONE I'VE SEEN UNTIL NOW!!

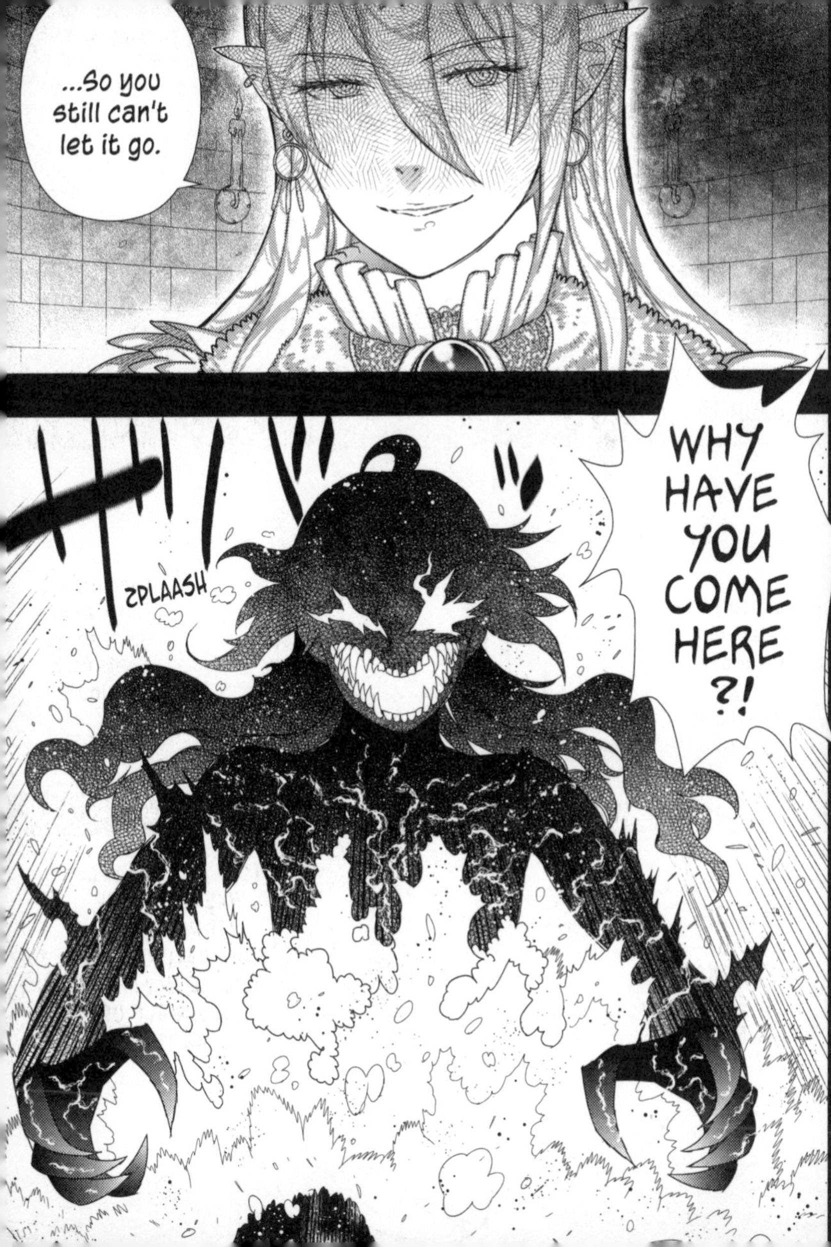
...So you still can't let it go.
WHY HAVE YOU COME HERE?!
ZPLAASH

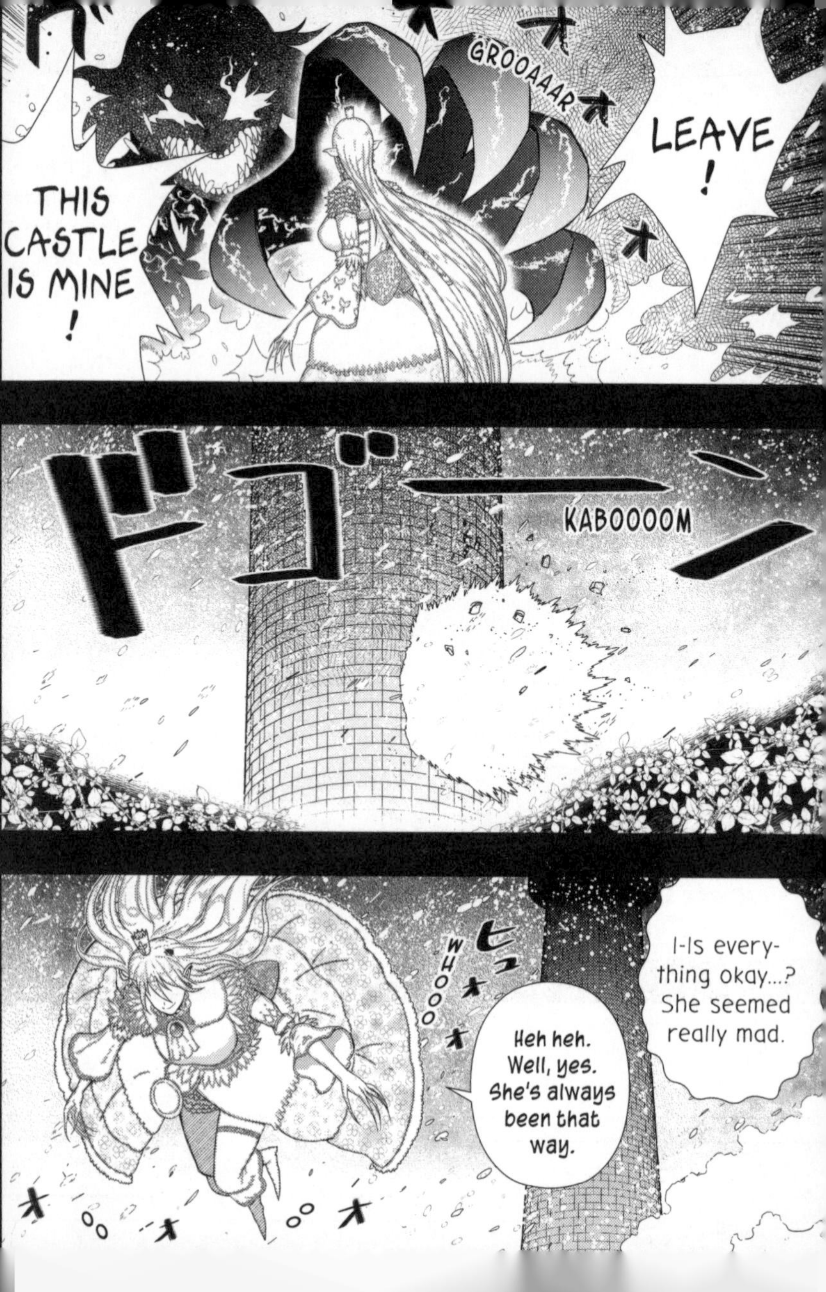
LEAVE!
GROOAAAR
THIS CASTLE IS MINE!
ドゴーン
KABOOOOM
I-Is everything okay...? She seemed really mad.
WHOOOO
Heh heh. Well, yes. She's always been that way.

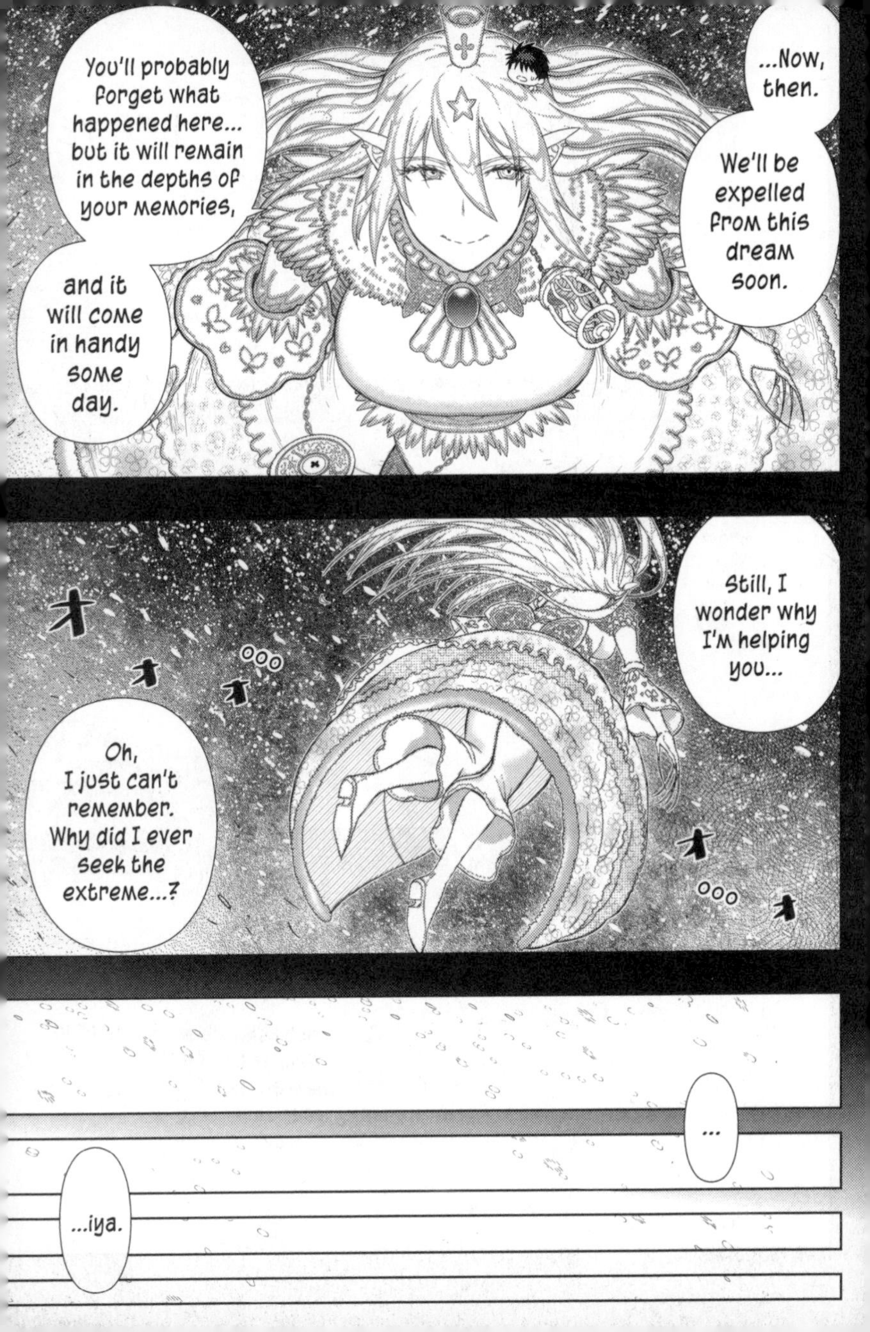
...Now, then.
We'll be expelled from this dream soon.
You'll probably forget what happened here... but it will remain in the depths of your memories,
and it will come in handy some day.
Still, I wonder why I'm helping you...
ooo
ooo
Oh, I just can't remember. Why did I ever seek the extreme...?
...
...iya.

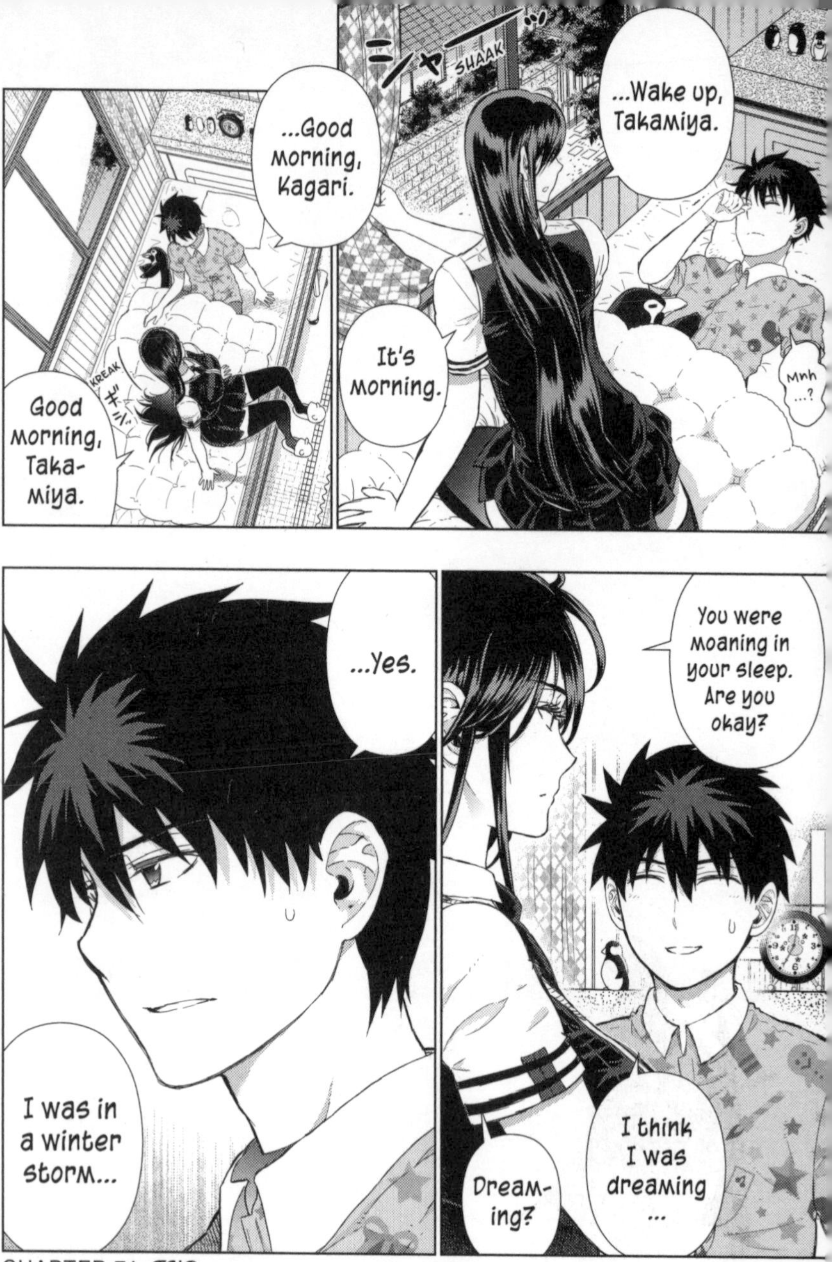
SHAAK
...Wake up, Takamiya.
Mnh ...?
It's morning.
...Good morning, Kagari.
KREAK
Good morning, Taka-miya.
You were moaning in your sleep. Are you okay?
I think I was dreaming ...
Dream-ing?
...Yes.
I was in a winter storm...

CHAPTER 74: *END*

Witchcraft Works

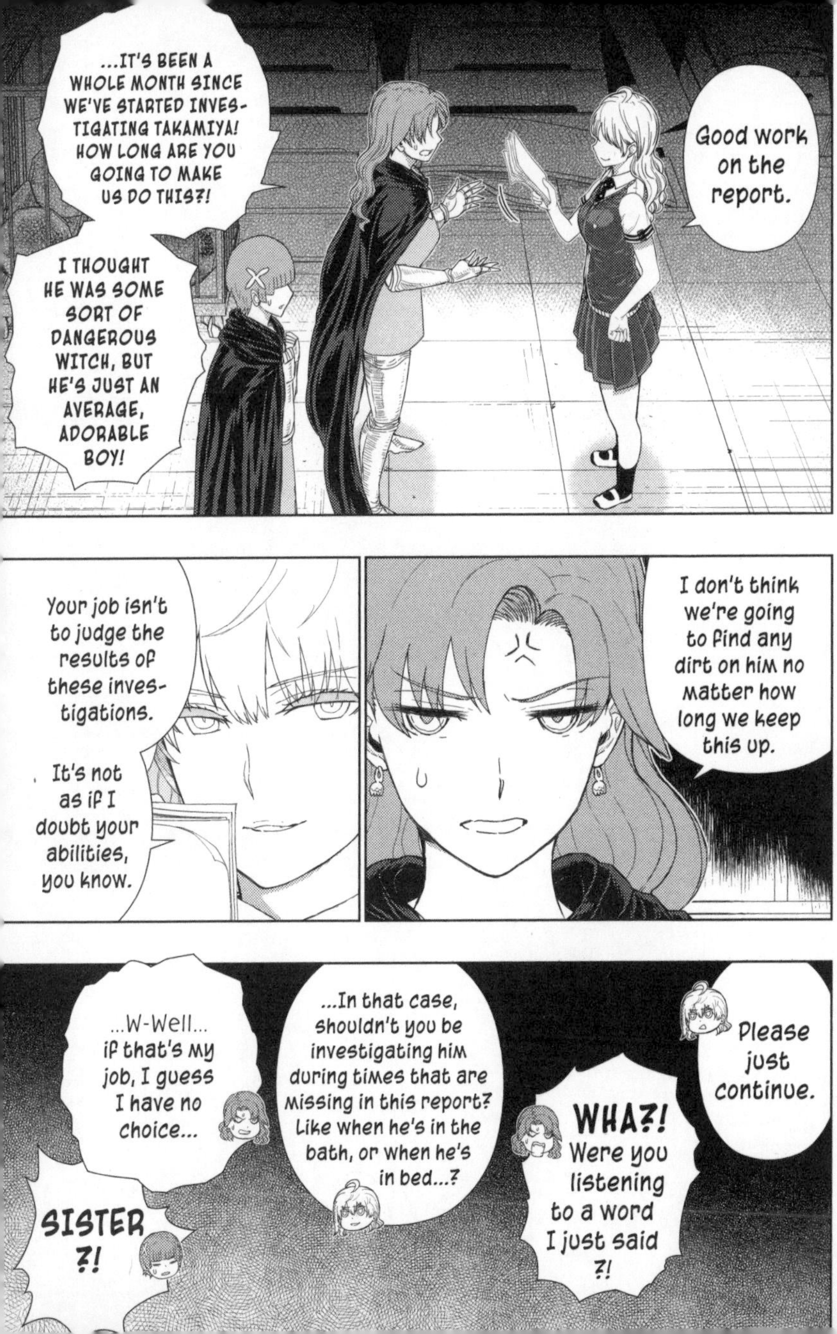
Good work on the report.
...IT'S BEEN A WHOLE MONTH SINCE WE'VE STARTED INVES-TIGATING TAKAMIYA! HOW LONG ARE YOU GOING TO MAKE US DO THIS?!
I THOUGHT HE WAS SOME SORT OF DANGEROUS WITCH, BUT HE'S JUST AN AVERAGE, ADORABLE BOY!
I don't think we're going to find any dirt on him no matter how long we keep this up.
Your job isn't to judge the results of these inves-tigations.
It's not as if I doubt your abilities, you know.
Please just continue.
...In that case, shouldn't you be investigating him during times that are missing in this report? Like when he's in the bath, or when he's in bed...?
...W-Well... if that's my job, I guess I have no choice...
WHA?! Were you listening to a word I just said?!
SISTER?!

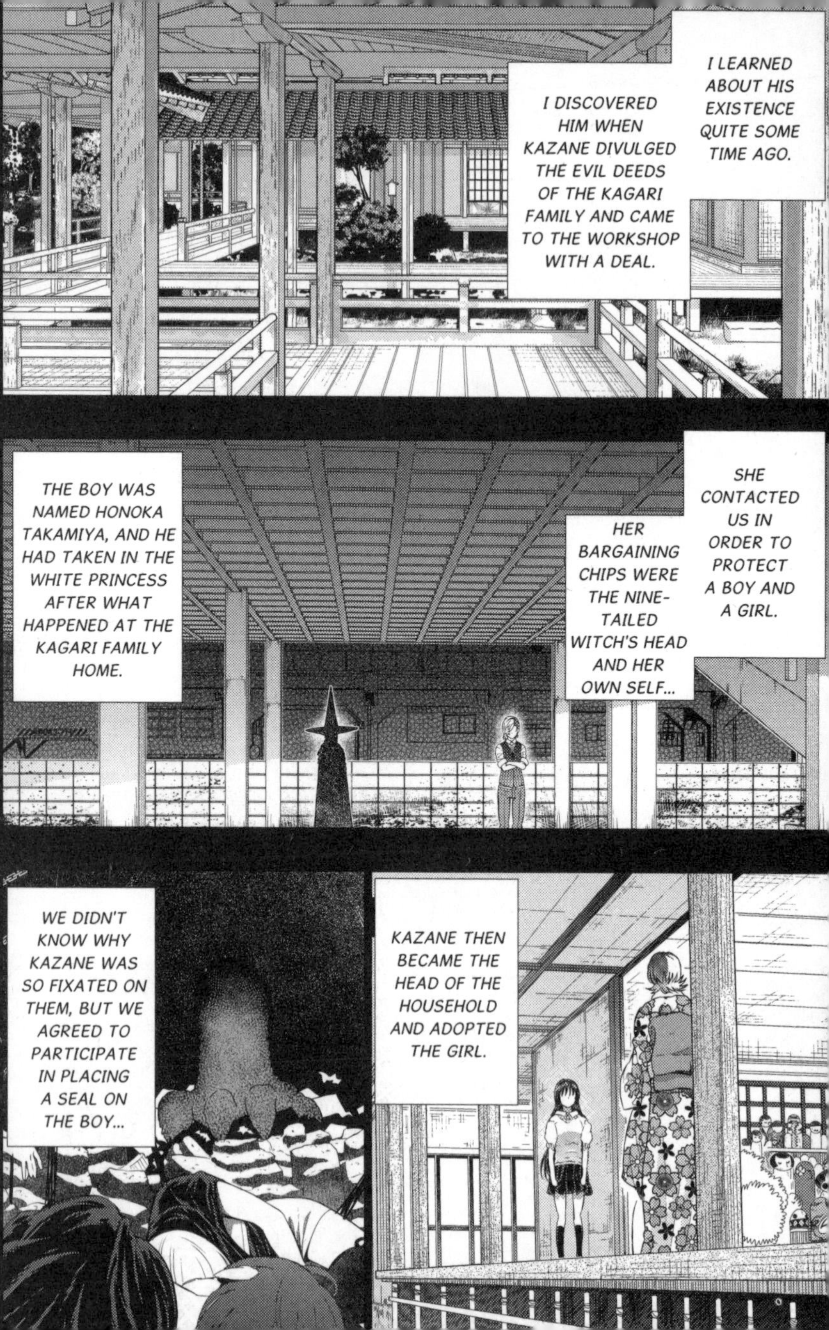
I LEARNED ABOUT HIS EXISTENCE QUITE SOME TIME AGO.
I DISCOVERED HIM WHEN KAZANE DIVULGED THE EVIL DEEDS OF THE KAGARI FAMILY AND CAME TO THE WORKSHOP WITH A DEAL.
SHE CONTACTED US IN ORDER TO PROTECT A BOY AND A GIRL.
HER BARGAINING CHIPS WERE THE NINE-TAILED WITCH'S HEAD AND HER OWN SELF...
THE BOY WAS NAMED HONOKA TAKAMIYA, AND HE HAD TAKEN IN THE WHITE PRINCESS AFTER WHAT HAPPENED AT THE KAGARI FAMILY HOME.
KAZANE THEN BECAME THE HEAD OF THE HOUSEHOLD AND ADOPTED THE GIRL.
WE DIDN'T KNOW WHY KAZANE WAS SO FIXATED ON THEM, BUT WE AGREED TO PARTICIPATE IN PLACING A SEAL ON THE BOY...

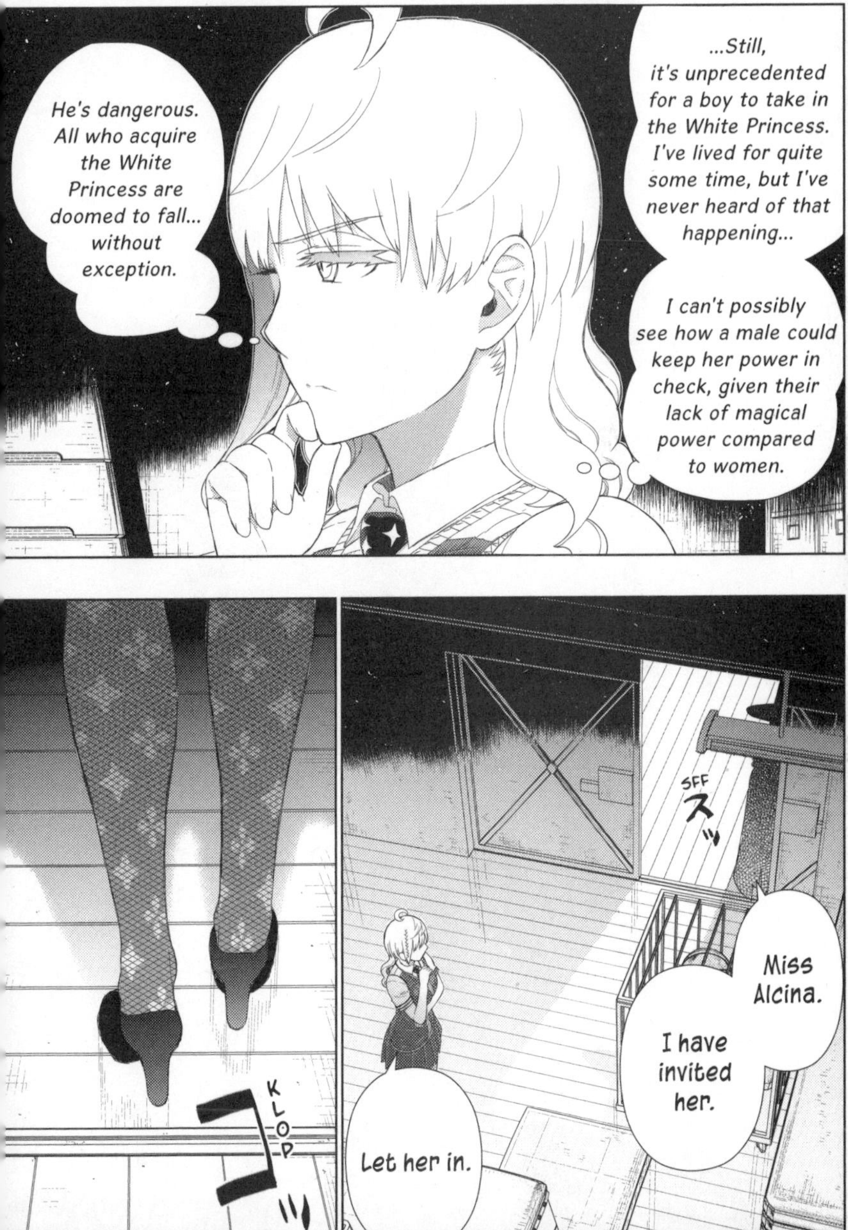
...Still, it's unprecedented for a boy to take in the White Princess. I've lived for quite some time, but I've never heard of that happening...
I can't possibly see how a male could keep her power in check, given their lack of magical power compared to women.
He's dangerous. All who acquire the White Princess are doomed to fall... without exception.
SFF
Miss Alcina.
I have invited her.
Let her in.
KLOP

CHAPTER 75 Takamiya and the Winter Storm's Test

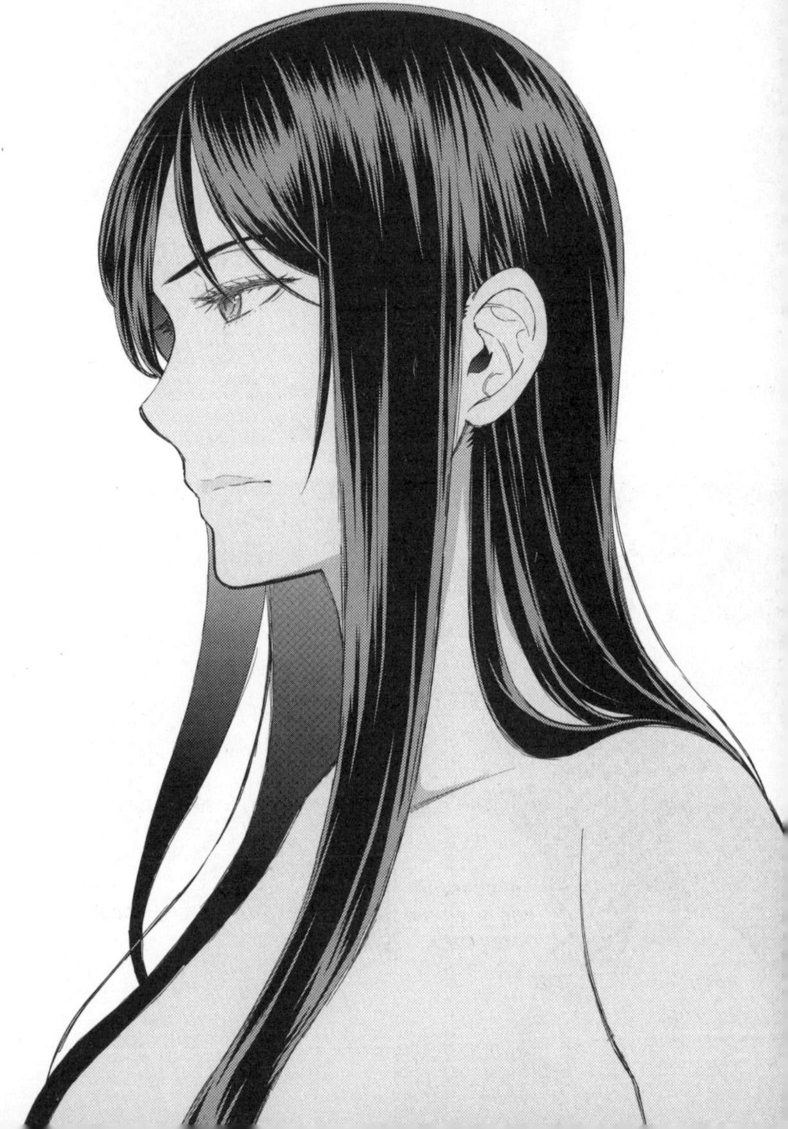

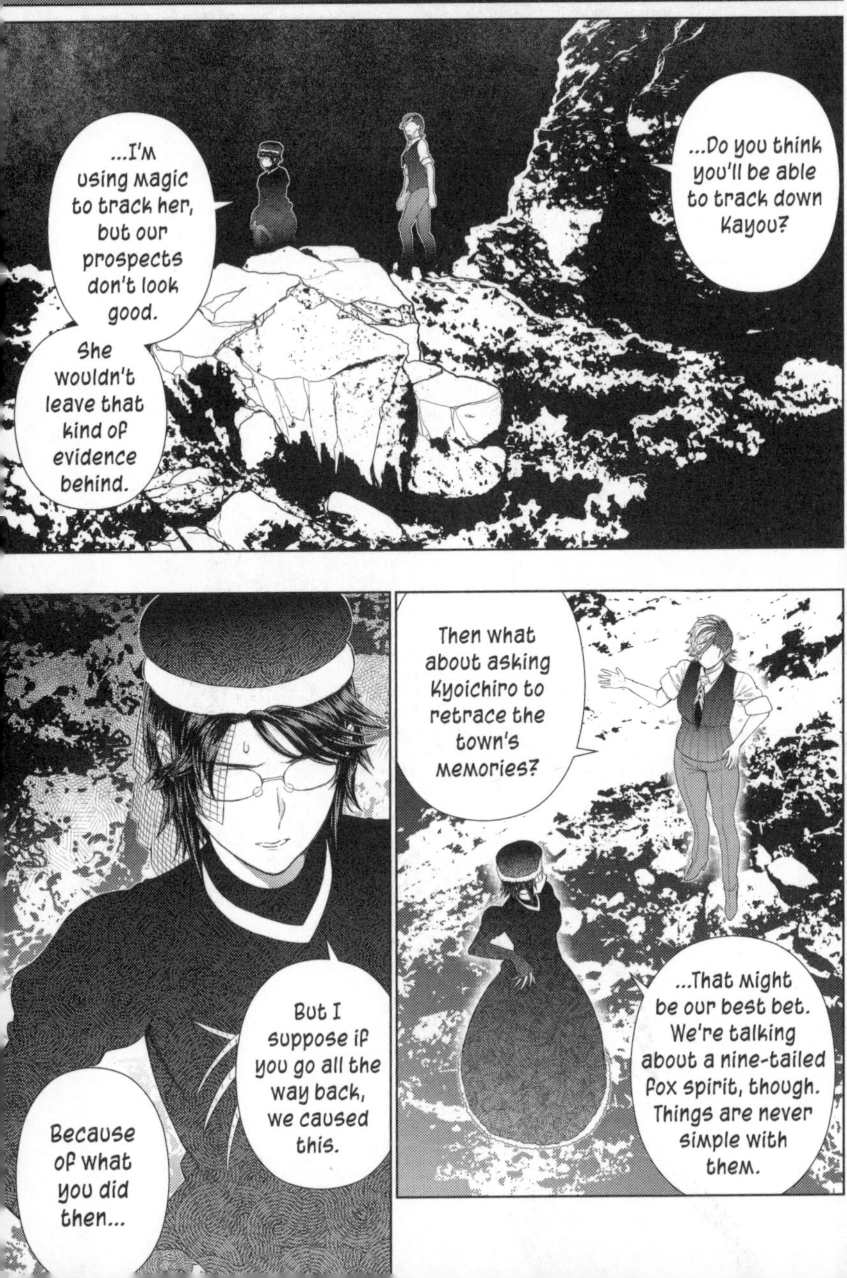
...Do you think you'll be able to track down Kayou?
...I'm using magic to track her, but our prospects don't look good.
She wouldn't leave that kind of evidence behind.
Then what about asking Kyoichiro to retrace the town's memories?
...That might be our best bet. We're talking about a nine-tailed fox spirit, though. Things are never simple with them.
But I suppose if you go all the way back, we caused this.
Because of what you did then...

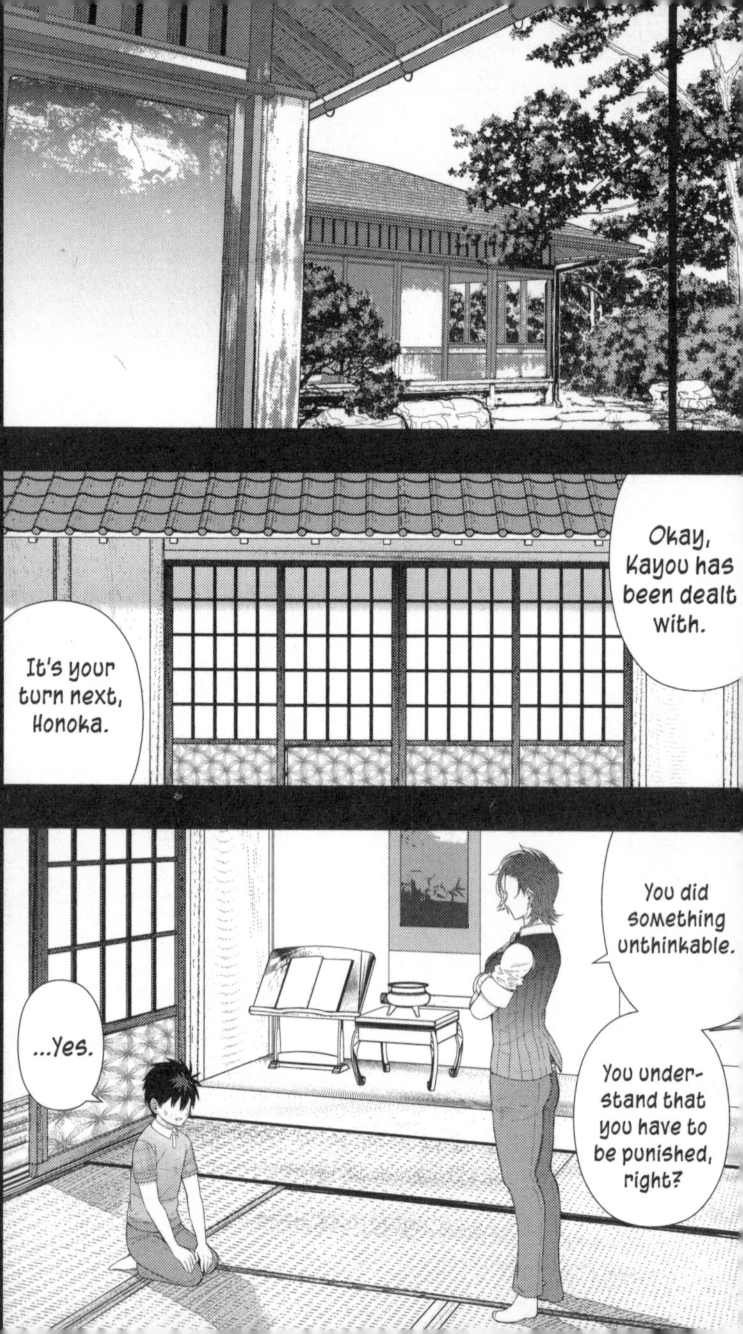
Okay, Kayou has been dealt with.
It's your turn next, Honoka.
You did something unthinkable.
You under-stand that you have to be punished, right?
...Yes.

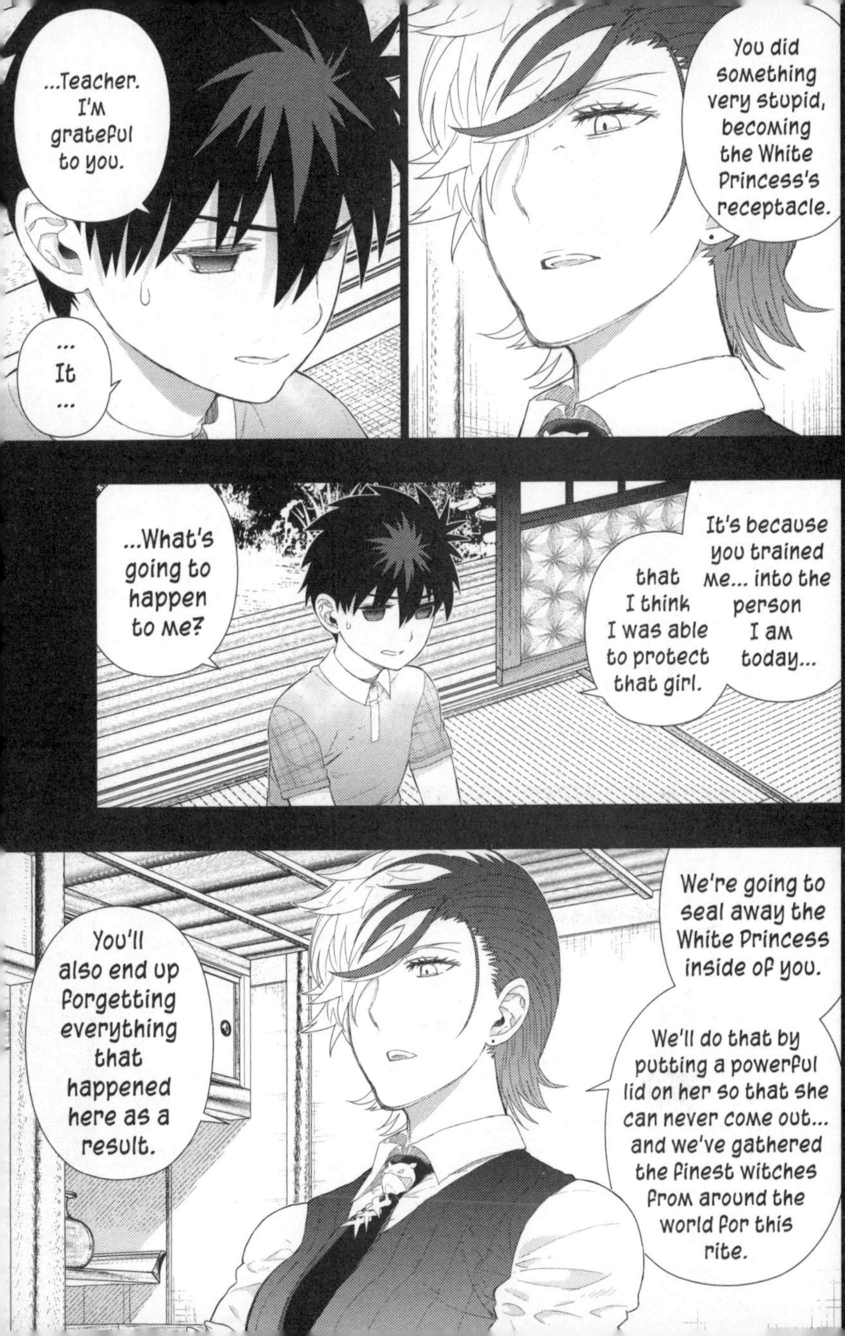

You did something very stupid, becoming the White Princess's receptacle.
...Teacher. I'm grateful to you.
... It ...
It's because you trained me... into the person I am today...
that I think I was able to protect that girl.
...What's going to happen to me?
We're going to seal away the White Princess inside of you.
We'll do that by putting a powerful lid on her so that she can never come out... and we've gathered the finest witches from around the world for this rite.
You'll also end up forgetting everything that happened here as a result.

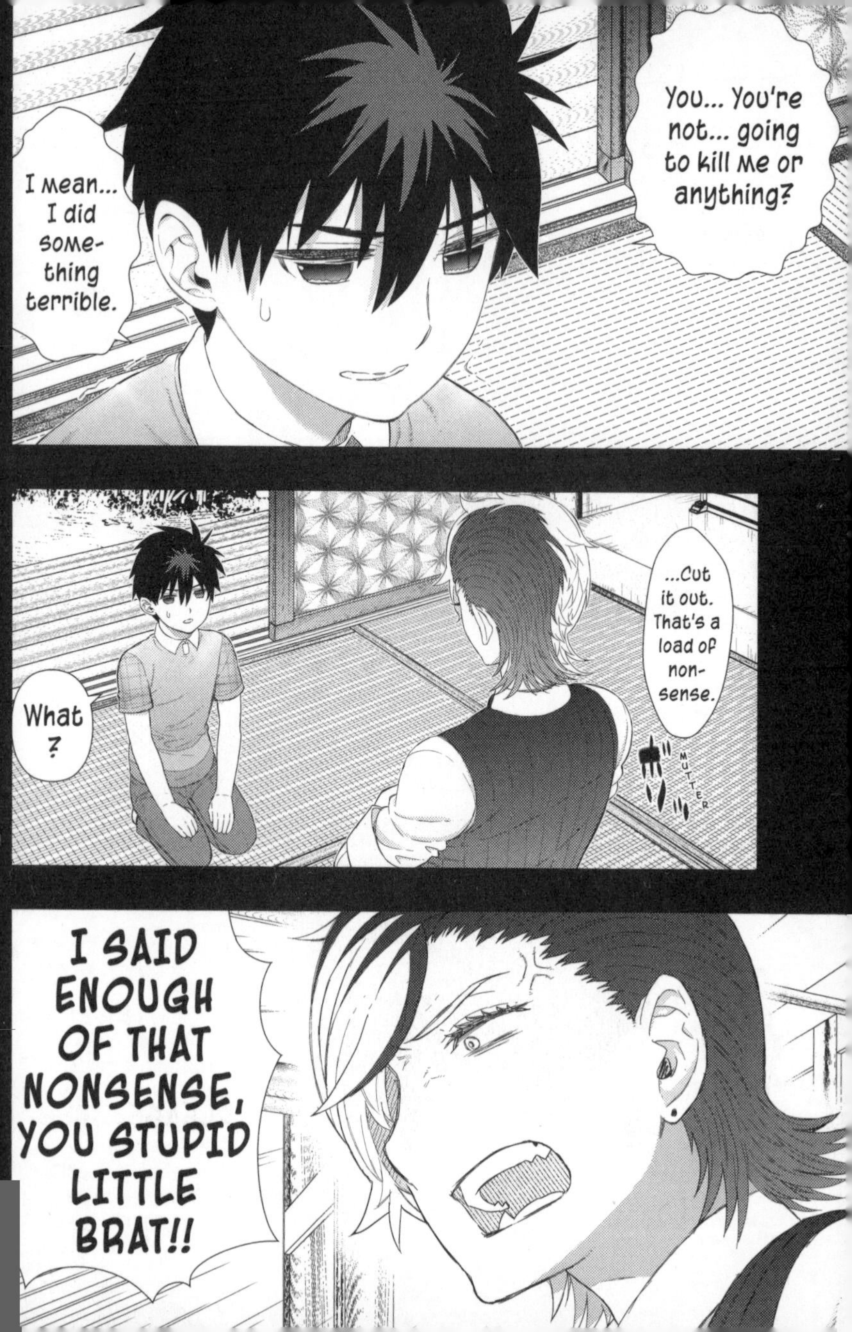
You... You're not... going to kill me or anything?
I mean... I did some-thing terrible.
...Cut it out. That's a load of non-sense.
MUTTER
What?
I SAID ENOUGH OF THAT NONSENSE, YOU STUPID LITTLE BRAT!!

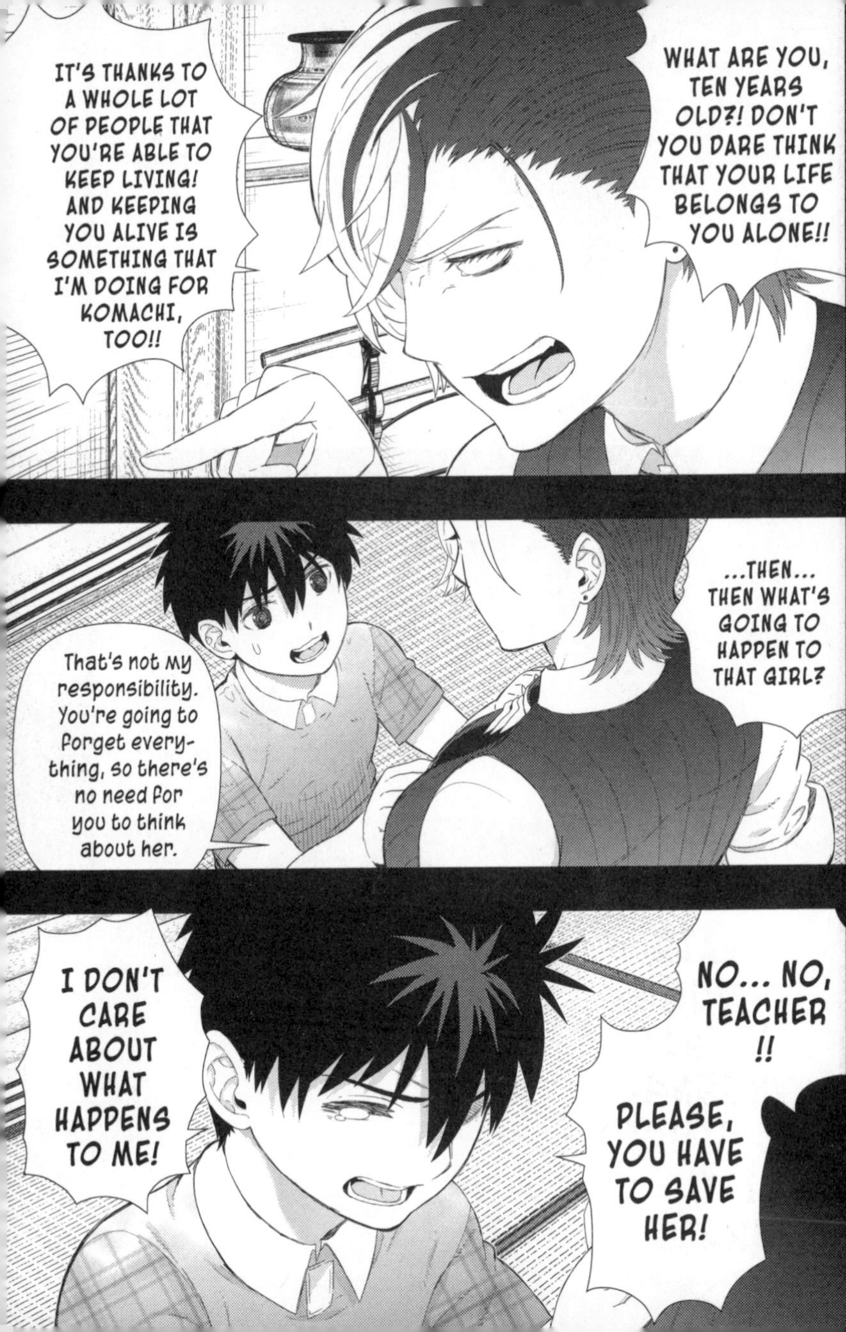
WHAT ARE YOU, TEN YEARS OLD?! DON'T YOU DARE THINK THAT YOUR LIFE BELONGS TO YOU ALONE!!
IT'S THANKS TO A WHOLE LOT OF PEOPLE THAT YOU'RE ABLE TO KEEP LIVING! AND KEEPING YOU ALIVE IS SOMETHING THAT I'M DOING FOR KOMACHI, TOO!!
...THEN... THEN WHAT'S GOING TO HAPPEN TO THAT GIRL?
That's not my responsibility. You're going to forget every-thing, so there's no need for you to think about her.
NO... NO, TEACHER !!
I DON'T CARE ABOUT WHAT HAPPENS TO ME!
PLEASE, YOU HAVE TO SAVE HER!

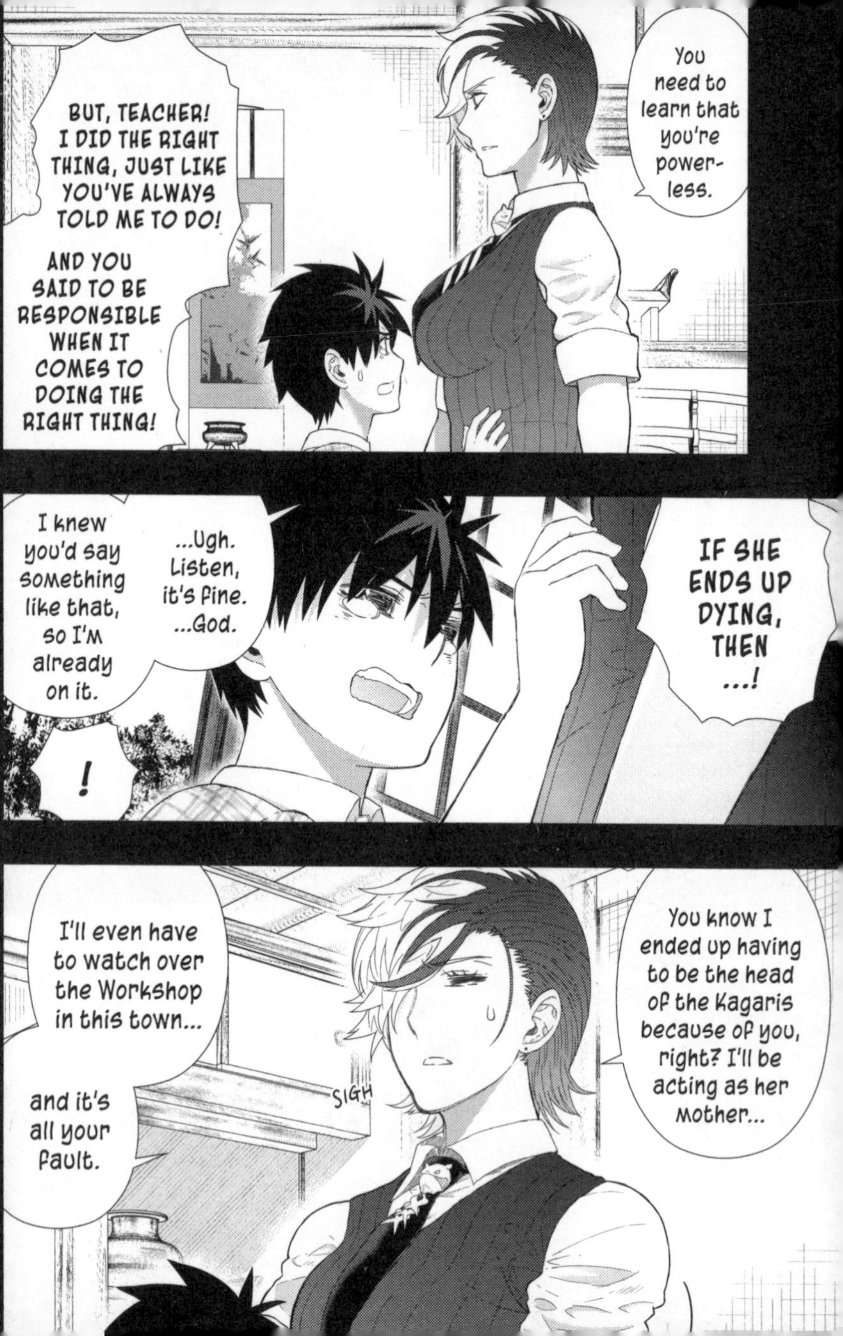
You need to learn that you're power-less.
BUT, TEACHER! I DID THE RIGHT THING, JUST LIKE YOU'VE ALWAYS TOLD ME TO DO!
AND YOU SAID TO BE RESPONSIBLE WHEN IT COMES TO DOING THE RIGHT THING!
IF SHE ENDS UP DYING, THEN ...!
...Ugh. Listen, it's fine. ...God.
I knew you'd say something like that, so I'm already on it.
!
You know I ended up having to be the head of the Kagaris because of you, right? I'll be acting as her mother...
SIGH
I'll even have to watch over the Workshop in this town...
and it's all your fault.

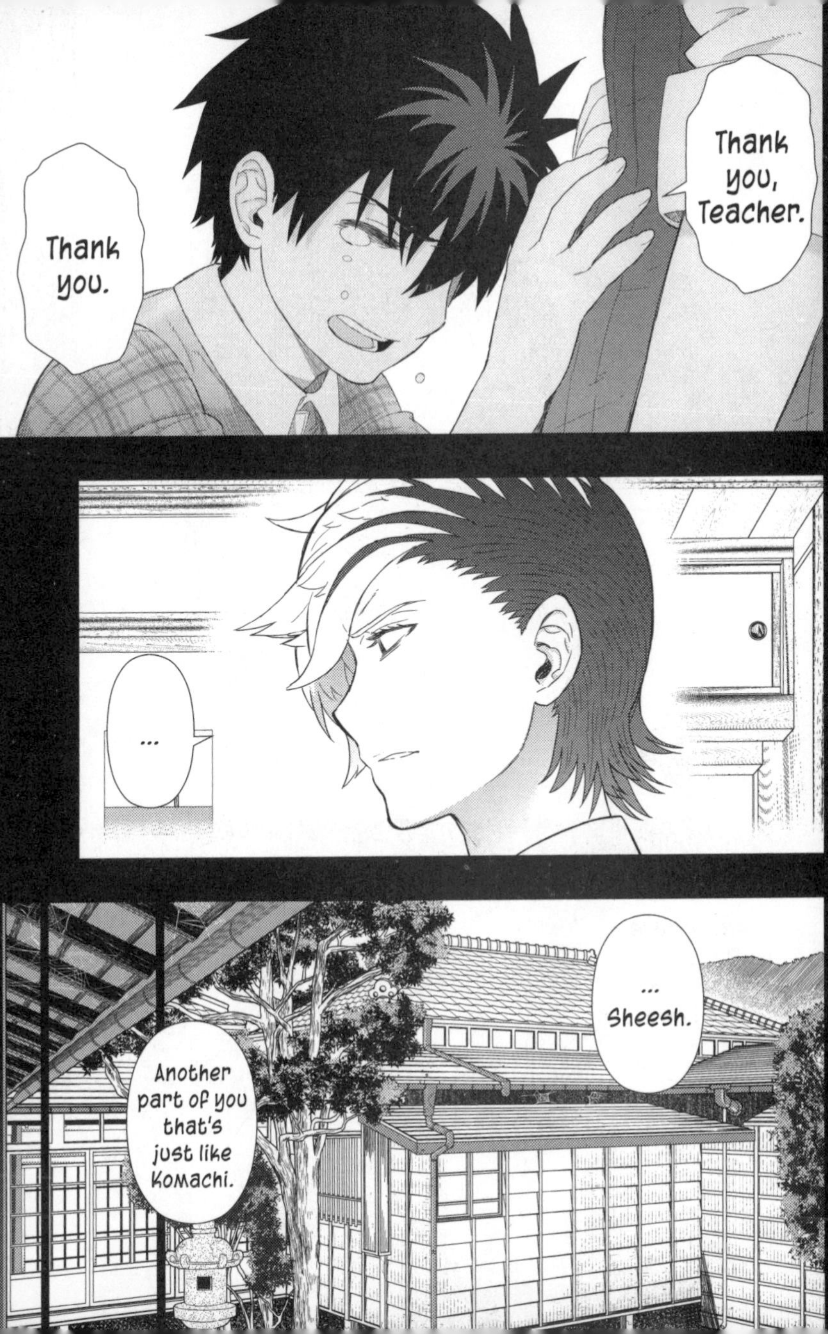
Thank you, Teacher.
Thank you.
...
... Sheesh.
Another part of you that's just like Komachi.

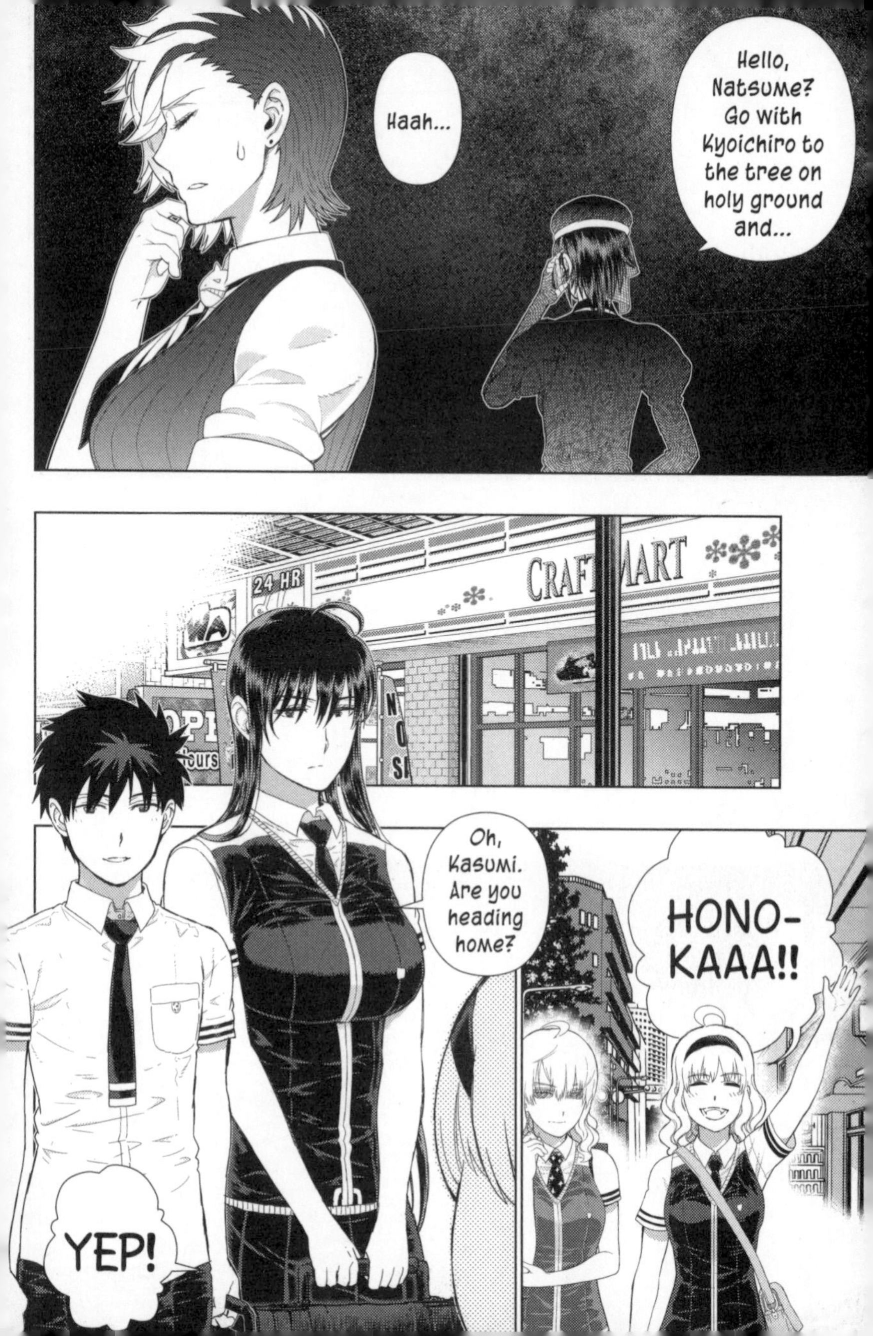
Hello, Natsume? Go with Kyoichiro to the tree on holy ground and...
Haah...
CRAFT MART
24 HR
HONO-KAAA!!
Oh, Kasumi. Are you heading home?
YEP!

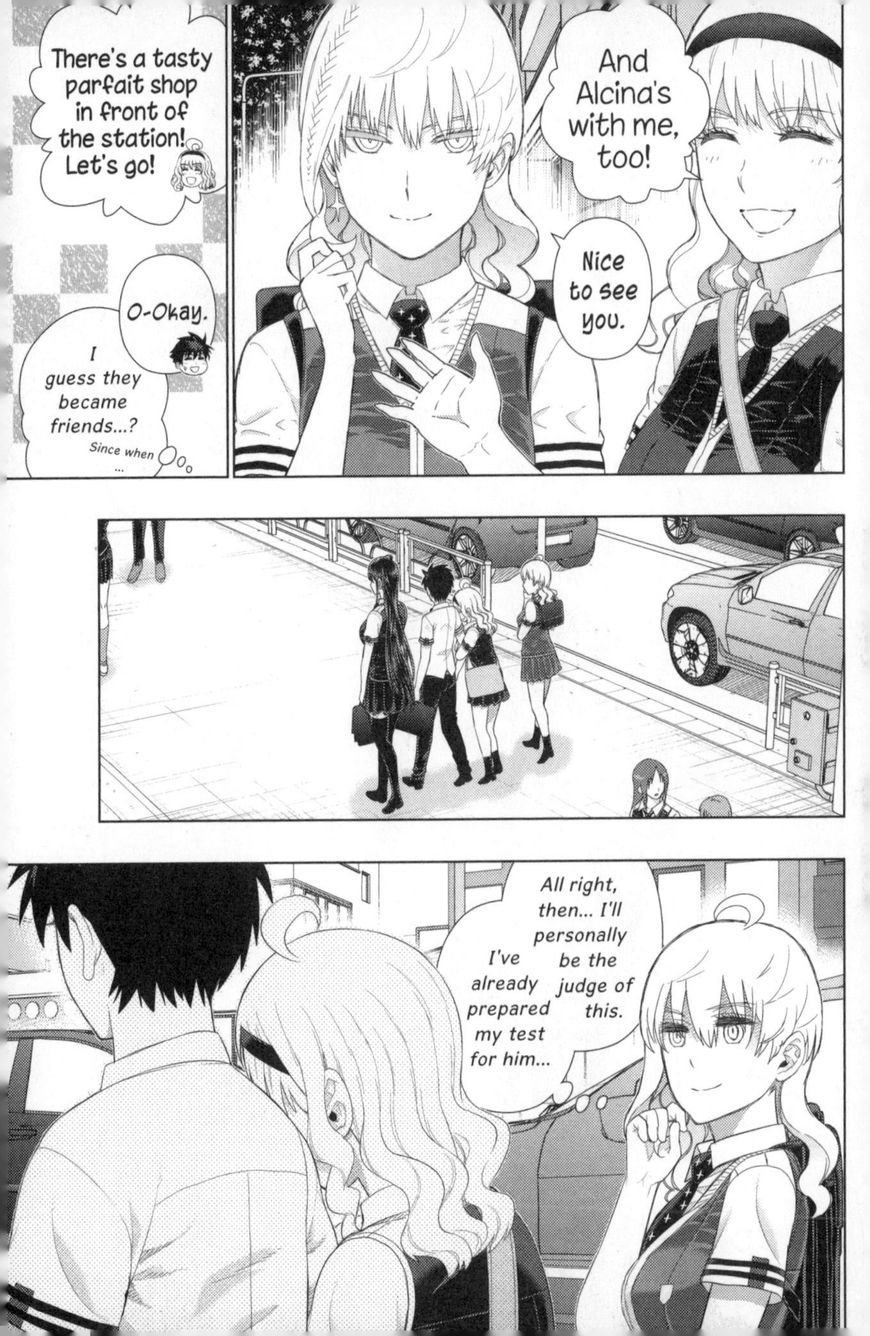

And Alcina's with me, too!
Nice to see you.
There's a tasty parfait shop in front of the station! Let's go!
O-Okay.
I guess they became friends...?
Since when ...
All right, then... I'll personally be the judge of this.
I've already prepared my test for him...

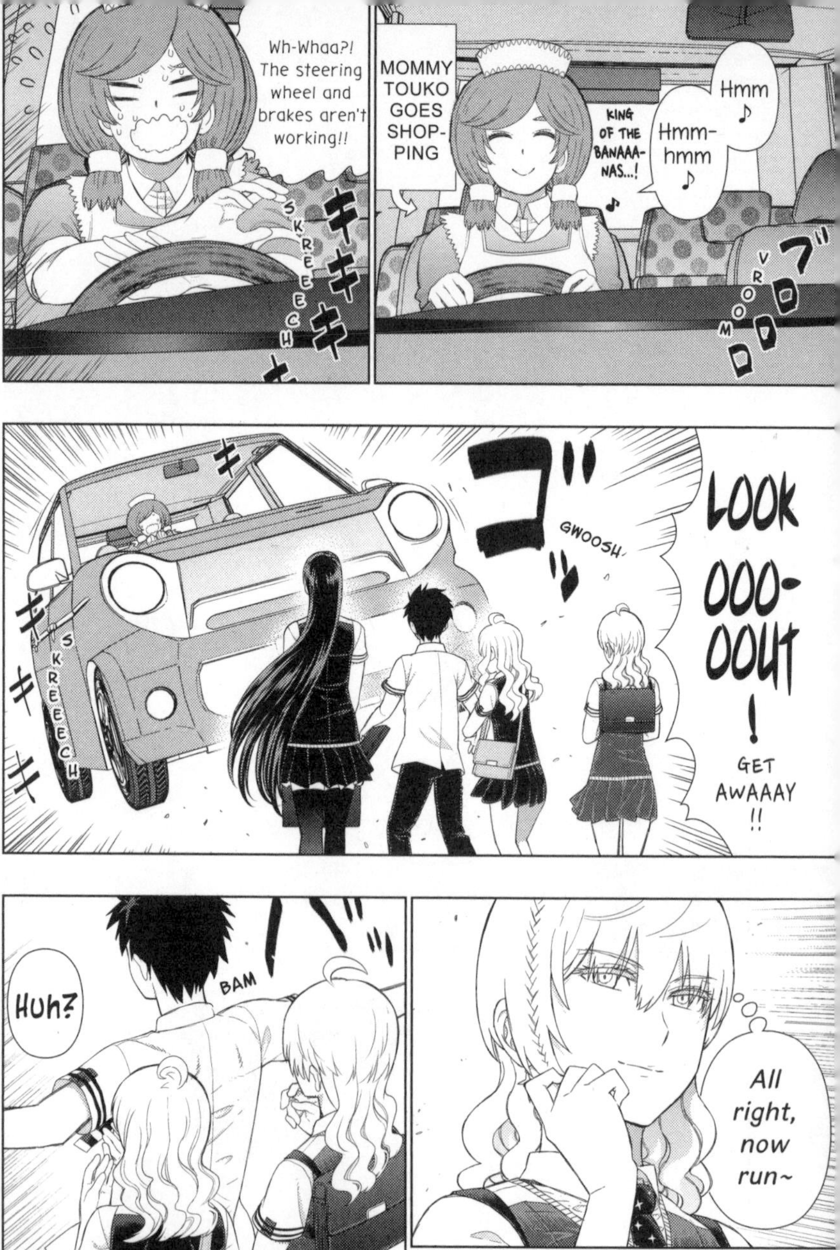

Hmm ♪
Hmm-hmm ♪
KING OF THE BANAAAA-NAS...!
MOMMY TOUKO GOES SHOP-PING
VROOM
Wh-Whaa?! The steering wheel and brakes aren't working!!
SKREEECH
LOOK OOOOOUT!
GET AWAAAY!!
GWOOSH
SKREEECH
All right, now run~
BAM
HUH?

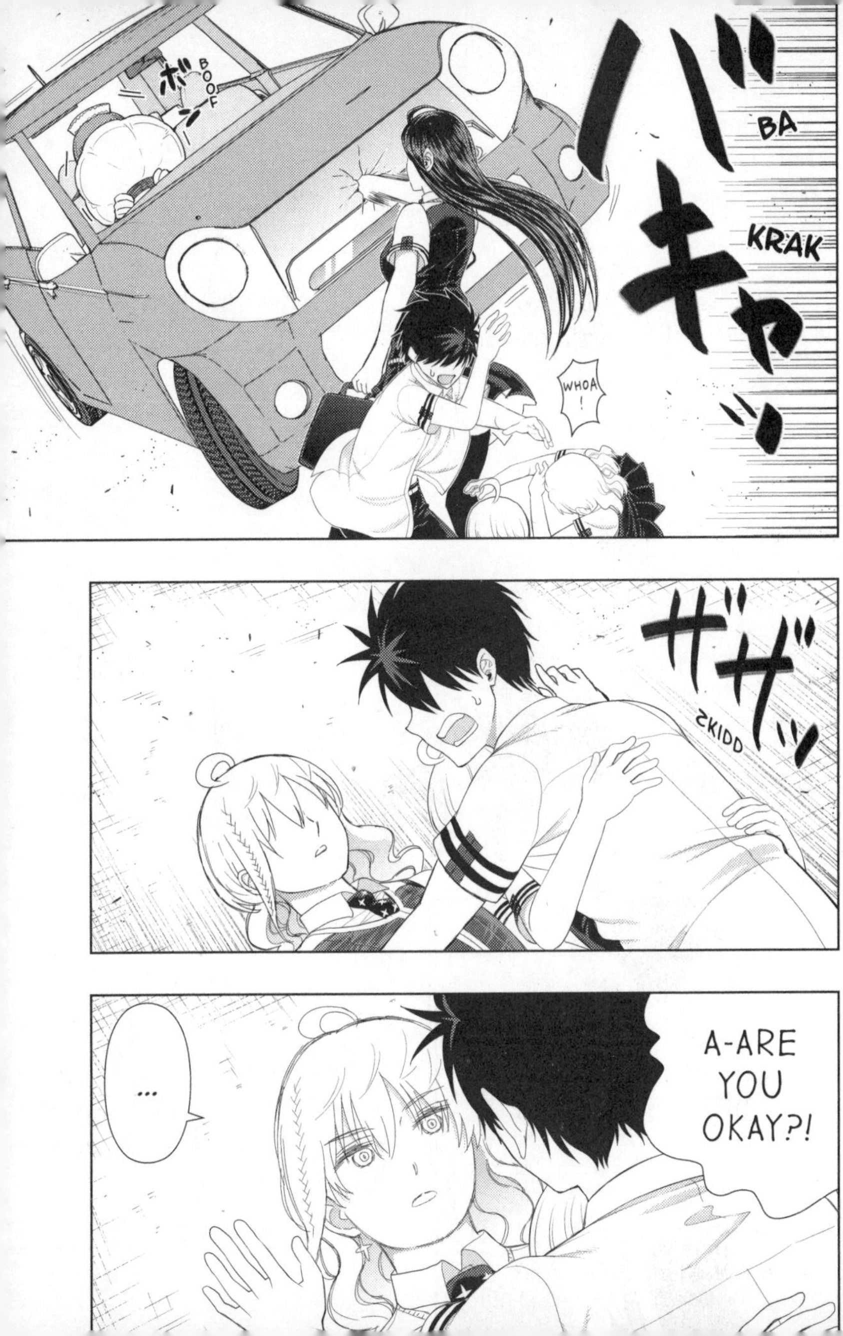
バキャッ
BA
KRAK
BOOF
WHOA!
ザザッ
ZKIDD
A-ARE YOU OKAY?!
...

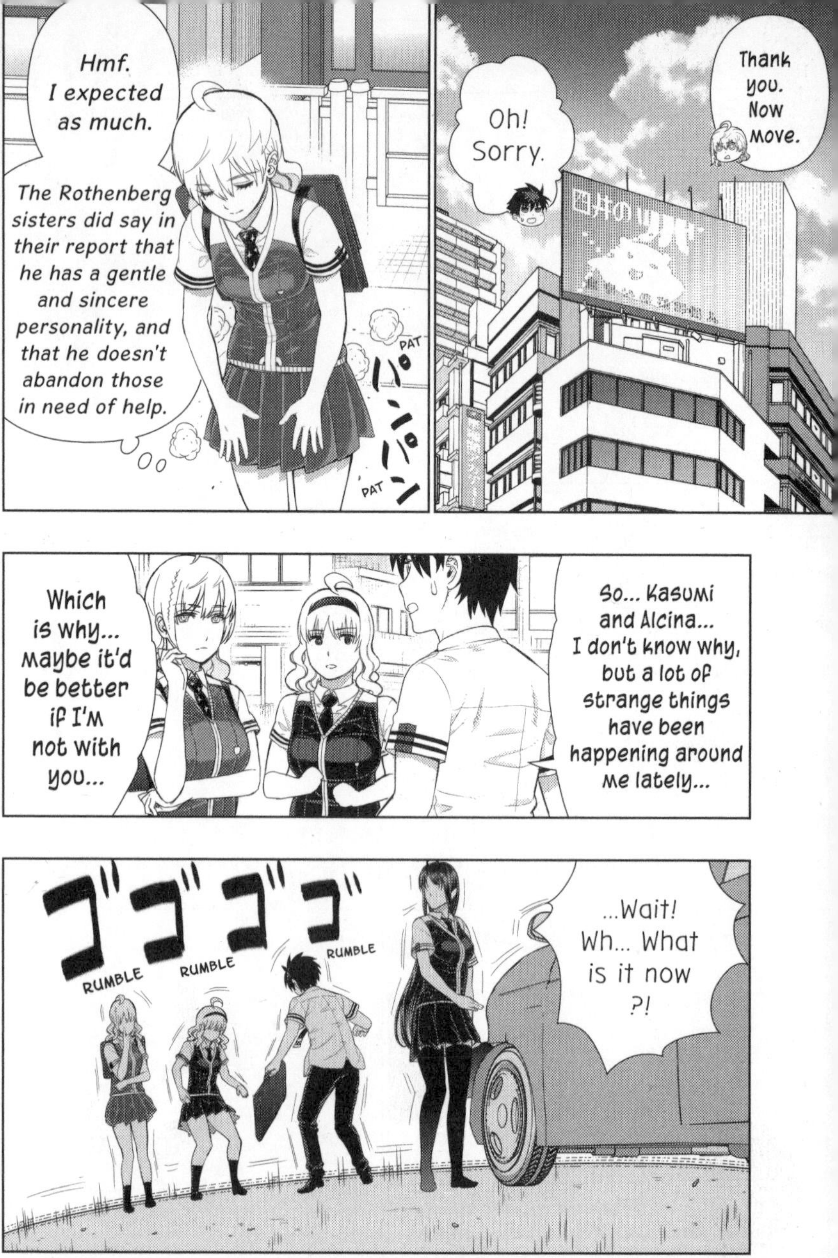
Thank you. Now move.
Oh! Sorry.
Hmf. I expected as much.
The Rothenberg sisters did say in their report that he has a gentle and sincere personality, and that he doesn't abandon those in need of help.
パンパン
PAT
PAT
So... Kasumi and Alcina... I don't know why, but a lot of strange things have been happening around me lately...
Which is why... maybe it'd be better if I'm not with you...
...Wait! Wh... What is it now ?!
ゴゴゴゴ
RUMBLE
RUMBLE
RUMBLE

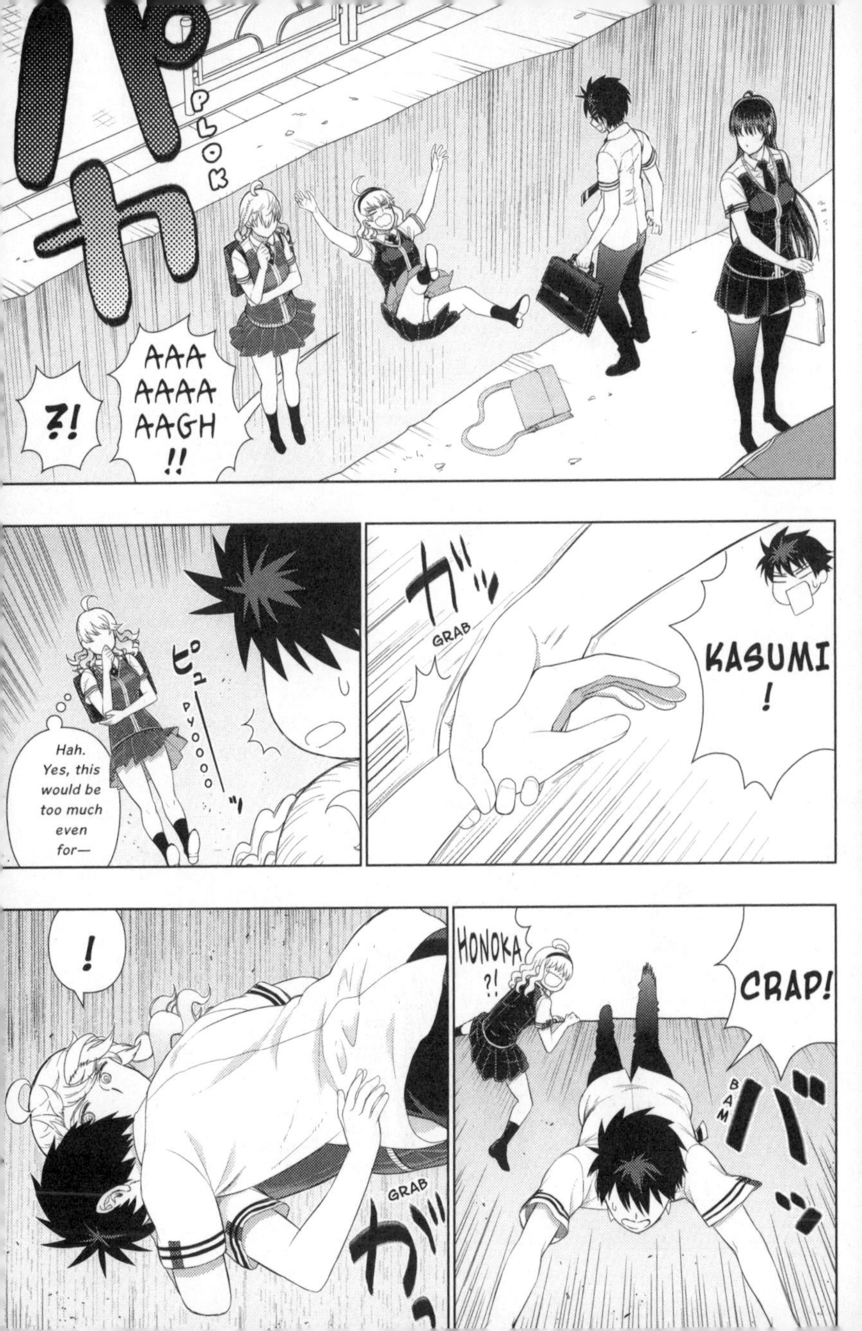
パッ
PLOK
AAA AAAA AAGH !!
?!
KASUMI !
ガッ
GRAB
ピュ
PYOOOOO
Hah. Yes, this would be too much even for—
CRAP!
HONOKA ?!
バッ
BAM
!
ガッ
GRAB

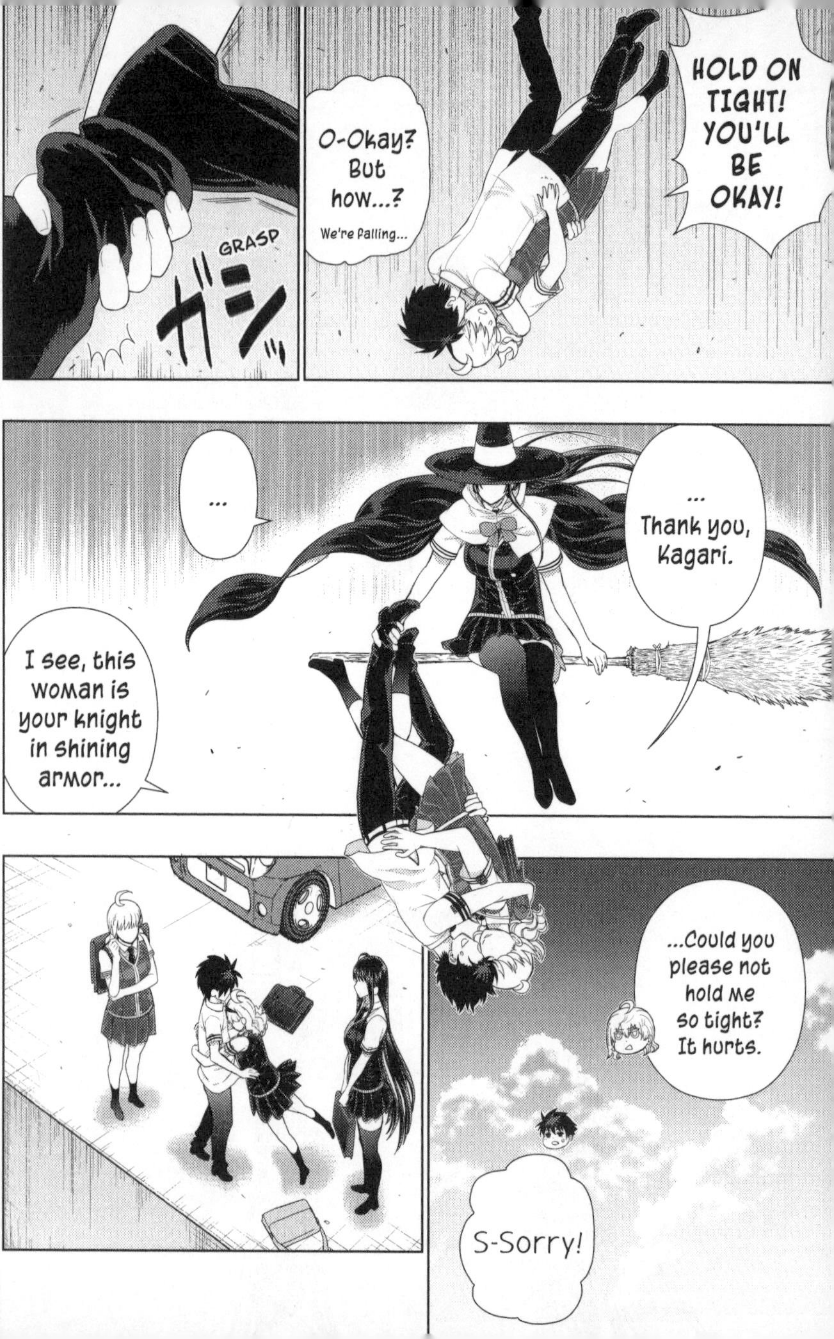
HOLD ON TIGHT! YOU'LL BE OKAY!
O-Okay? But how...?
We're falling...
GRASP
ガシ
...
Thank you, Kagari.
...
I see, this woman is your knight in shining armor...
...Could you please not hold me so tight? It hurts.
S-Sorry!

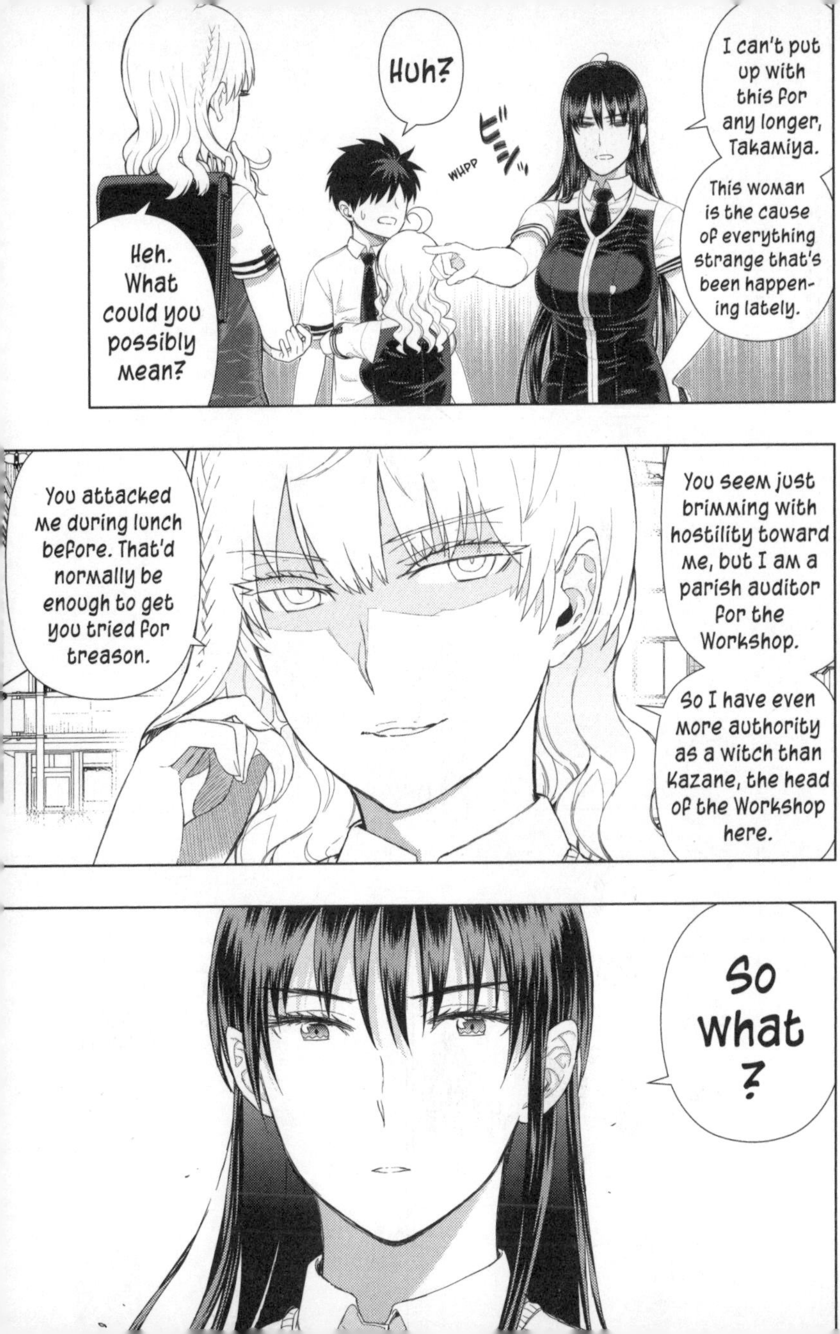
I can't put up with this for any longer, Takamiya.
This woman is the cause of everything strange that's been happening lately.
Huh?
WHPP
Heh. What could you possibly mean?
You seem just brimming with hostility toward me, but I am a parish auditor for the Workshop.
So I have even more authority as a witch than Kazane, the head of the Workshop here.
You attacked me during lunch before. That'd normally be enough to get you tried for treason.
So what?

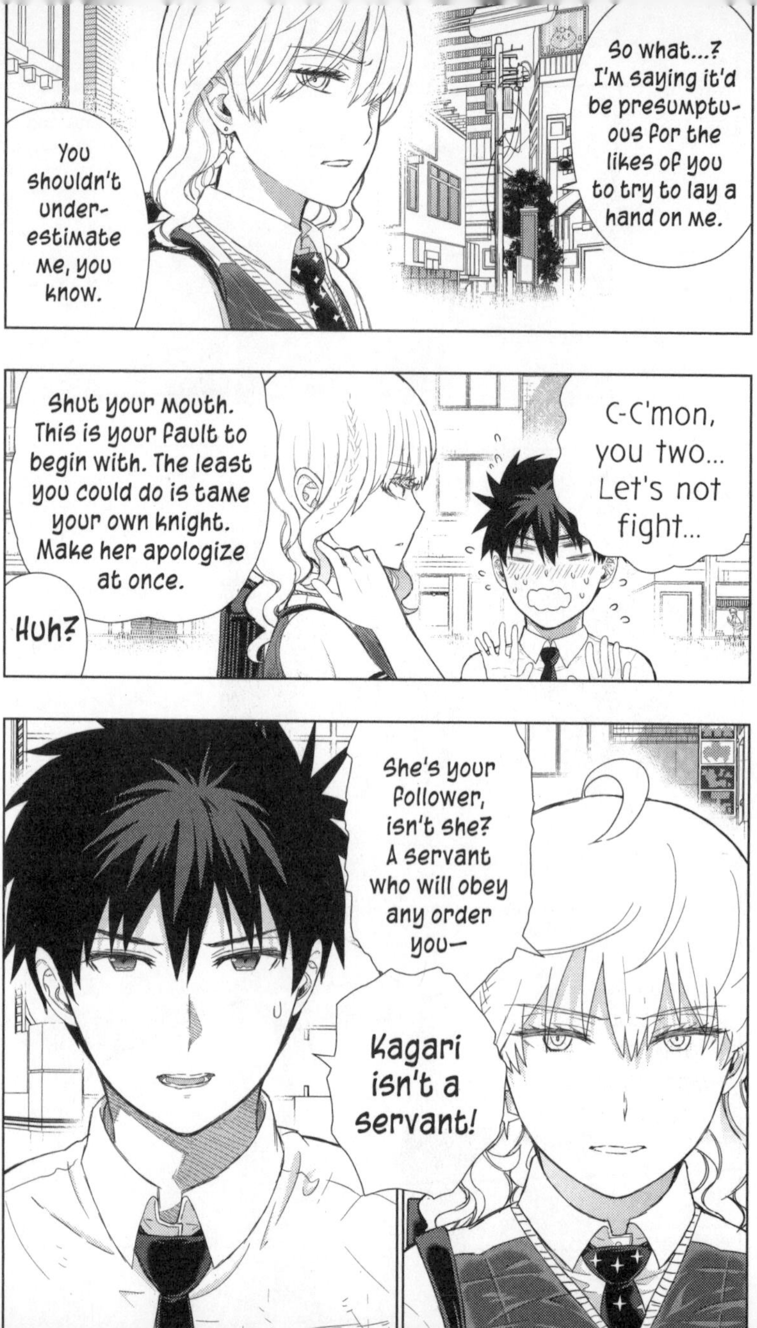
So what...? I'm saying it'd be presumptuous for the likes of you to try to lay a hand on me.
You shouldn't underestimate me, you know.
C-C'mon, you two... Let's not fight...
Shut your mouth. This is your fault to begin with. The least you could do is tame your own knight. Make her apologize at once.
Huh?
She's your follower, isn't she? A servant who will obey any order you—
Kagari isn't a servant!

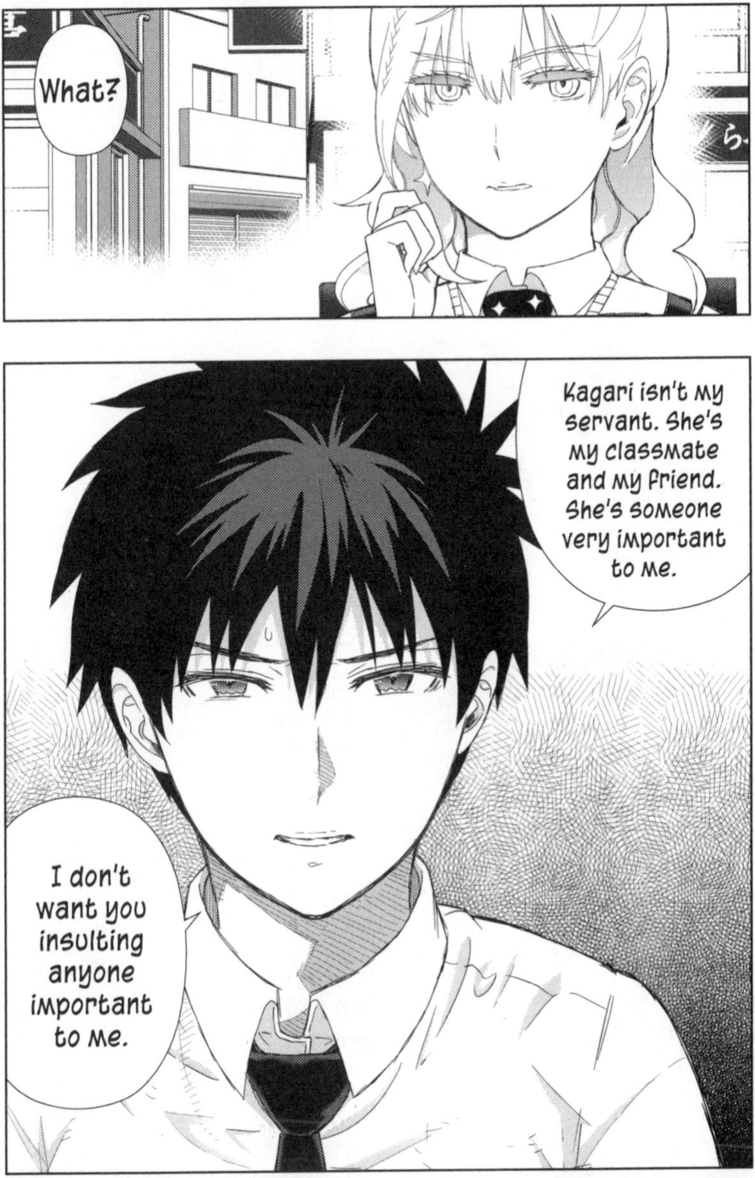
What?
Kagari isn't my servant. She's my classmate and my friend. She's someone very important to me.
I don't want you insulting anyone important to me.

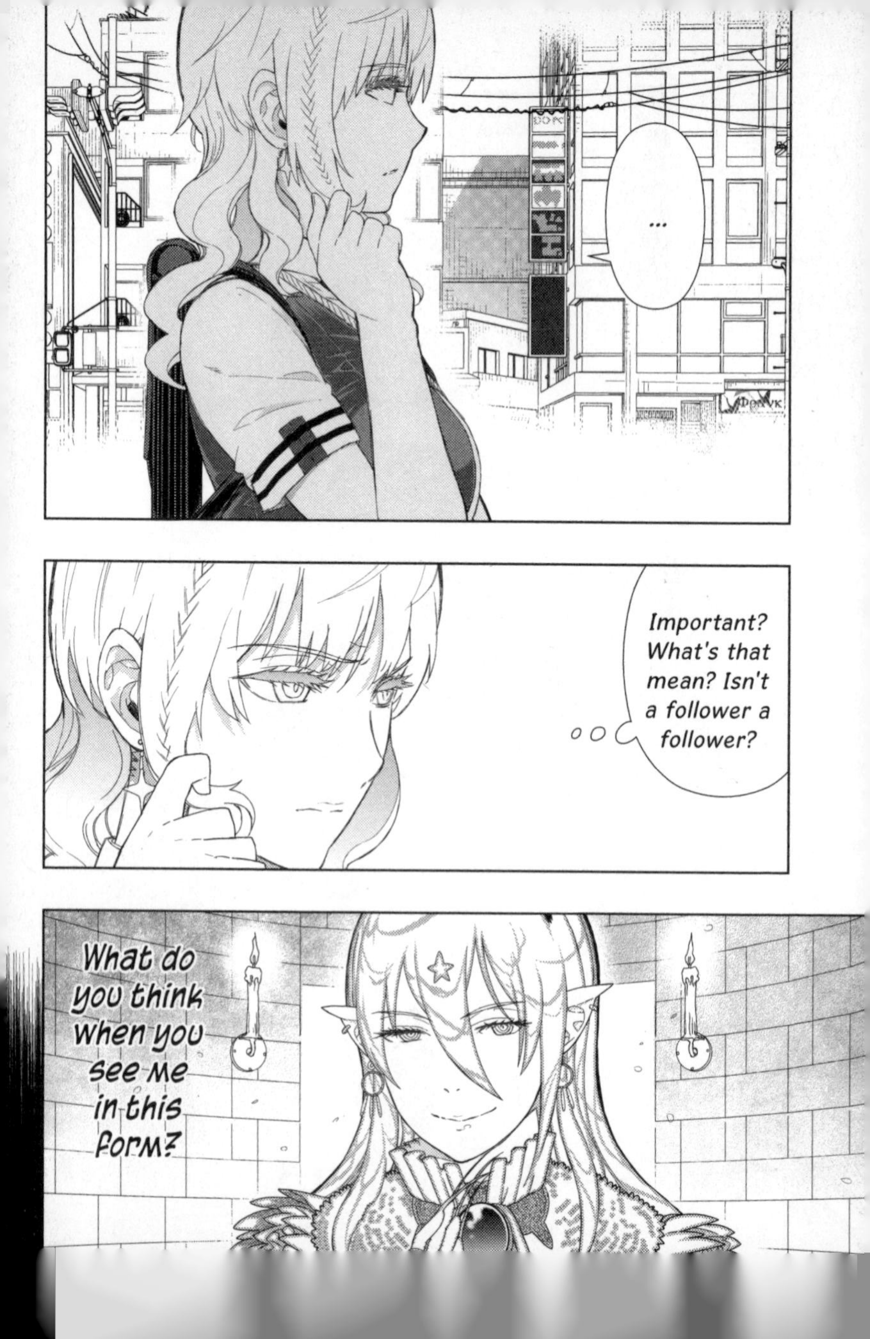
...
Important? What's that mean? Isn't a follower a follower?
What do you think when you see me in this form?

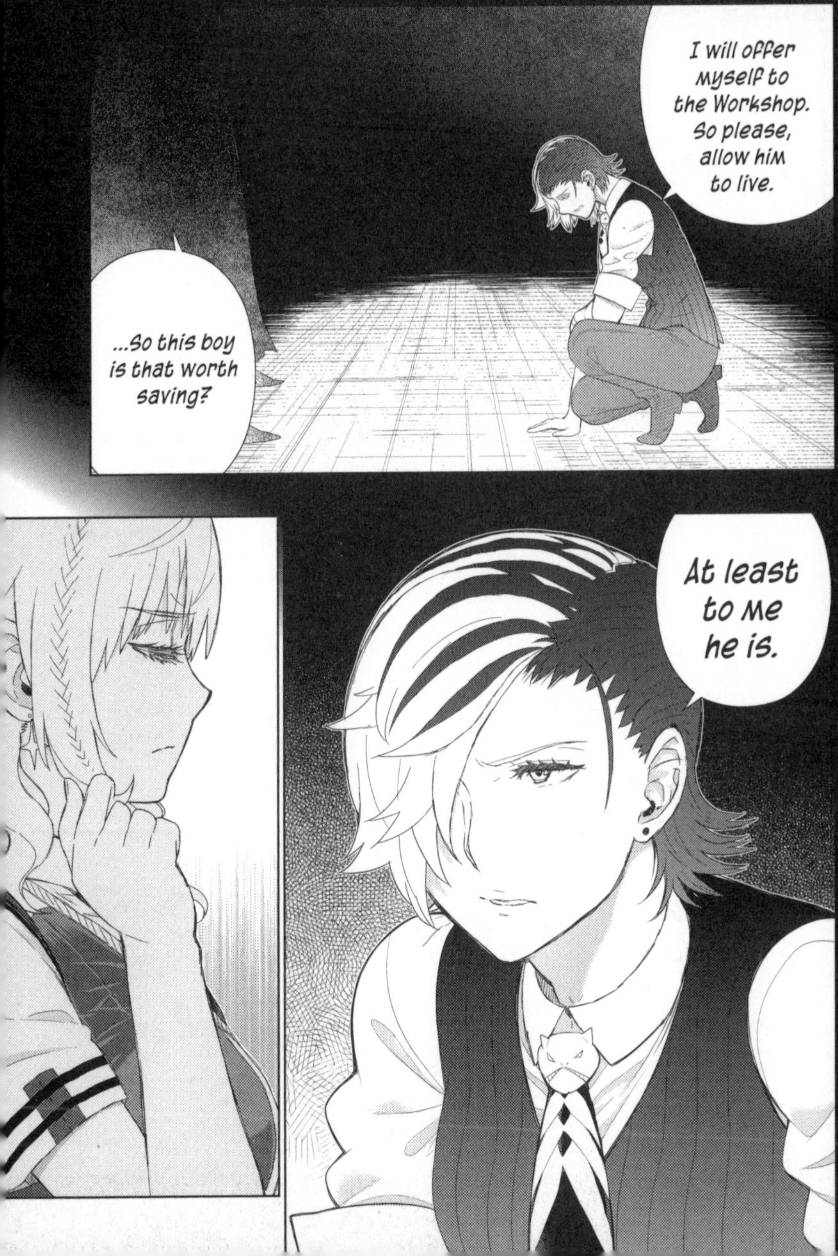
I will offer myself to the Workshop. So please, allow him to live.
...So this boy is that worth saving?
At least to me he is.

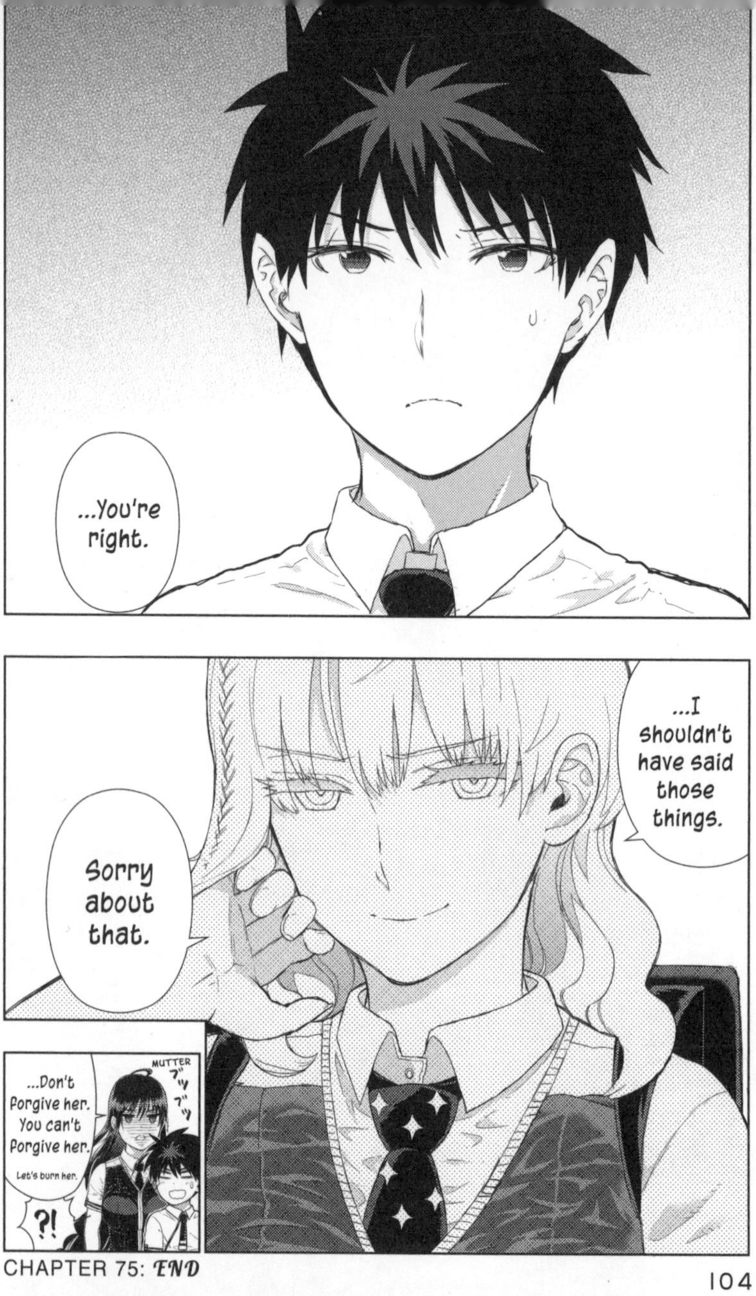
...You're right.
...I shouldn't have said those things.
Sorry about that.
MUTTER
ブツブツ
...Don't forgive her. You can't forgive her.
Let's burn her.
?!

CHAPTER 75: *END*

Witchcraft Works

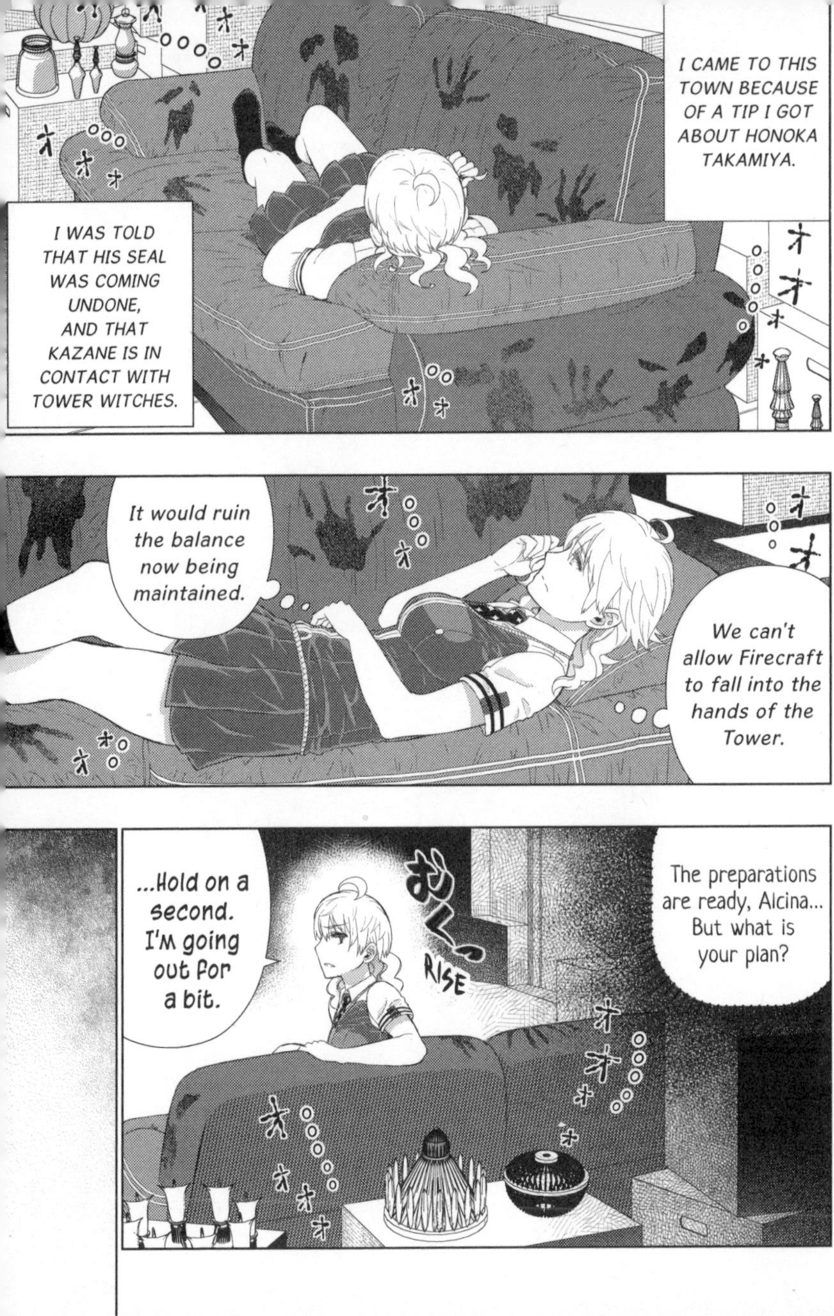
I CAME TO THIS TOWN BECAUSE OF A TIP I GOT ABOUT HONOKA TAKAMIYA.
I WAS TOLD THAT HIS SEAL WAS COMING UNDONE, AND THAT KAZANE IS IN CONTACT WITH TOWER WITCHES.
We can't allow Firecraft to fall into the hands of the Tower.
It would ruin the balance now being maintained.
The preparations are ready, Alcina... But what is your plan?
RISE
...Hold on a second. I'm going out for a bit.

CHAPTER 76 Takamiya and Alcina's Decision

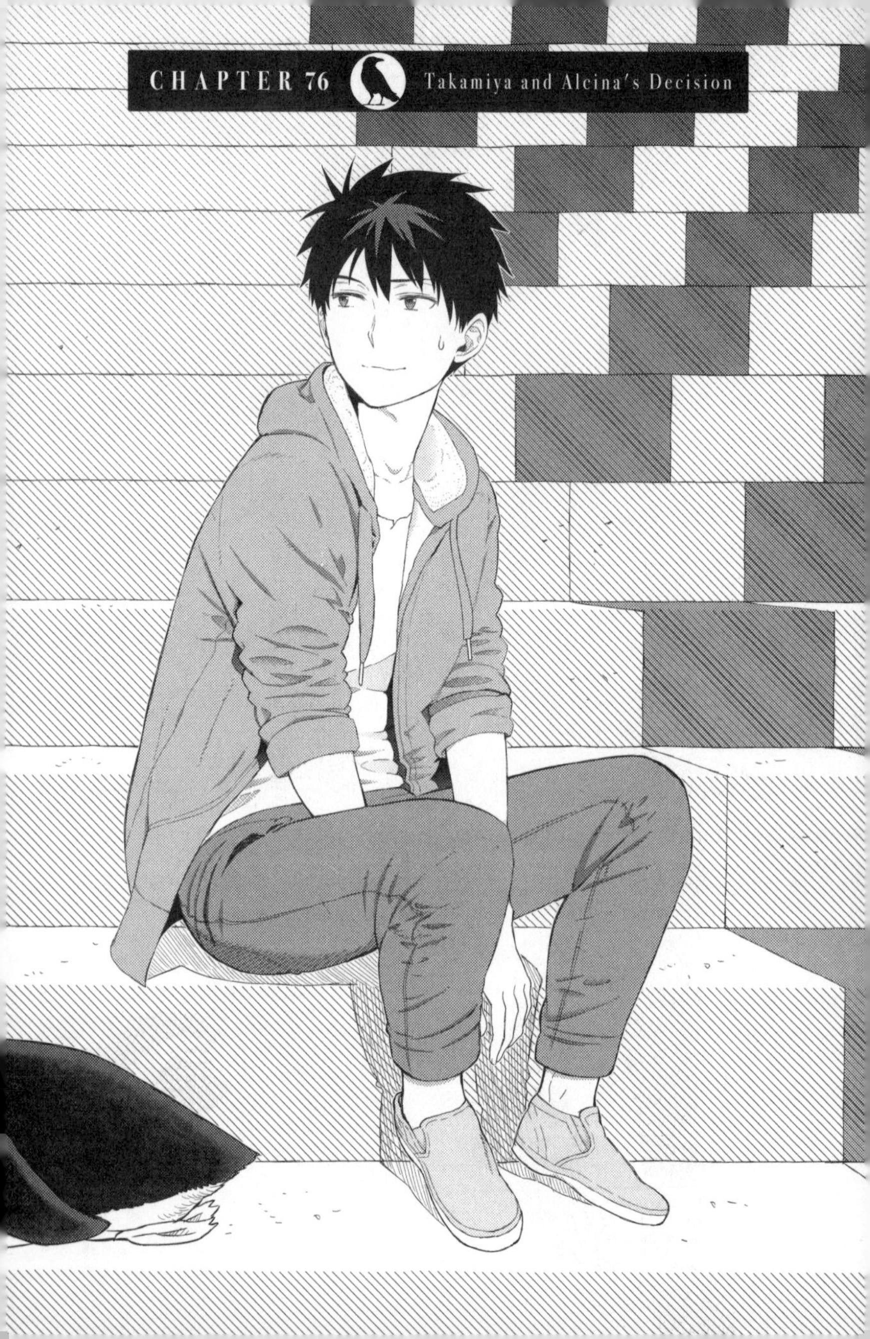

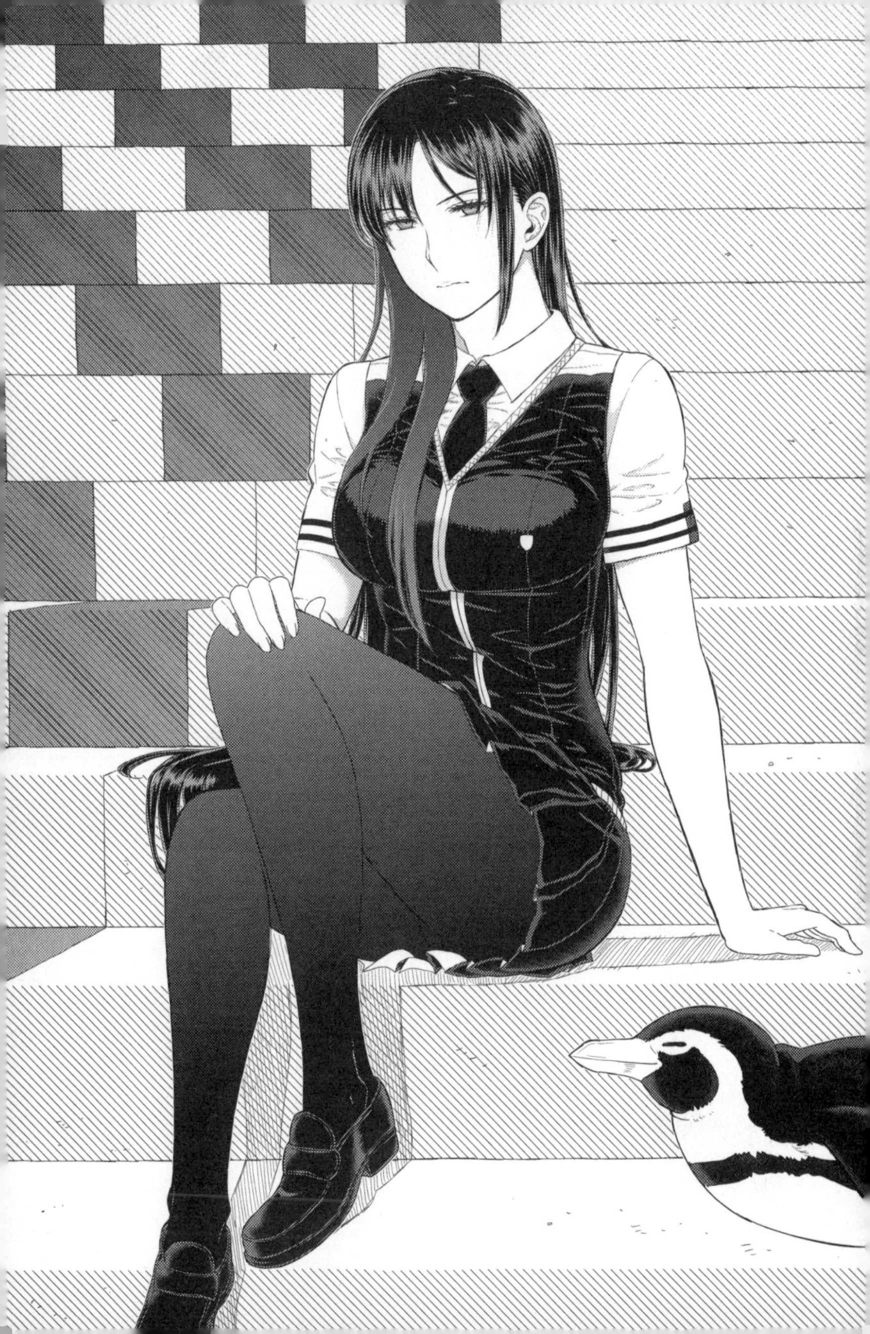

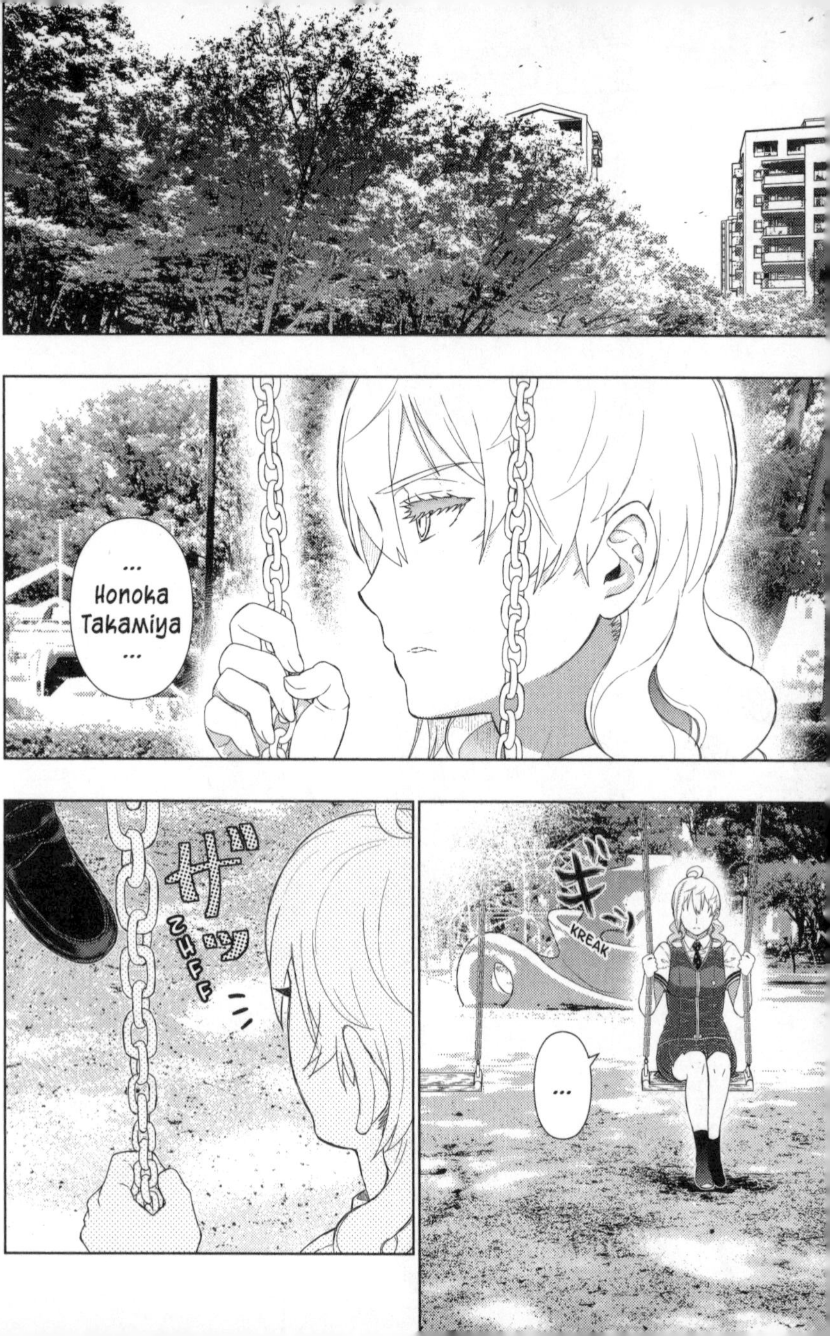

... Honoka Takamiya ...
ギッ
KREAK
...
ザッ
ZHFF

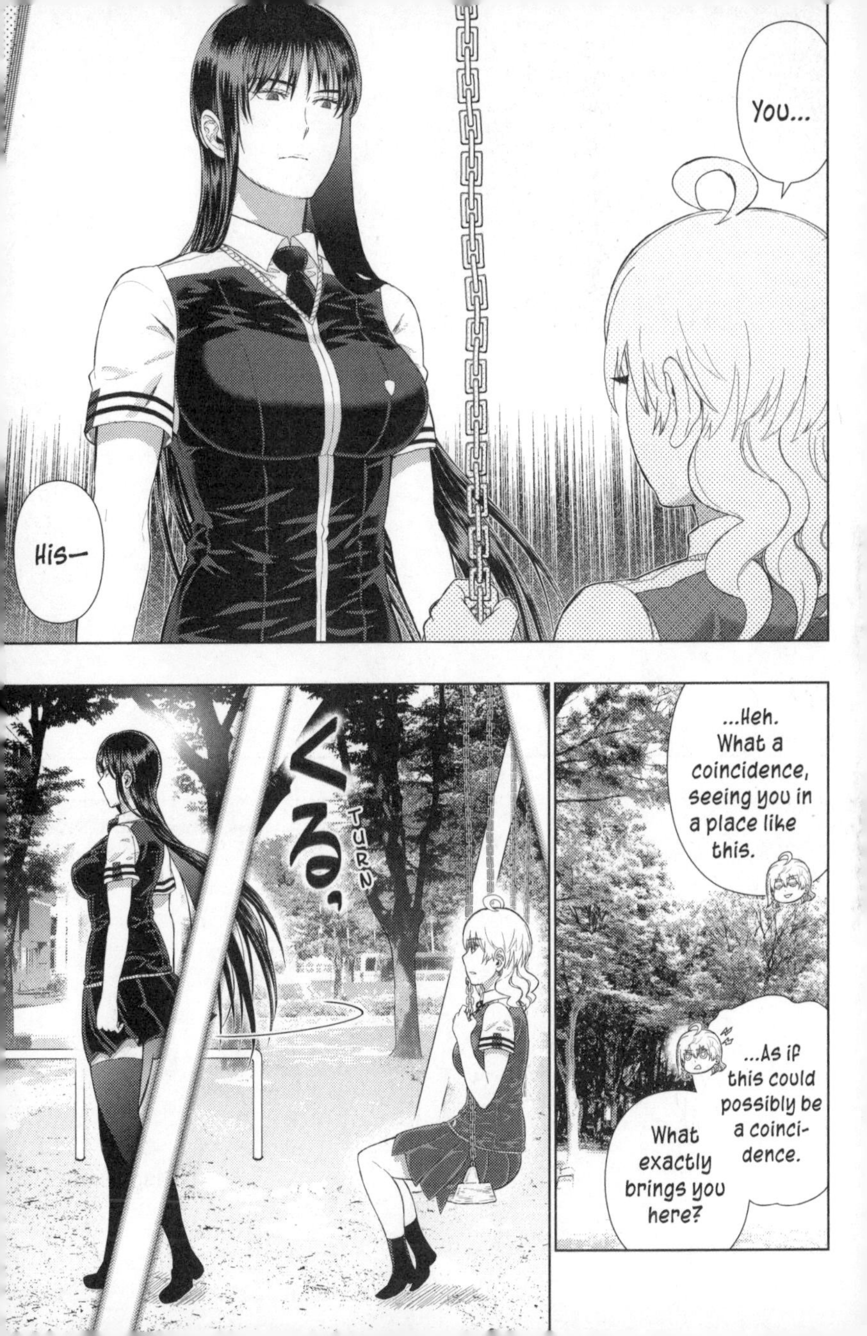
You...
His—
...Heh. What a coincidence, seeing you in a place like this.
...As if this could possibly be a coincidence.
What exactly brings you here?
TURN

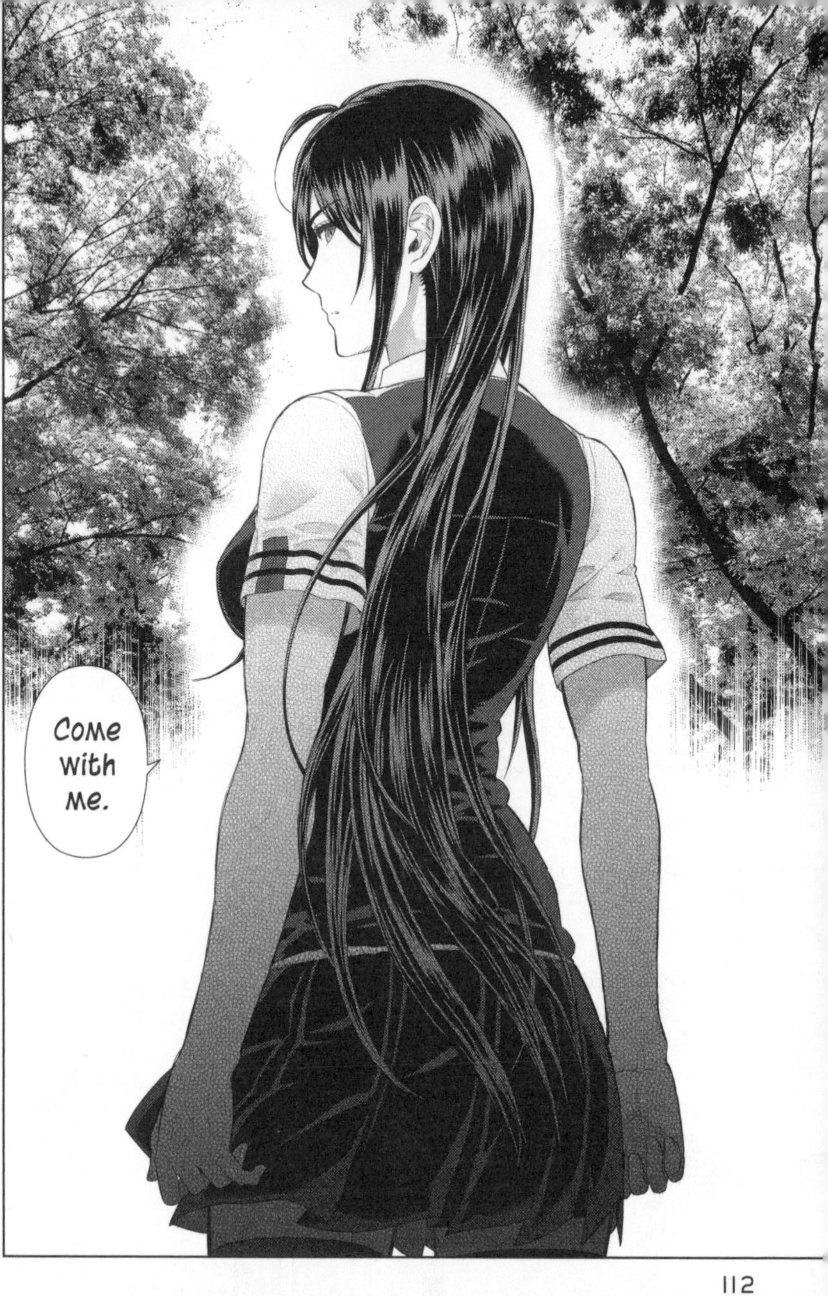
Come with me.

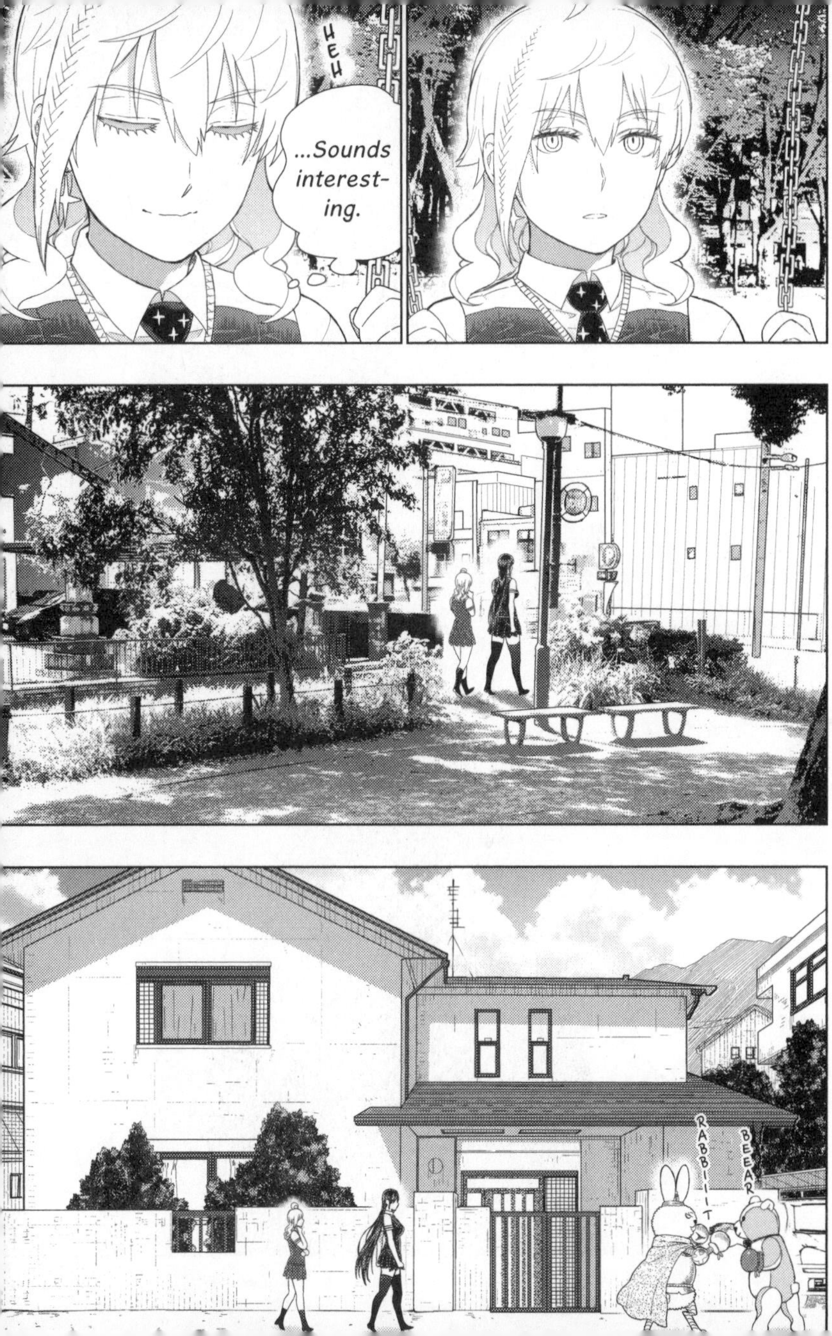
HEH
...Sounds interest-ing.
BEEAR
RABBIIT

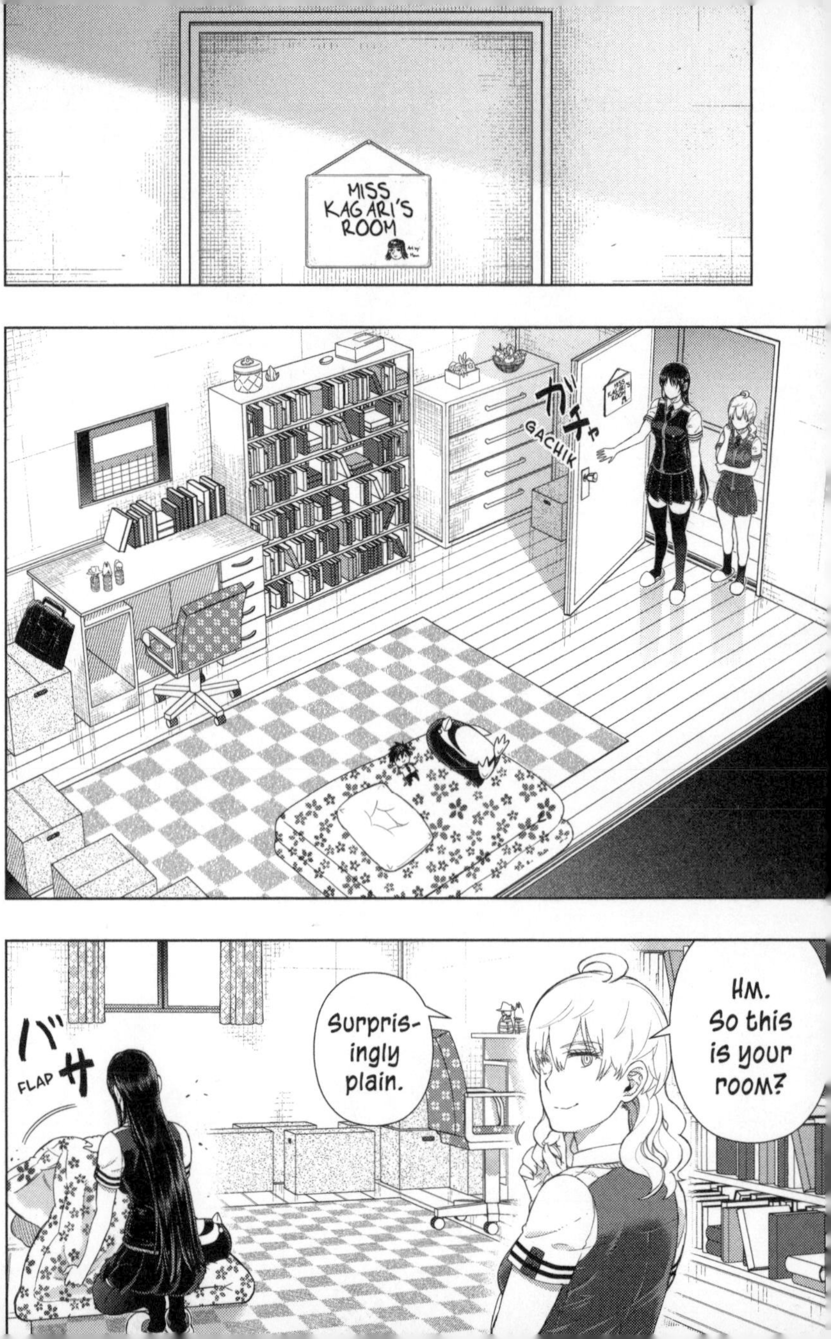
MISS KAGARI'S ROOM
ガチャ
GACHIK
HM. So this is your room?
Surpris-ingly plain.
バサ
FLAP

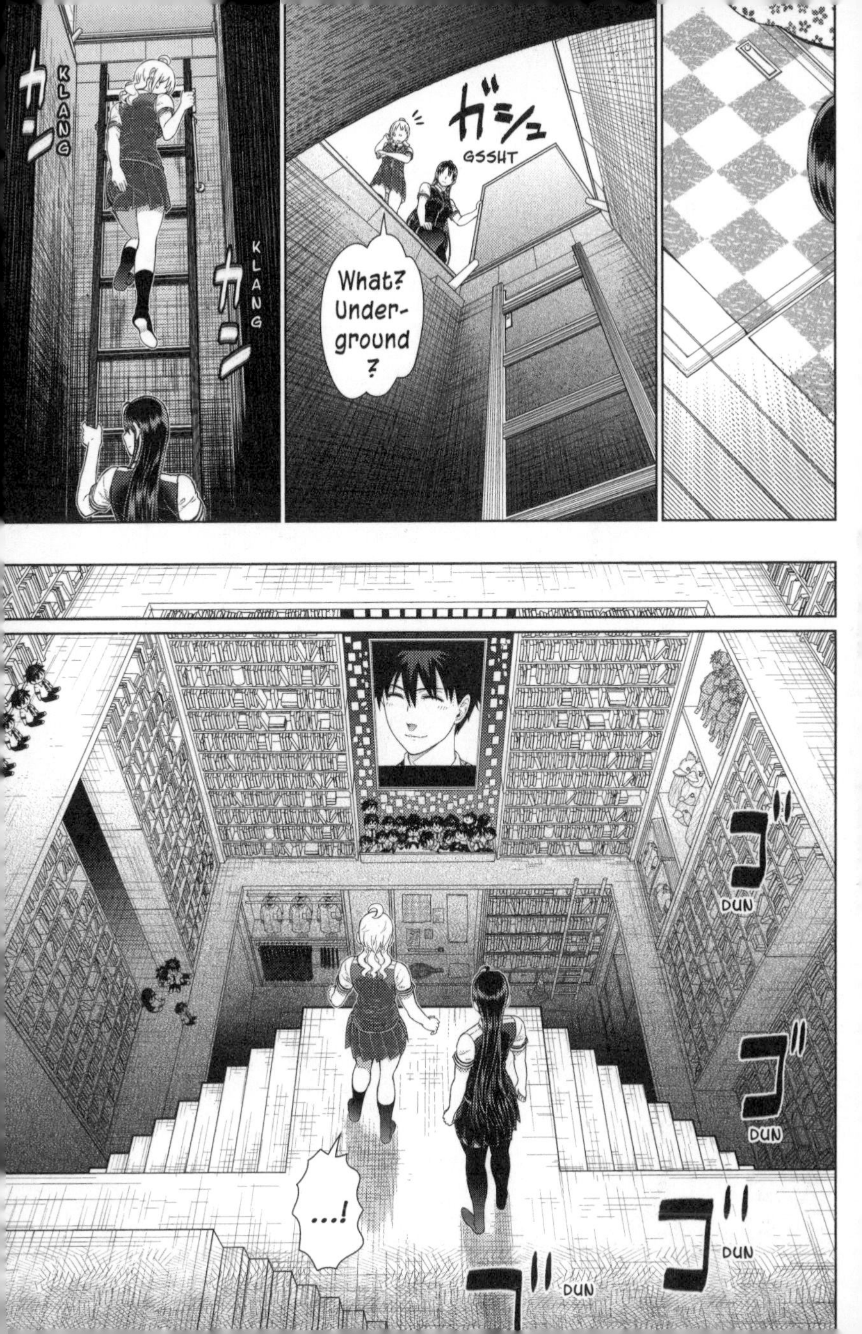
ガシュ
GSSHT
What? Under-ground?
カーン
KLANG
カーン
KLANG
ゴ
DUN
ゴ
DUN
...!
ゴ
DUN
ゴ
DUN

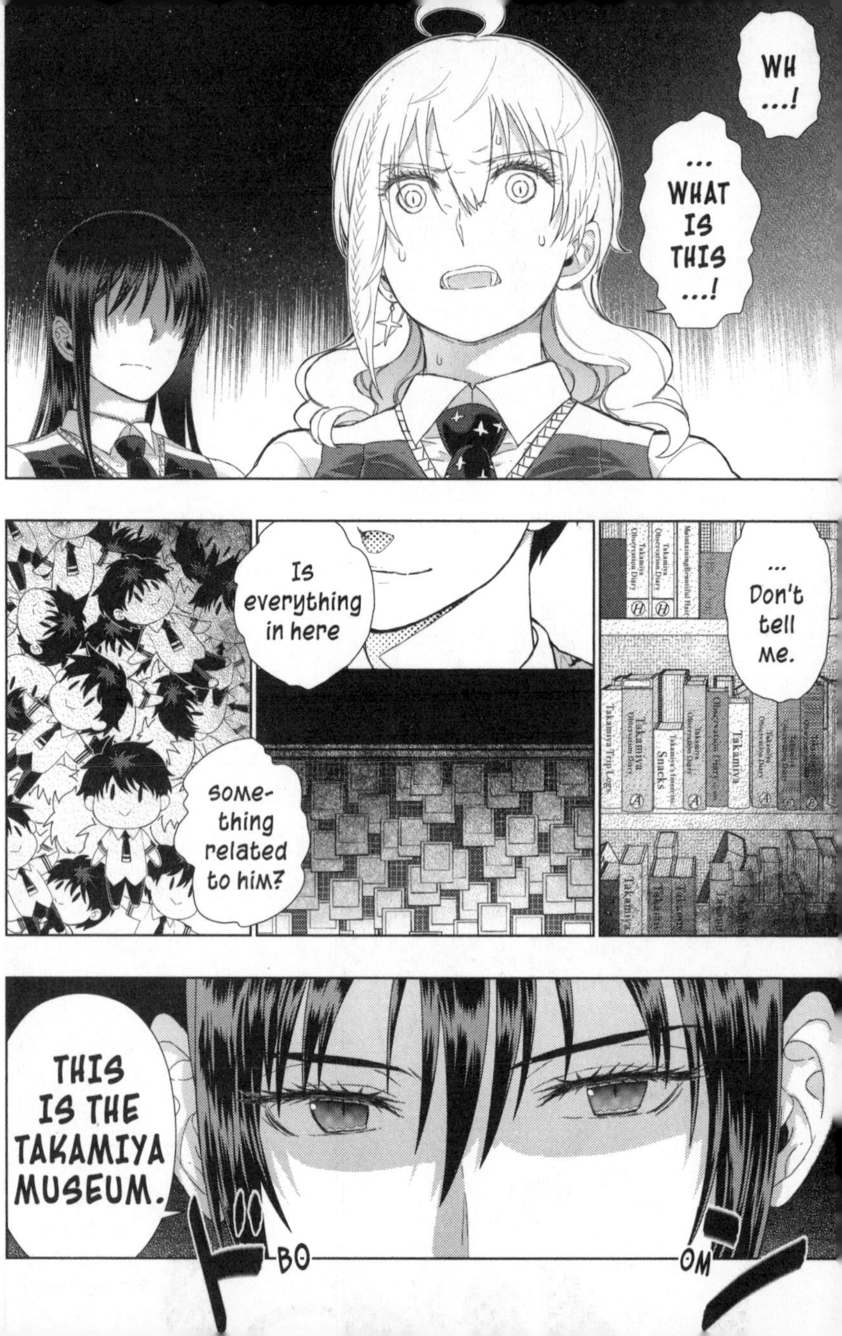
WH ...!
... WHAT IS THIS ...!
... Don't tell me.
Is everything in here
some-thing related to him?
THIS IS THE TAKAMIYA MUSEUM.
BO—OM

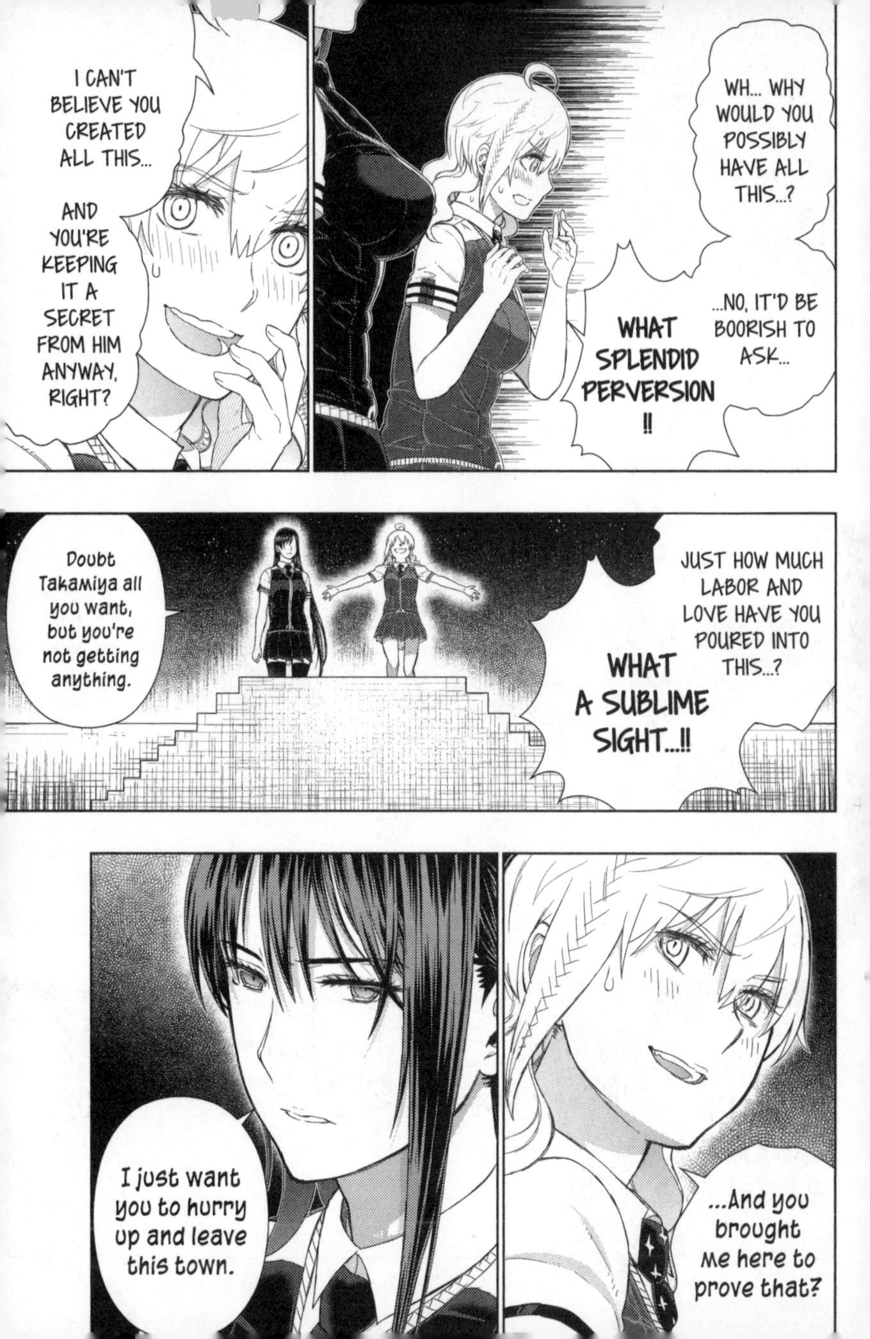
WH... WHY WOULD YOU POSSIBLY HAVE ALL THIS...?
...NO, IT'D BE BOORISH TO ASK...
WHAT SPLENDID PERVERSION !!
I CAN'T BELIEVE YOU CREATED ALL THIS...
AND YOU'RE KEEPING IT A SECRET FROM HIM ANYWAY, RIGHT?
JUST HOW MUCH LABOR AND LOVE HAVE YOU POURED INTO THIS...?
WHAT A SUBLIME SIGHT...!!
Doubt Takamiya all you want, but you're not getting anything.
...And you brought me here to prove that?
I just want you to hurry up and leave this town.

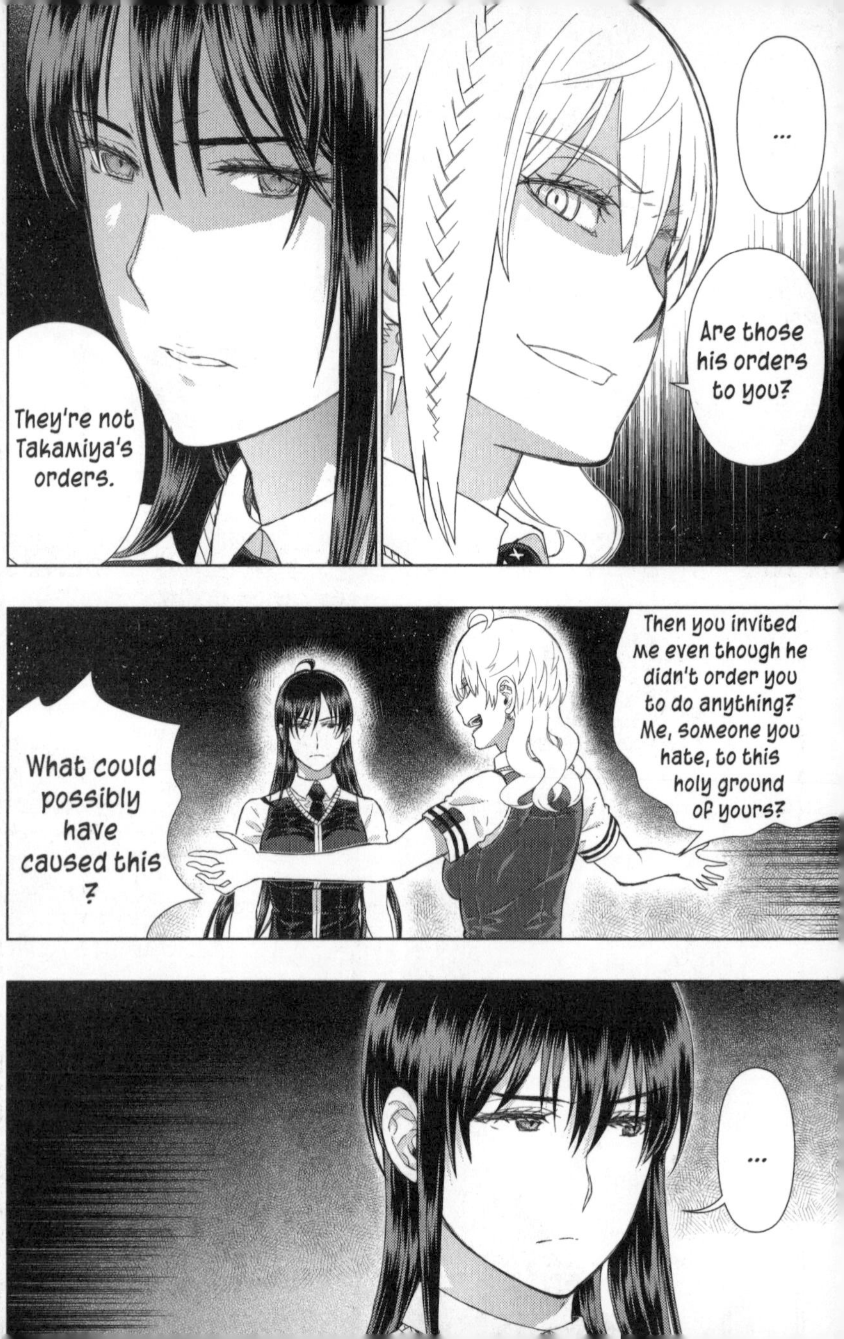
...
Are those his orders to you?
They're not Takamiya's orders.
Then you invited me even though he didn't order you to do anything? Me, someone you hate, to this holy ground of yours?
What could possibly have caused this ?
...

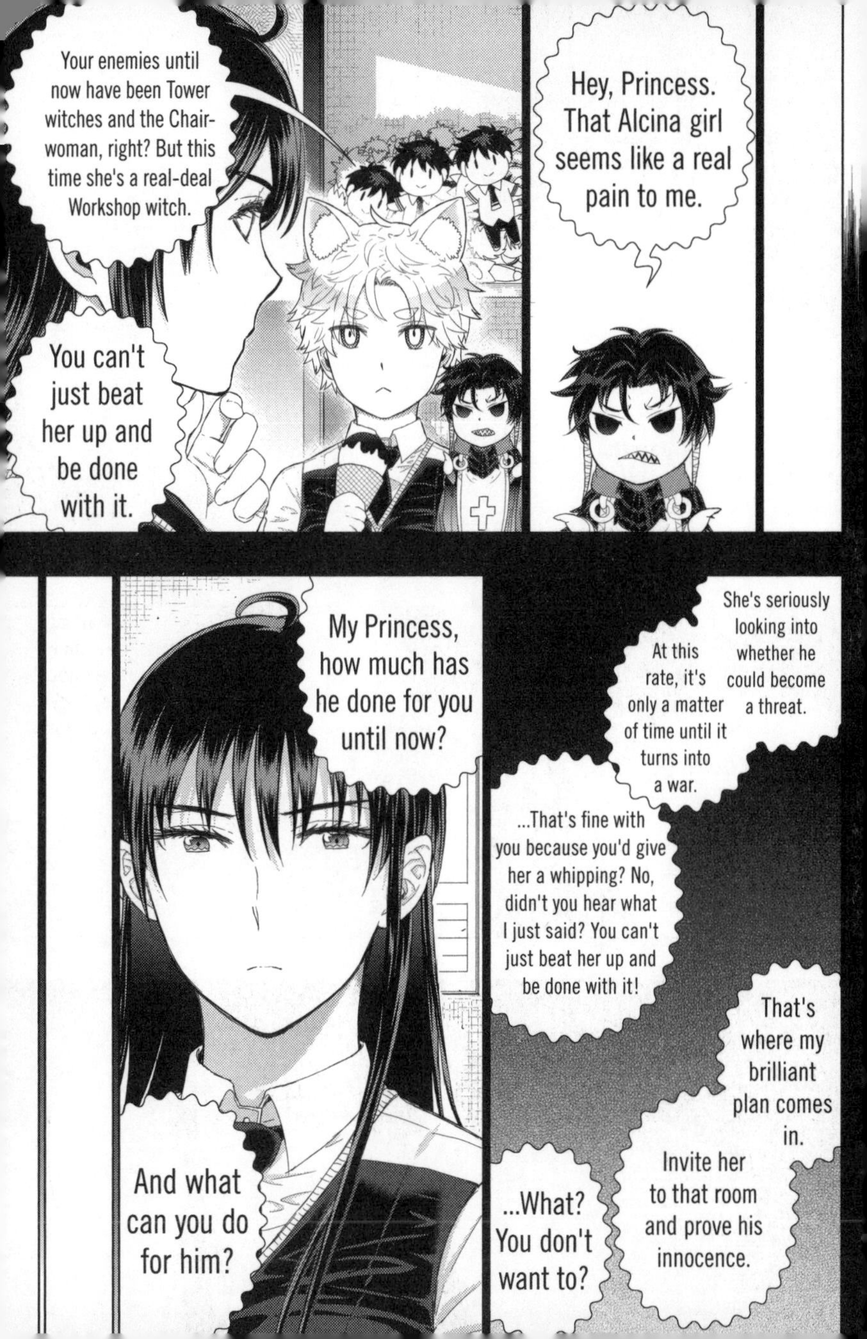
Hey, Princess. That Alcina girl seems like a real pain to me.
Your enemies until now have been Tower witches and the Chair-woman, right? But this time she's a real-deal Workshop witch.
You can't just beat her up and be done with it.
She's seriously looking into whether he could become a threat.
At this rate, it's only a matter of time until it turns into a war.
...That's fine with you because you'd give her a whipping? No, didn't you hear what I just said? You can't just beat her up and be done with it!
That's where my brilliant plan comes in.
Invite her to that room and prove his innocence.
...What? You don't want to?
My Princess, how much has he done for you until now?
And what can you do for him?

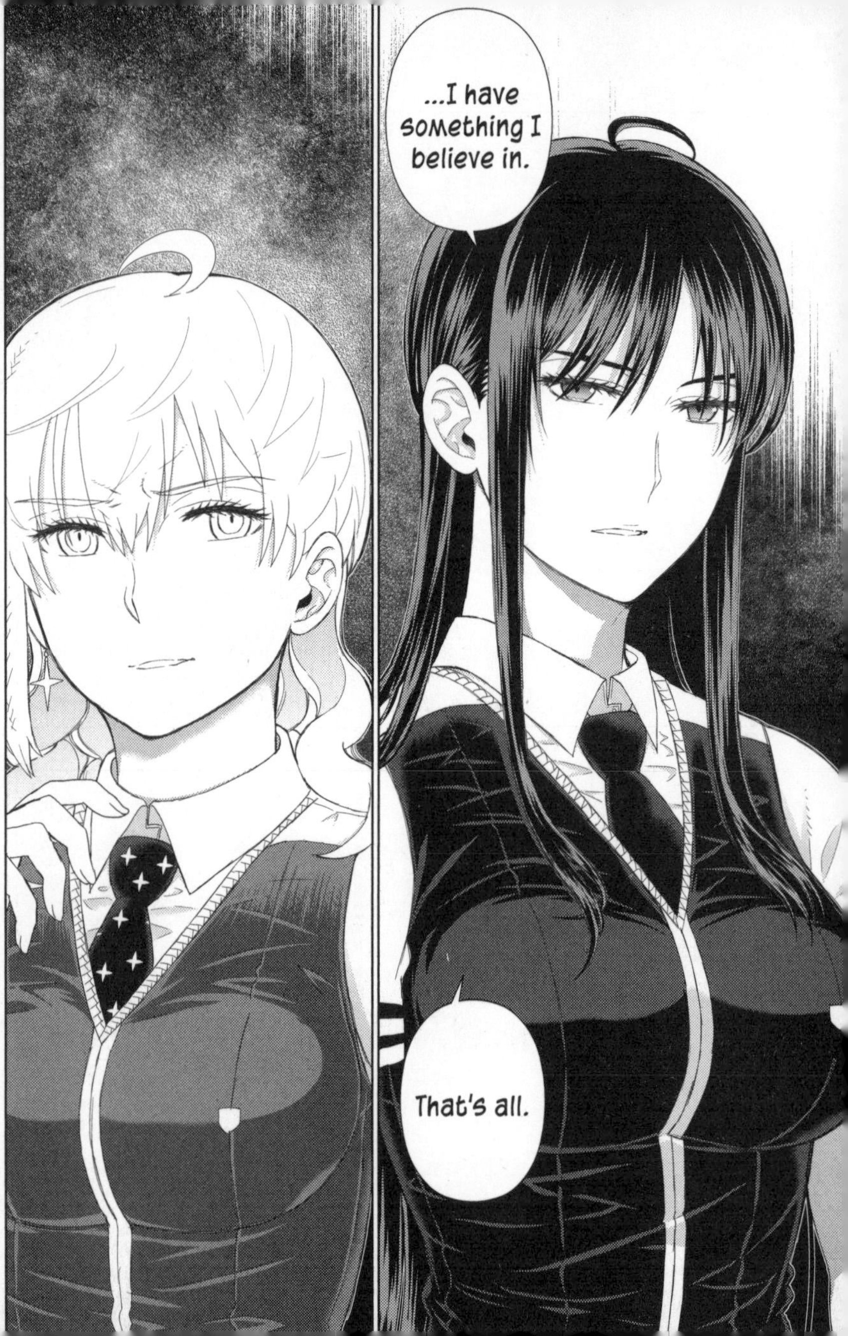
...I have something I believe in.
That's all.

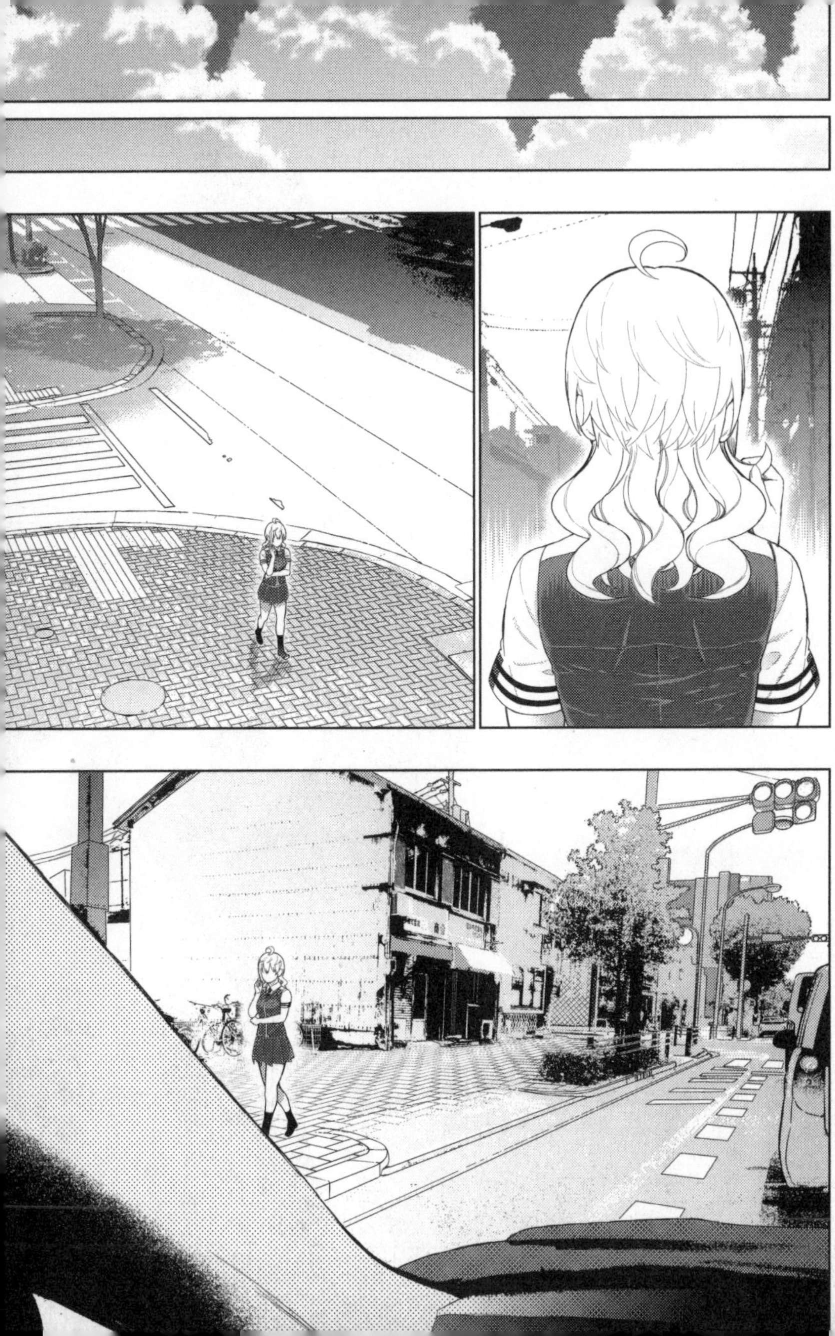

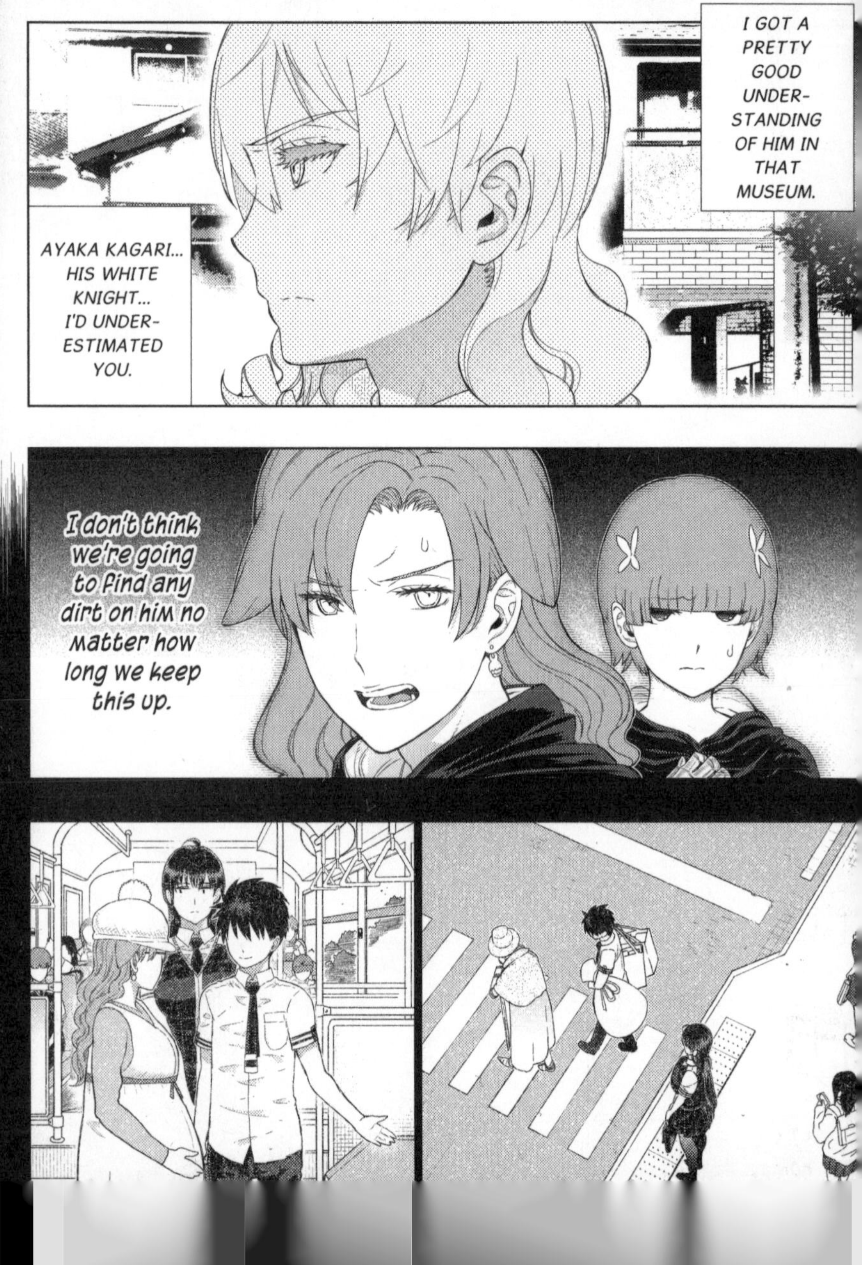
I GOT A PRETTY GOOD UNDER-STANDING OF HIM IN THAT MUSEUM.
AYAKA KAGARI... HIS WHITE KNIGHT... I'D UNDER-ESTIMATED YOU.
I don't think we're going to find any dirt on him no matter how long we keep this up.

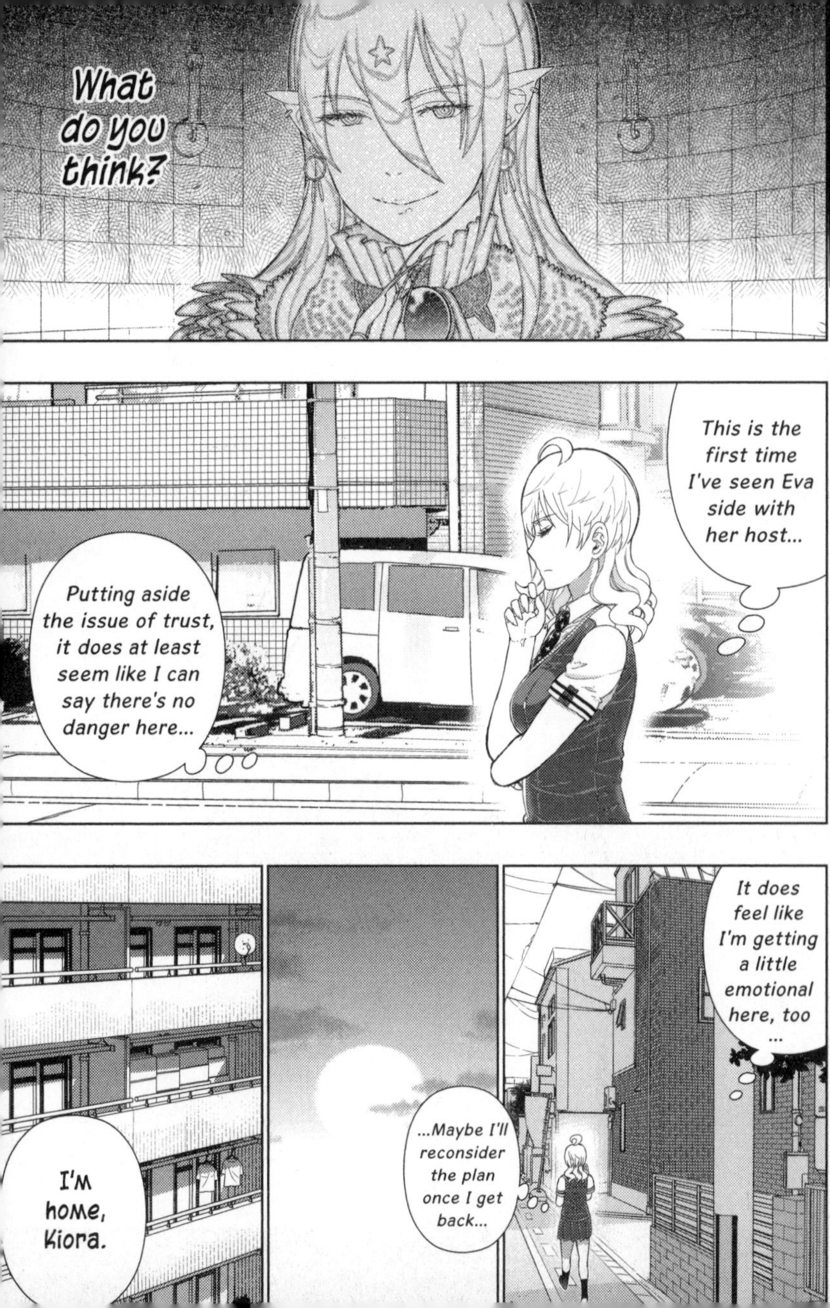
What do you think?
This is the first time I've seen Eva side with her host...
Putting aside the issue of trust, it does at least seem like I can say there's no danger here...
It does feel like I'm getting a little emotional here, too ...
...Maybe I'll reconsider the plan once I get back...
I'm home, Kiora.

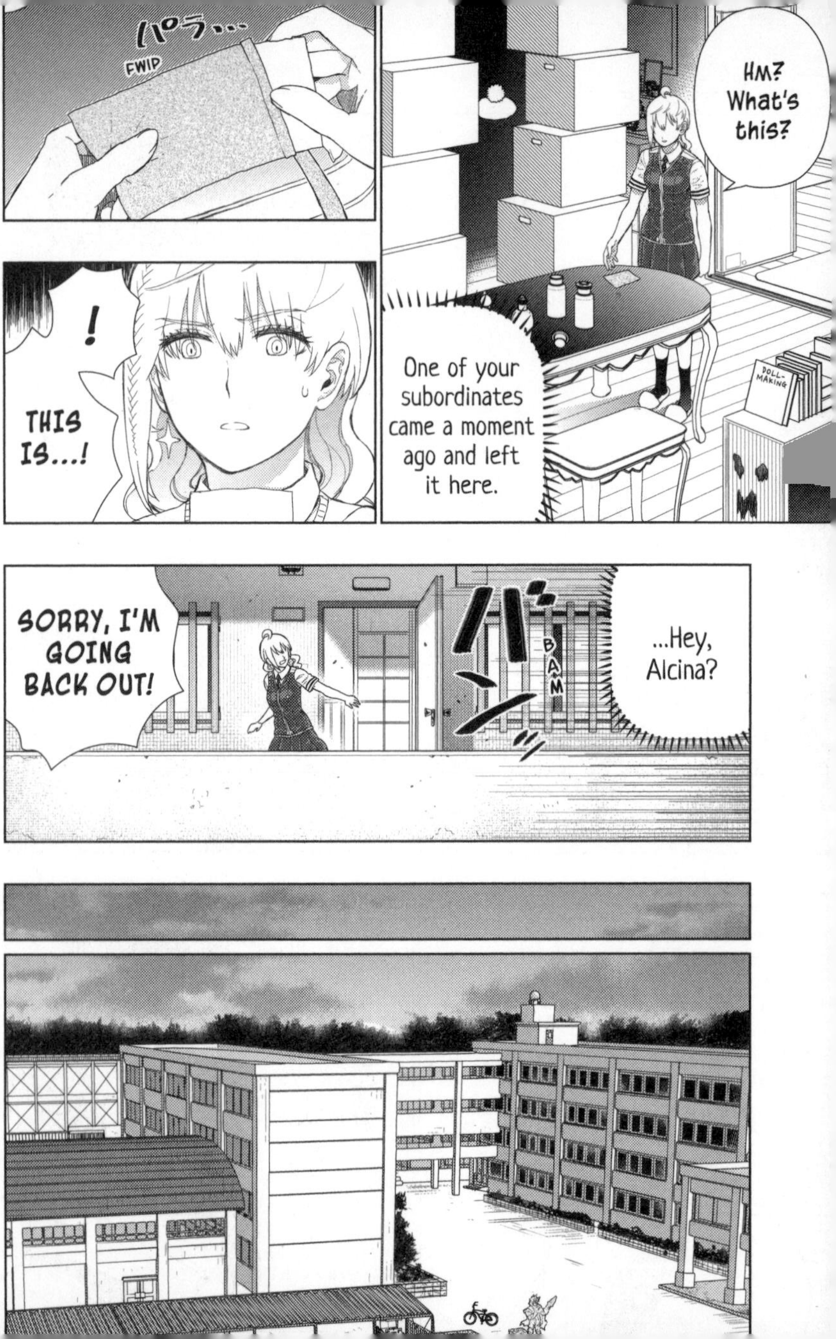
HM? What's this?
DOLL-MAKING
One of your subordinates came a moment ago and left it here.
パラ…
FWIP
!
THIS IS...!
...Hey, Alcina?
バン
BAM
SORRY, I'M GOING BACK OUT!

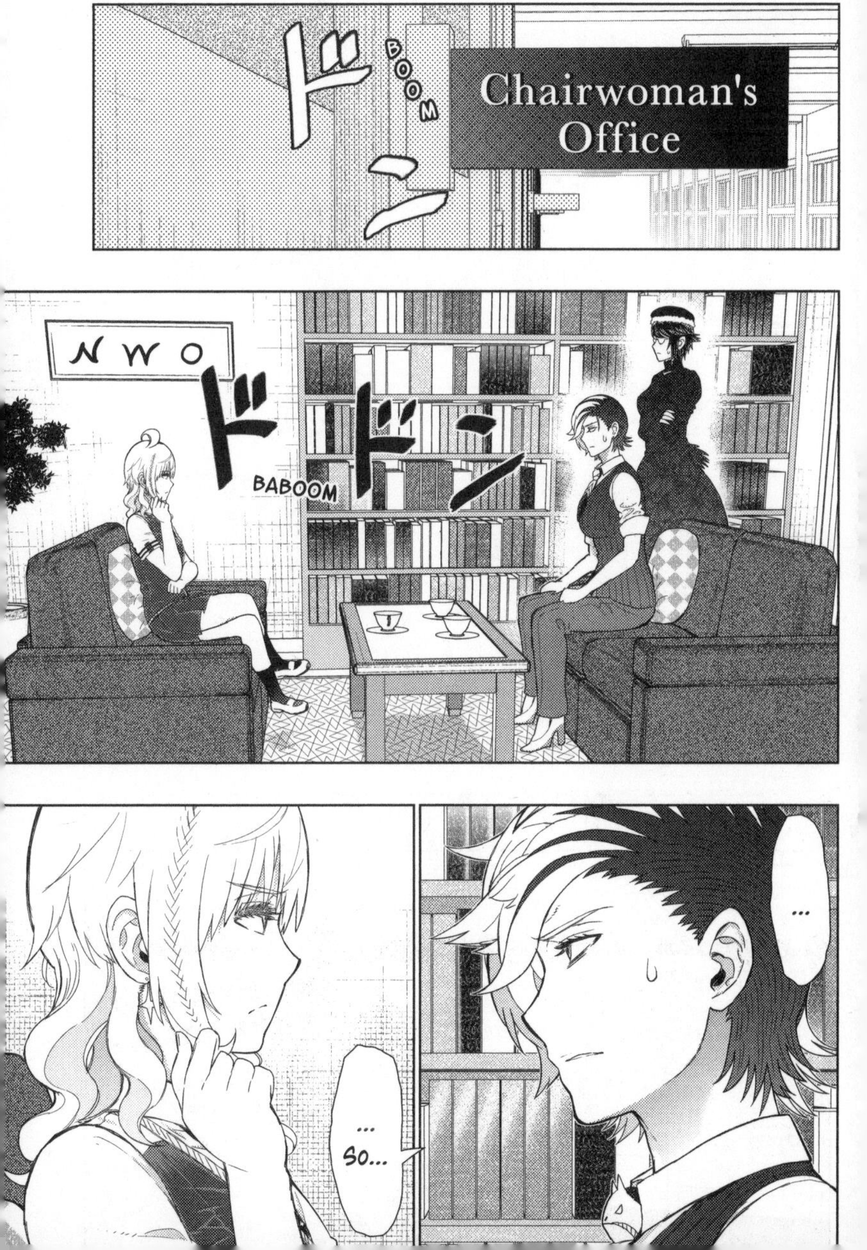

Chairwoman's Office
BOOM
NWO
BABOOM
...
... so...

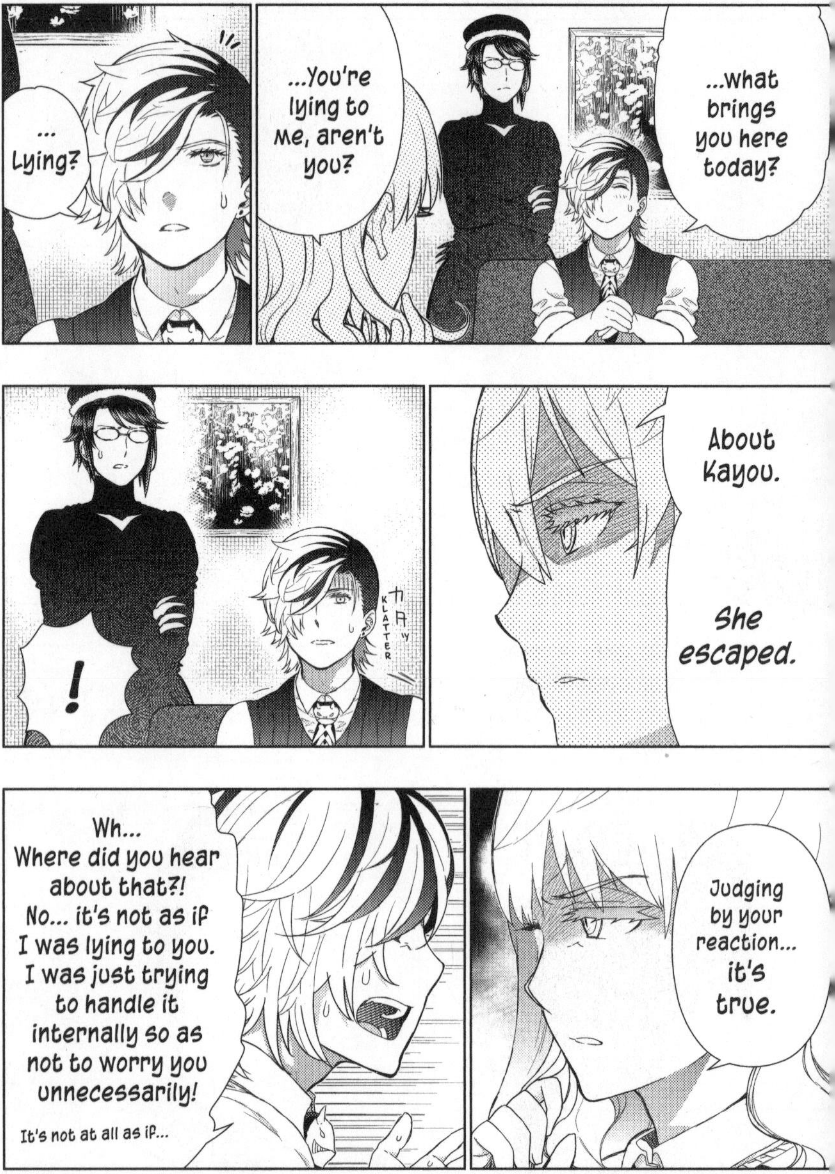
...what brings you here today?
...You're lying to me, aren't you?
... Lying?
About Kayou.
She escaped.
KLATTER
!
Judging by your reaction... it's true.
Wh... Where did you hear about that?! No... it's not as if I was lying to you. I was just trying to handle it internally so as not to worry you unnecessarily!
It's not at all as if...

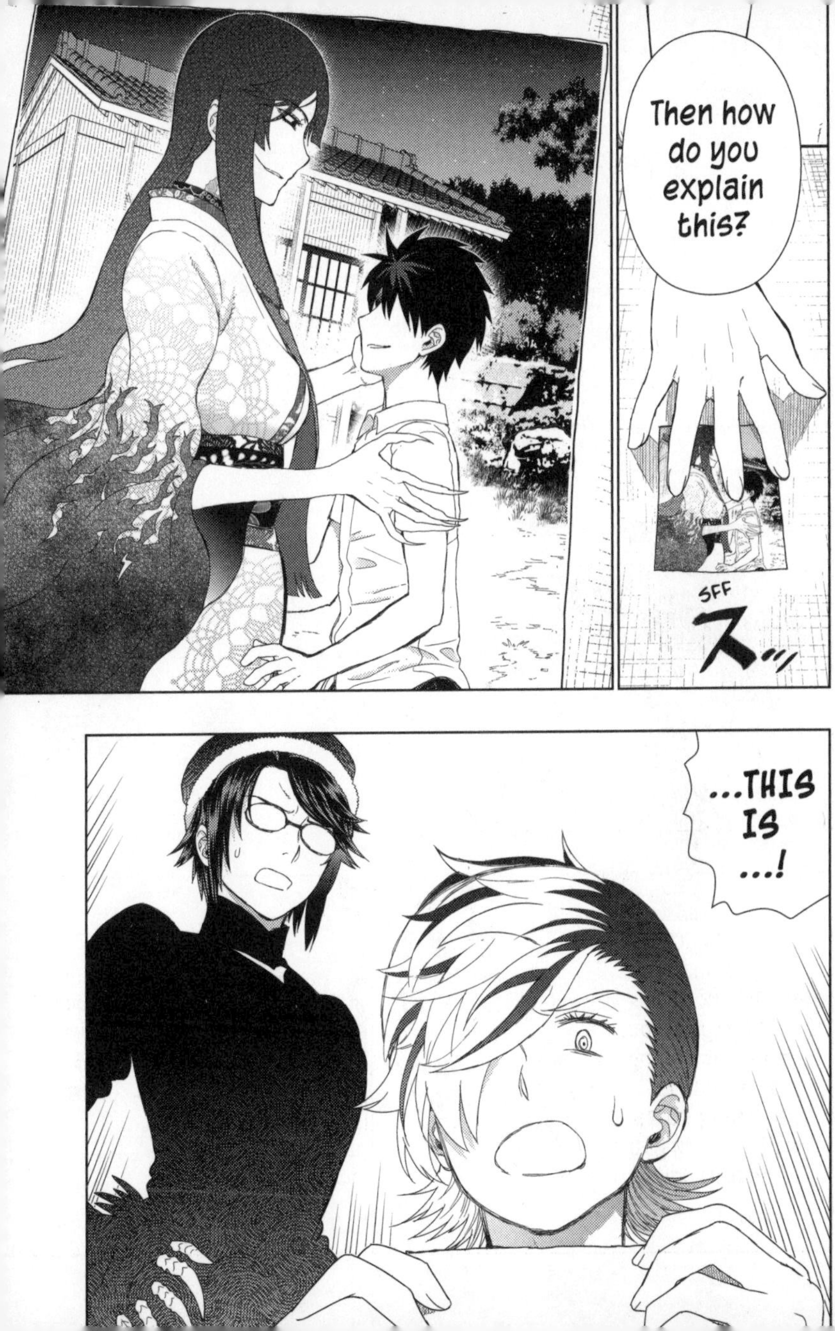
Then how do you explain this?
SFF
スッ
...THIS IS ...!

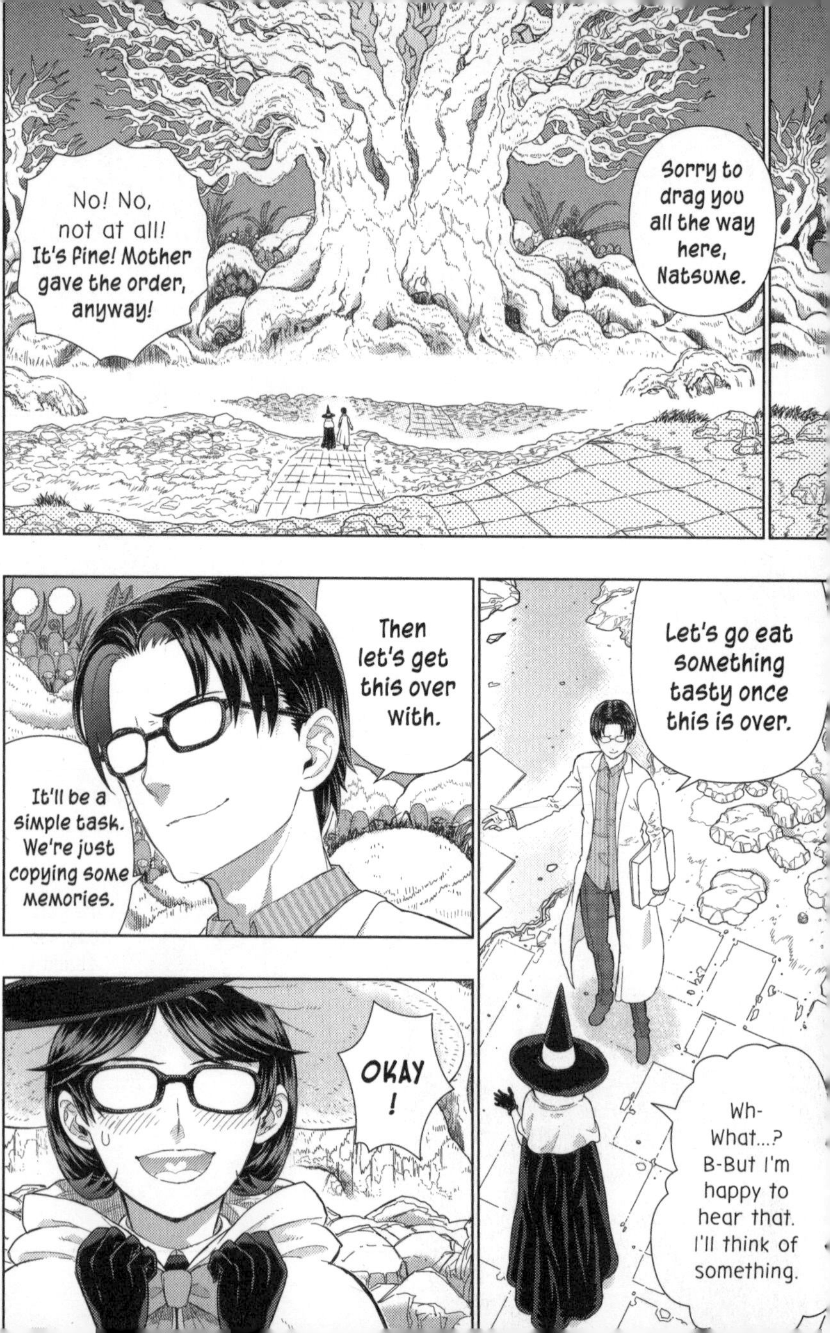

Sorry to drag you all the way here, Natsume.
No! No, not at all! It's fine! Mother gave the order, anyway!
Let's go eat something tasty once this is over.
Wh- What...? B-But I'm happy to hear that. I'll think of something.
Then let's get this over with.
It'll be a simple task. We're just copying some memories.
OKAY!

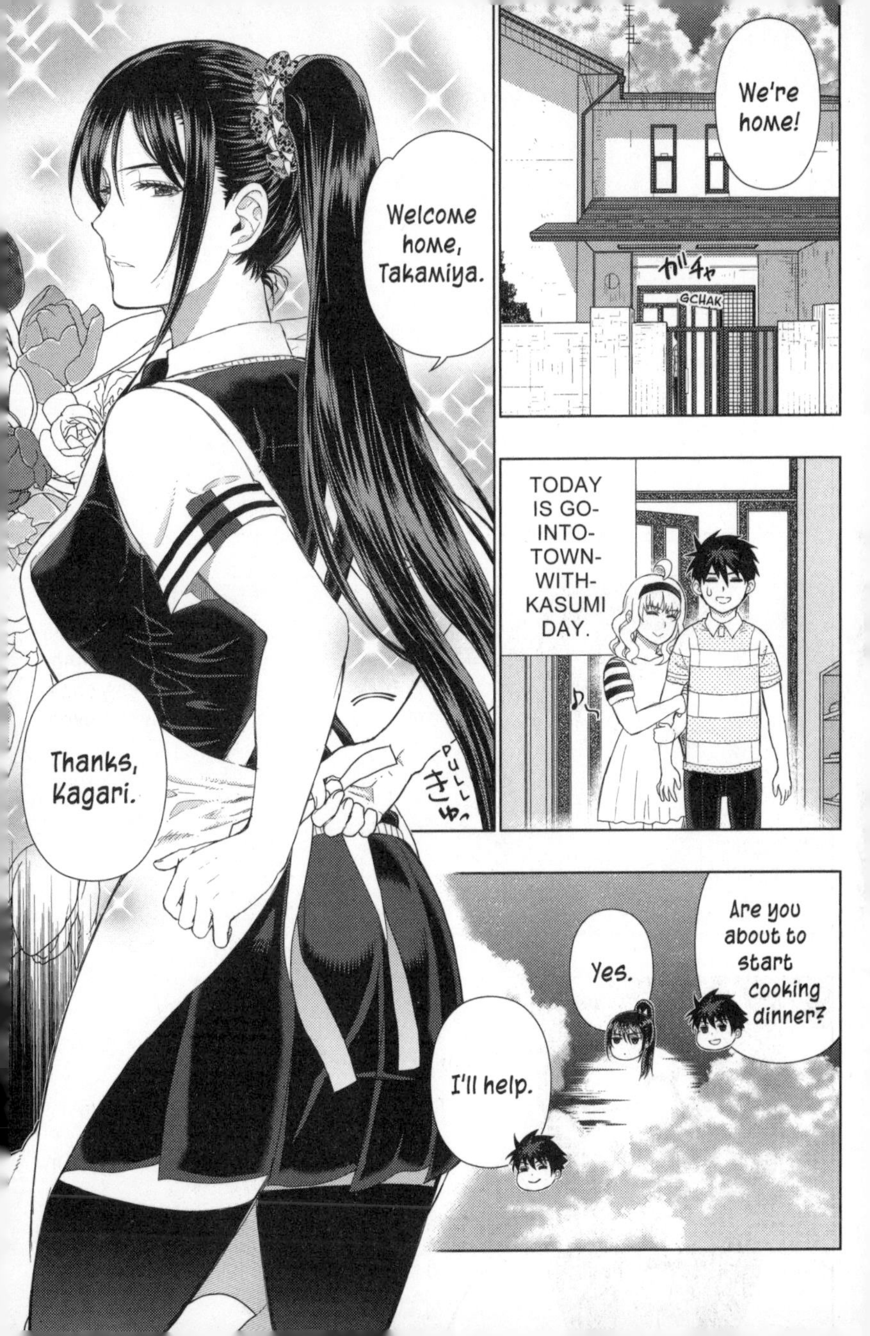
We're home!
ガチャ
GCHAK
TODAY IS GO-INTO-TOWN-WITH-KASUMI DAY.
♪
Are you about to start cooking dinner?
Yes.
I'll help.
Welcome home, Takamiya.
Thanks, Kagari.
PULL
きゅ

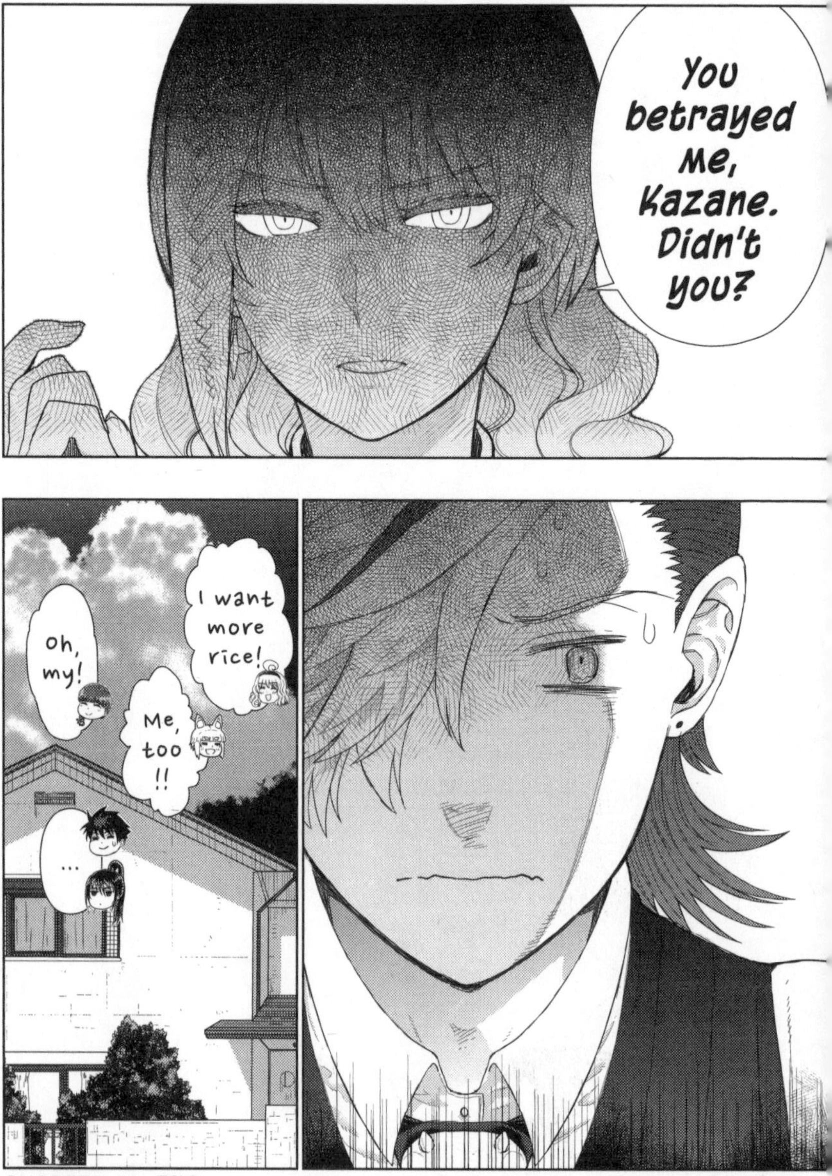
You betrayed me, Kazane. Didn't you?
I want more rice!
Oh, my!
Me, too!!
...

CHAPTER 76: END

Witchcraft Works

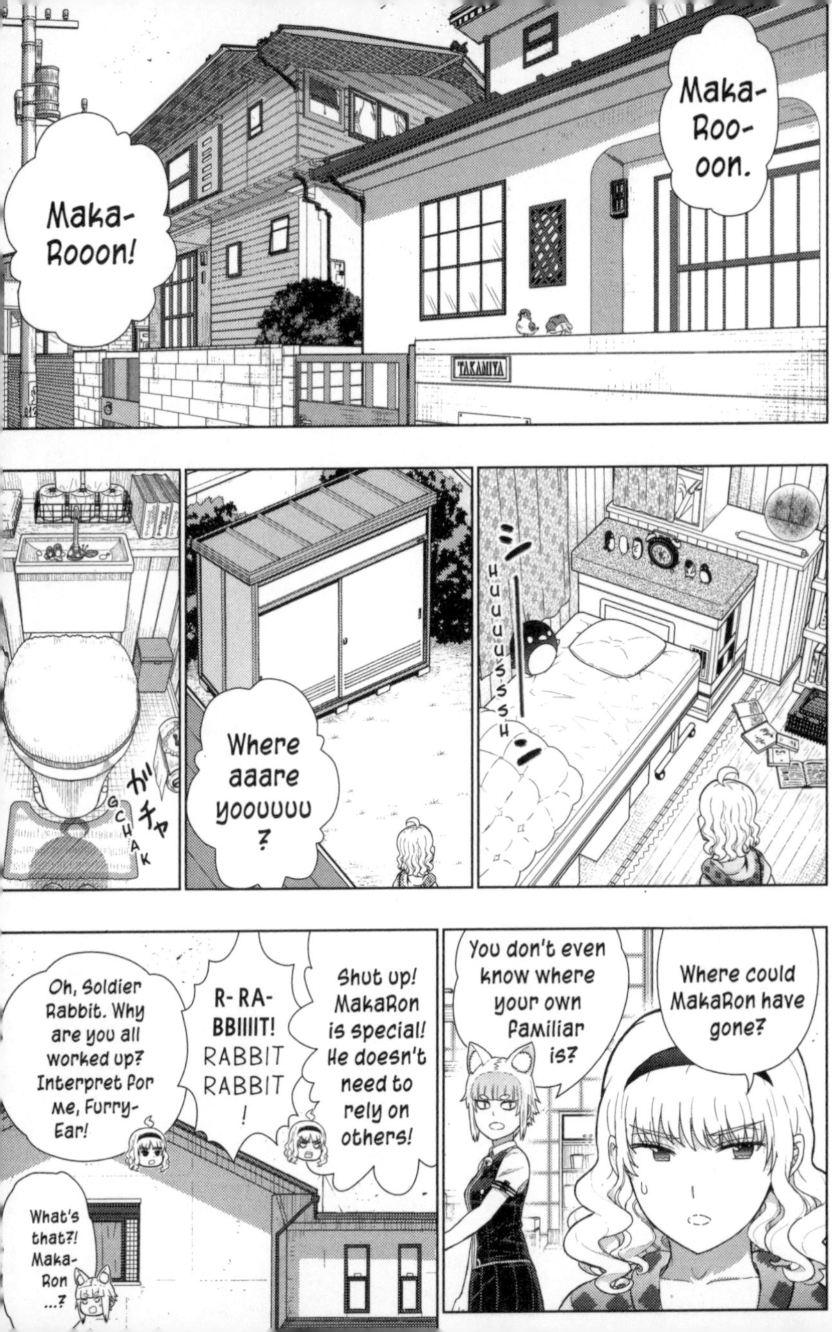

Maka-Roooon.
Maka-Rooon!
TAKAMIYA
シーン
HUUUUUSSSH
Where aaare youuuuu?
ガチャ
GCHAK
Where could MakaRon have gone?
You don't even know where your own familiar is?
Shut up! MakaRon is special! He doesn't need to rely on others!
R- RA- BBIIIIT! RABBIT RABBIT!
Oh, Soldier Rabbit. Why are you all worked up? Interpret for me, Furry-Ear!
What's that?! Maka-Ron ...?

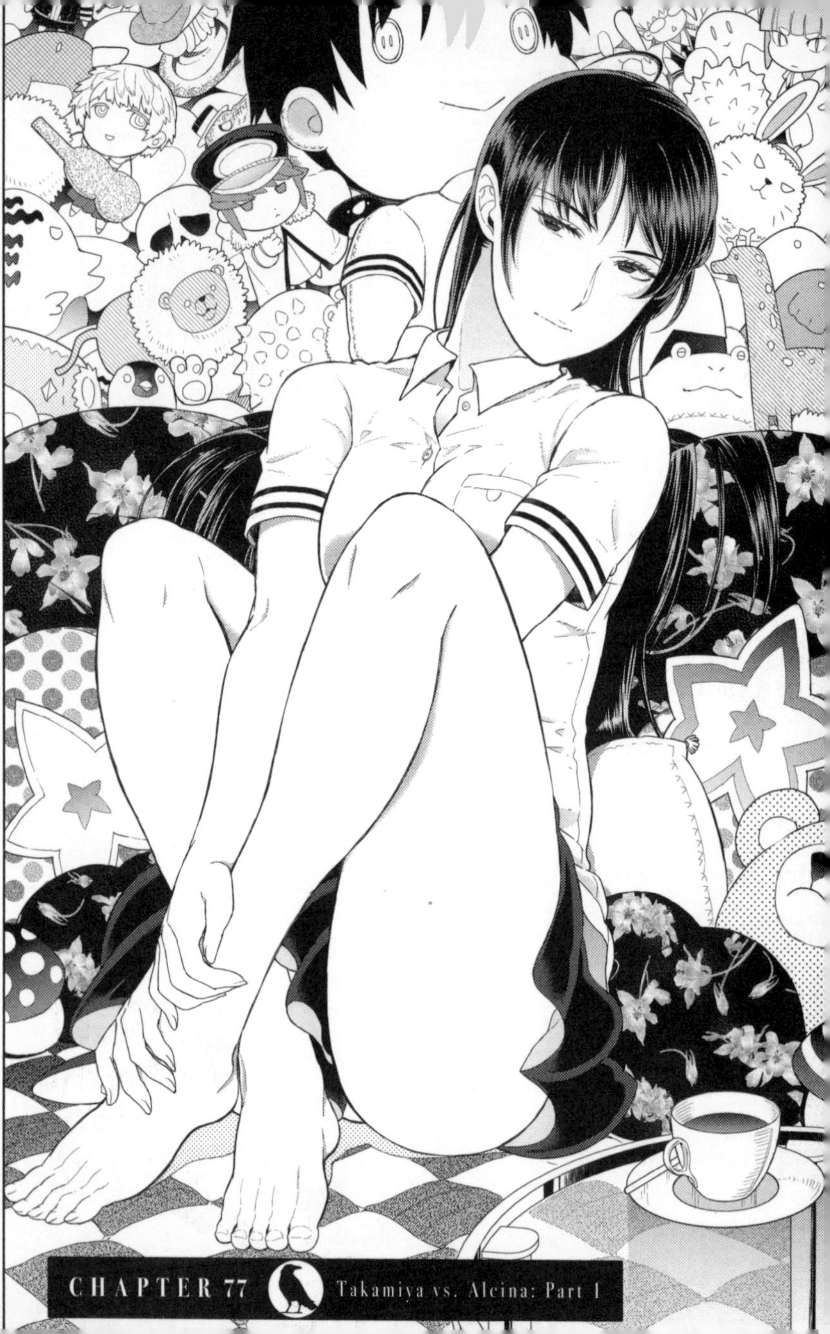
CHAPTER 77
Takamiya vs. Alcina: Part 1

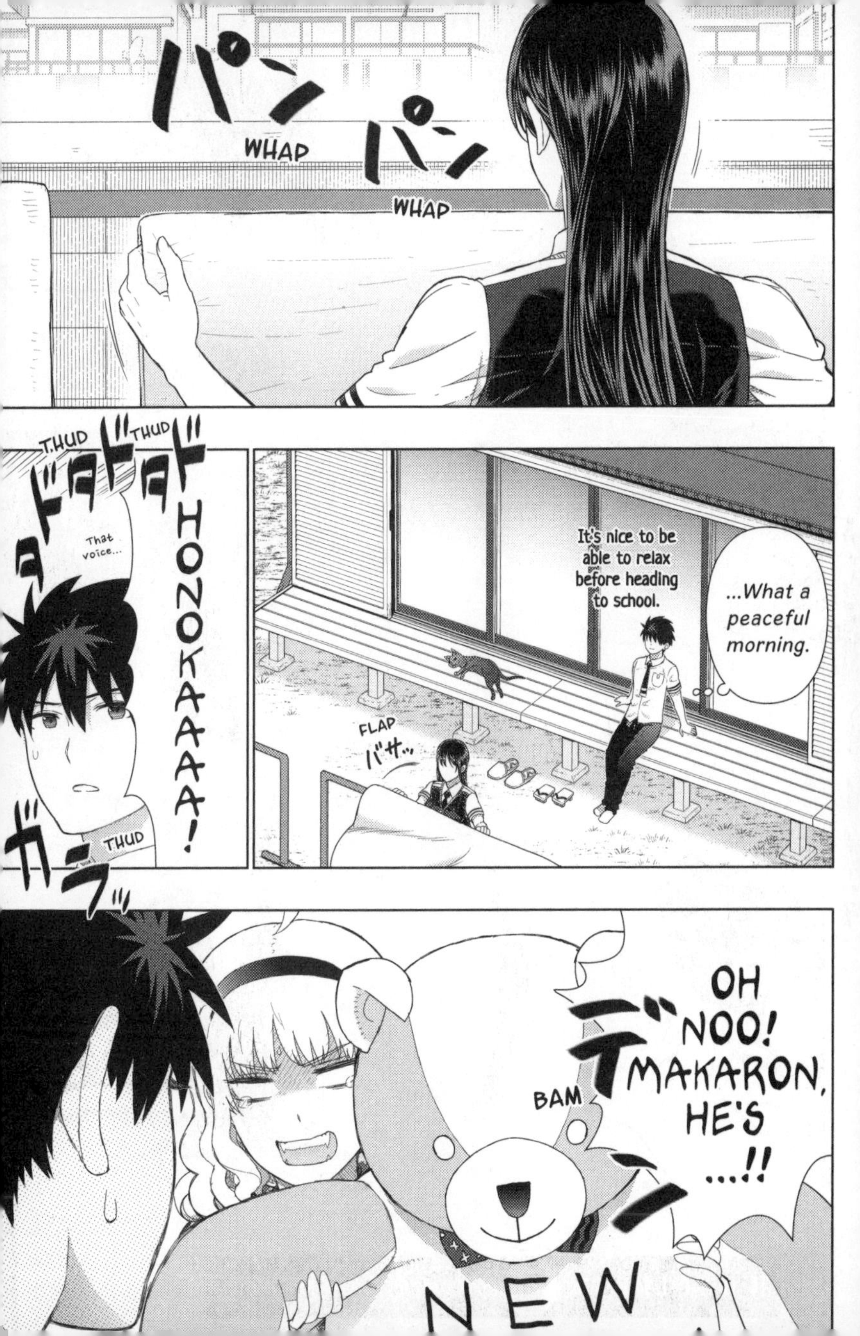

パン
WHAP
パン
WHAP
...What a peaceful morning.
It's nice to be able to relax before heading to school.
バサッ
FLAP
ダドダドダ
T.THUD THUD
HONOKAAAA!
That voice...
ガラッ
THUD
OH NOO! MAKARON, HE'S ...!!
デーー
BAM
NEW

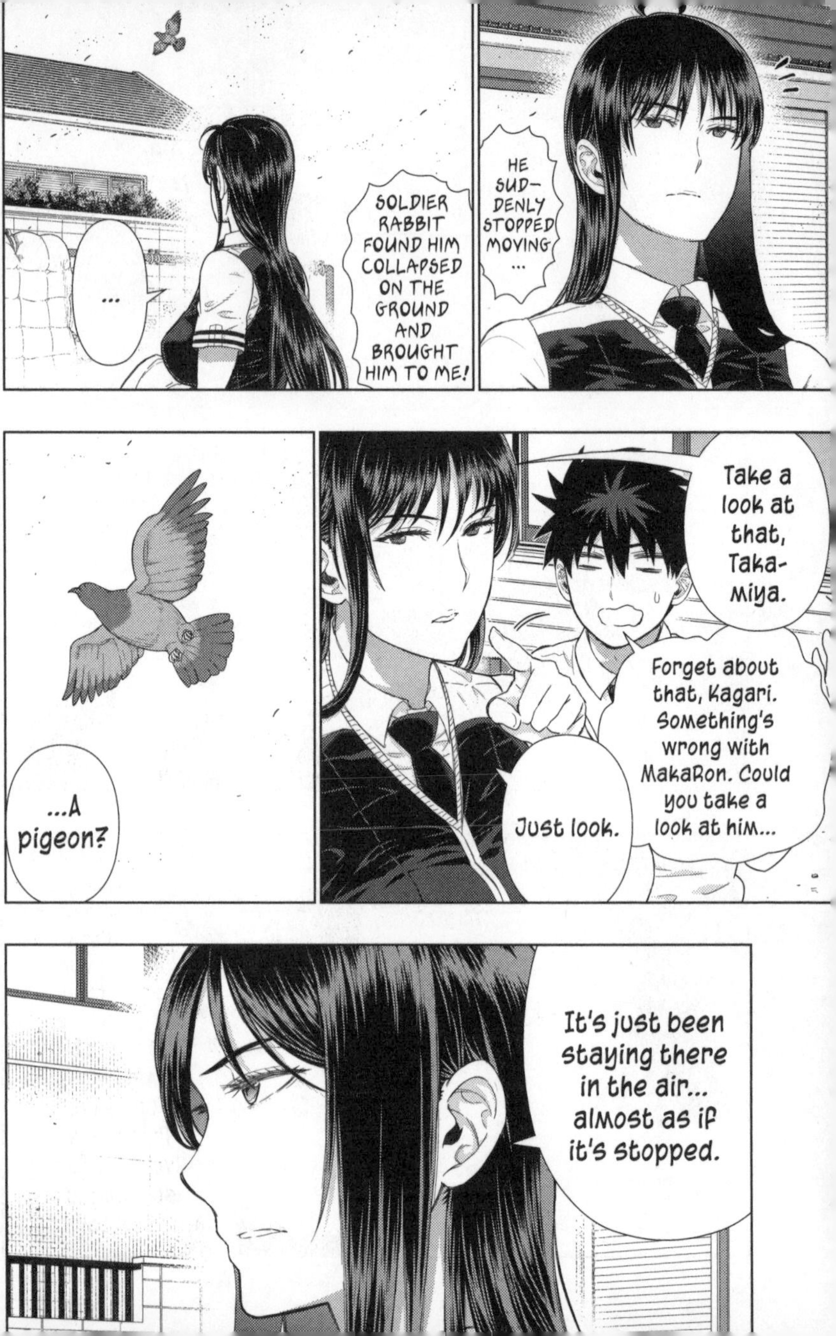
HE SUDDENLY STOPPED MOVING...
SOLDIER RABBIT FOUND HIM COLLAPSED ON THE GROUND AND BROUGHT HIM TO ME!
...
Take a look at that, Takamiya.
Forget about that, Kagari. Something's wrong with MakaRon. Could you take a look at him...
Just look.
...A pigeon?
It's just been staying there in the air... almost as if it's stopped.

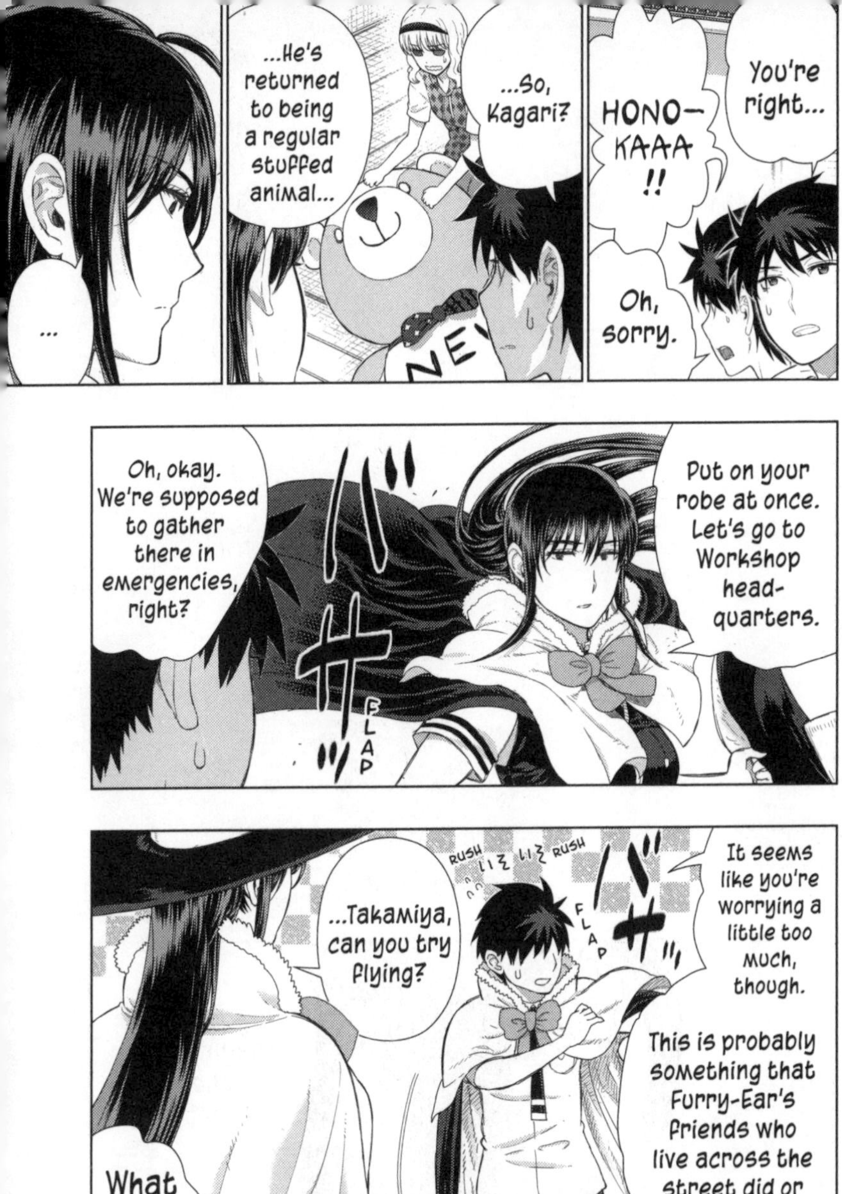

You're right...
HONO-KAAA!!
Oh, sorry.
...So, Kagari?
...He's returned to being a regular stuffed animal...
...
Put on your robe at once. Let's go to Workshop head-quarters.
FLAP
Oh, okay. We're supposed to gather there in emergencies, right?
It seems like you're worrying a little too much, though.
RUSH RUSH
FLAP
This is probably something that Furry-Ear's friends who live across the street did or someth—
...Takamiya, can you try flying?
What?

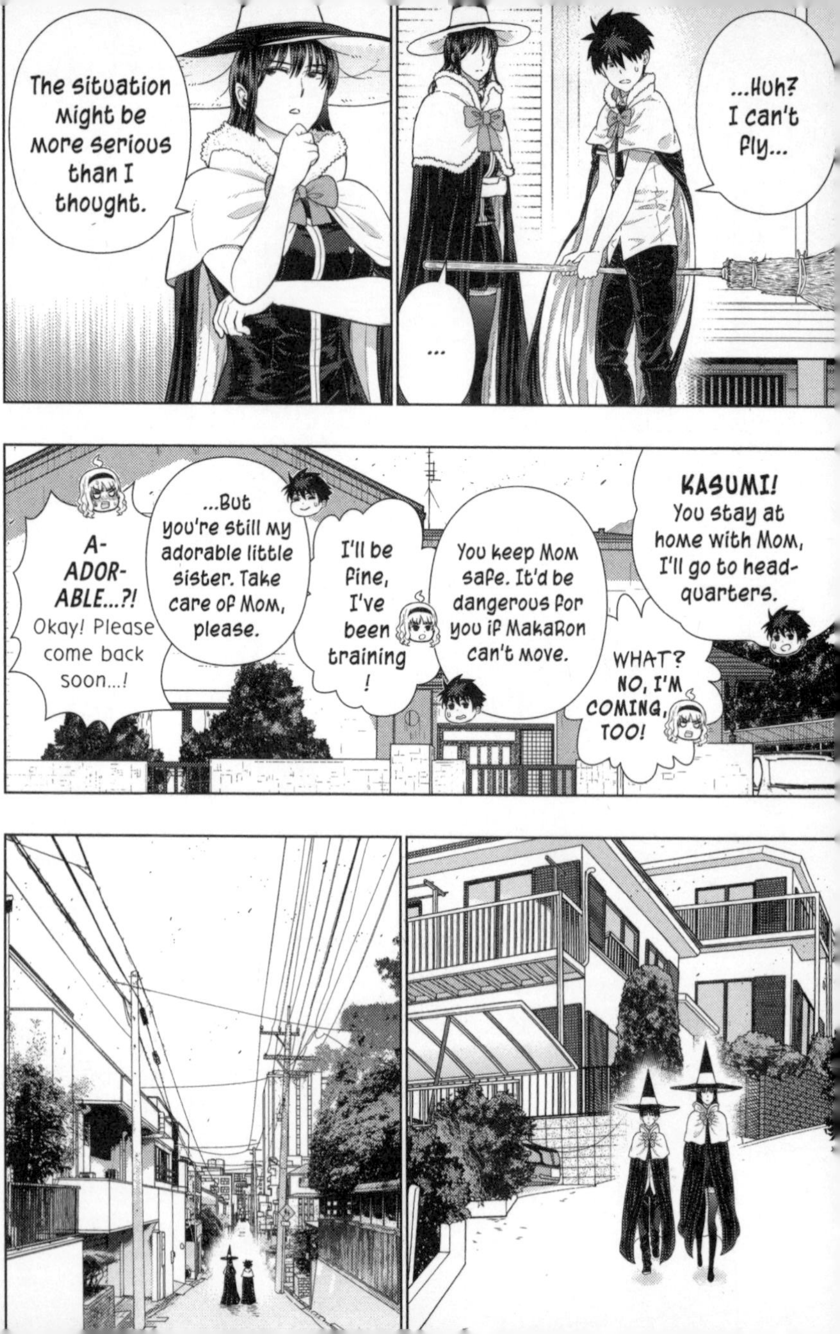
...Huh? I can't fly...
...
The situation might be more serious than I thought.
KASUMI! You stay at home with Mom, I'll go to head-quarters.
WHAT? NO, I'M COMING, TOO!
You keep Mom safe. It'd be dangerous for you if MakaRon can't move.
I'll be fine, I've been training!
...But you're still my adorable little sister. Take care of Mom, please.
A-ADORABLE...?! Okay! Please come back soon...!

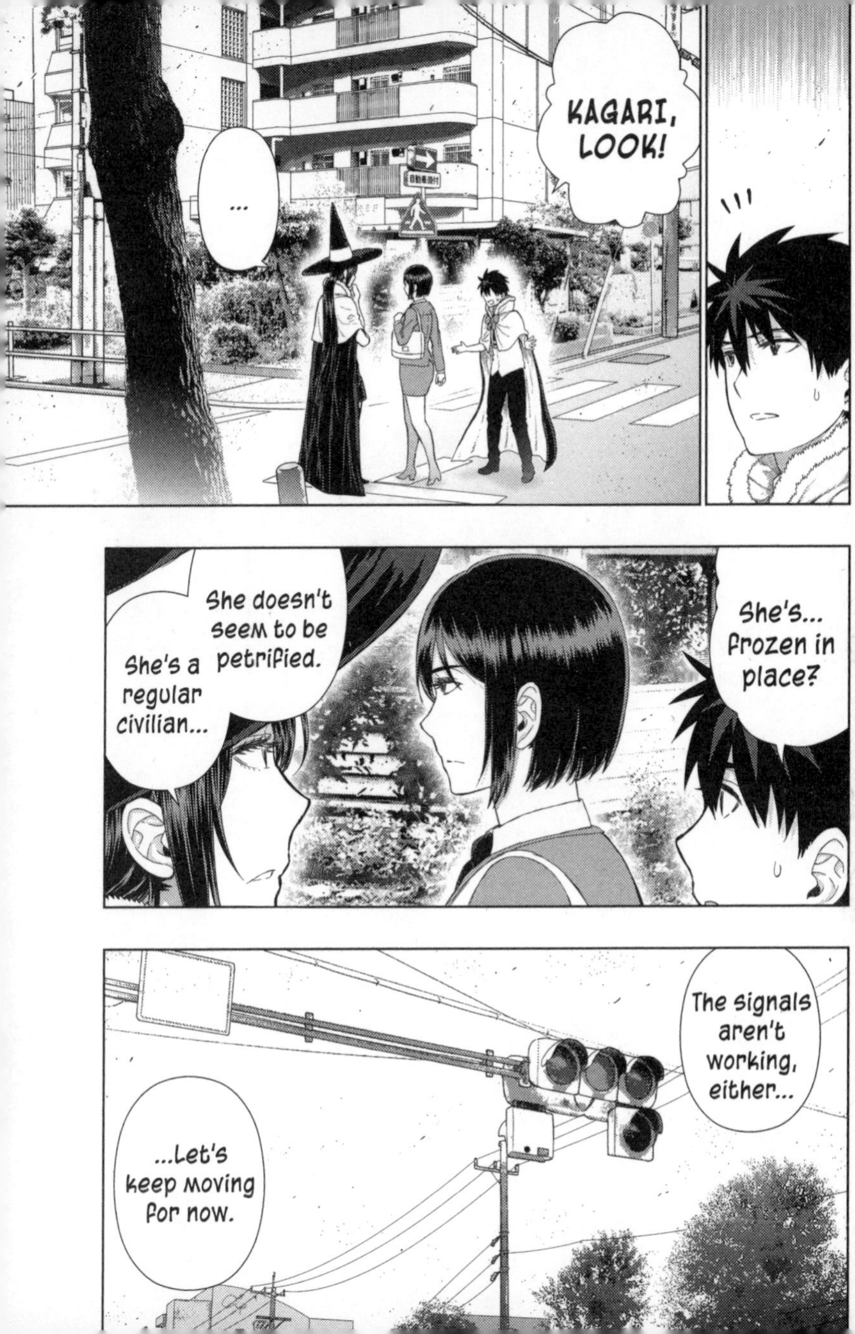
KAGARI, LOOK!
...
She's... frozen in place?
She doesn't seem to be petrified.
She's a regular civilian...
The signals aren't working, either...
...Let's keep moving for now.

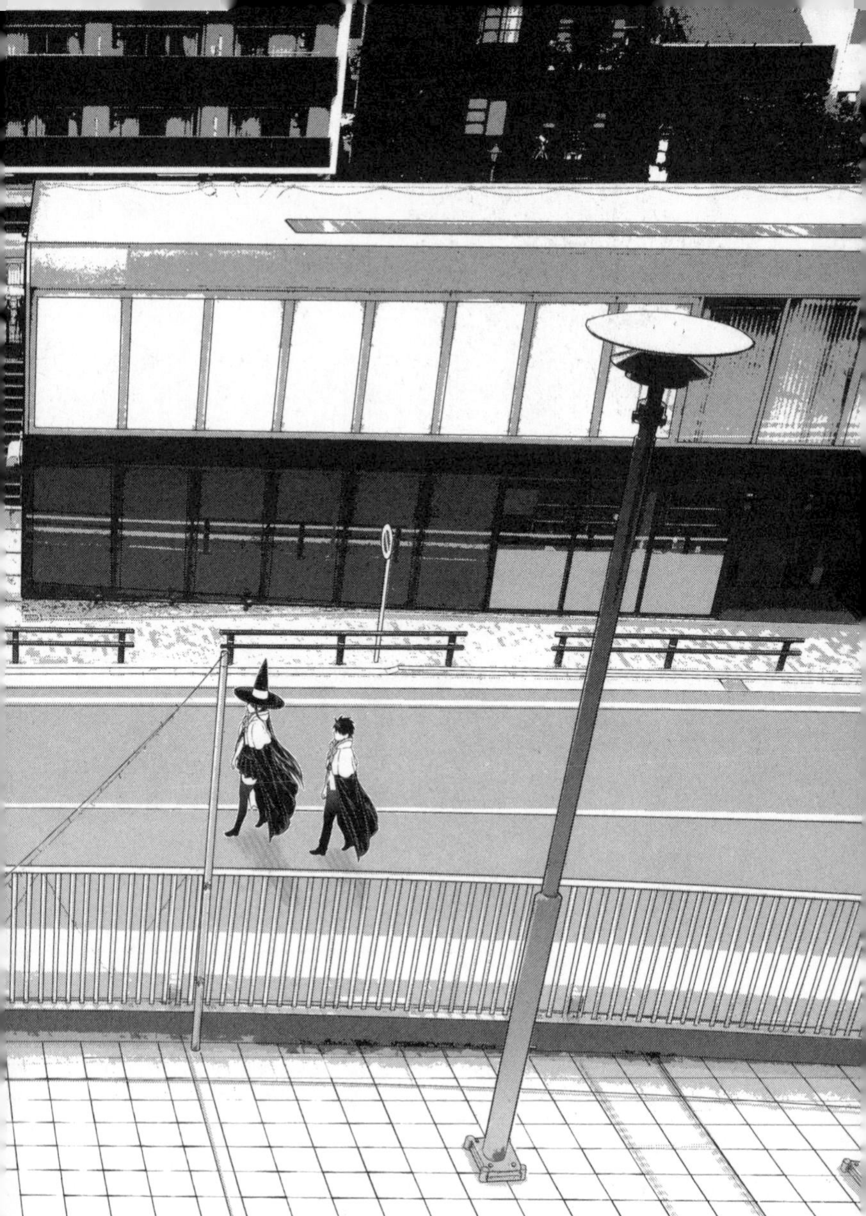

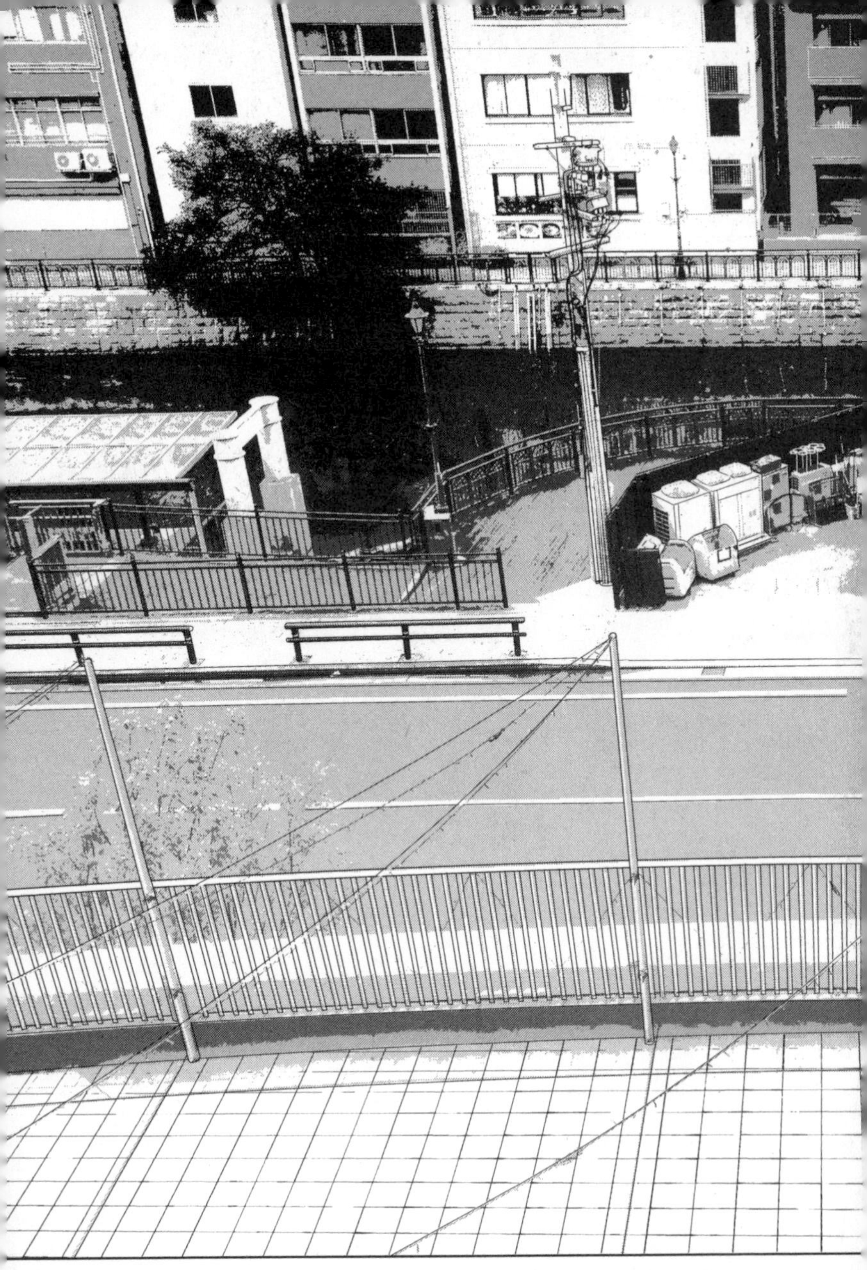

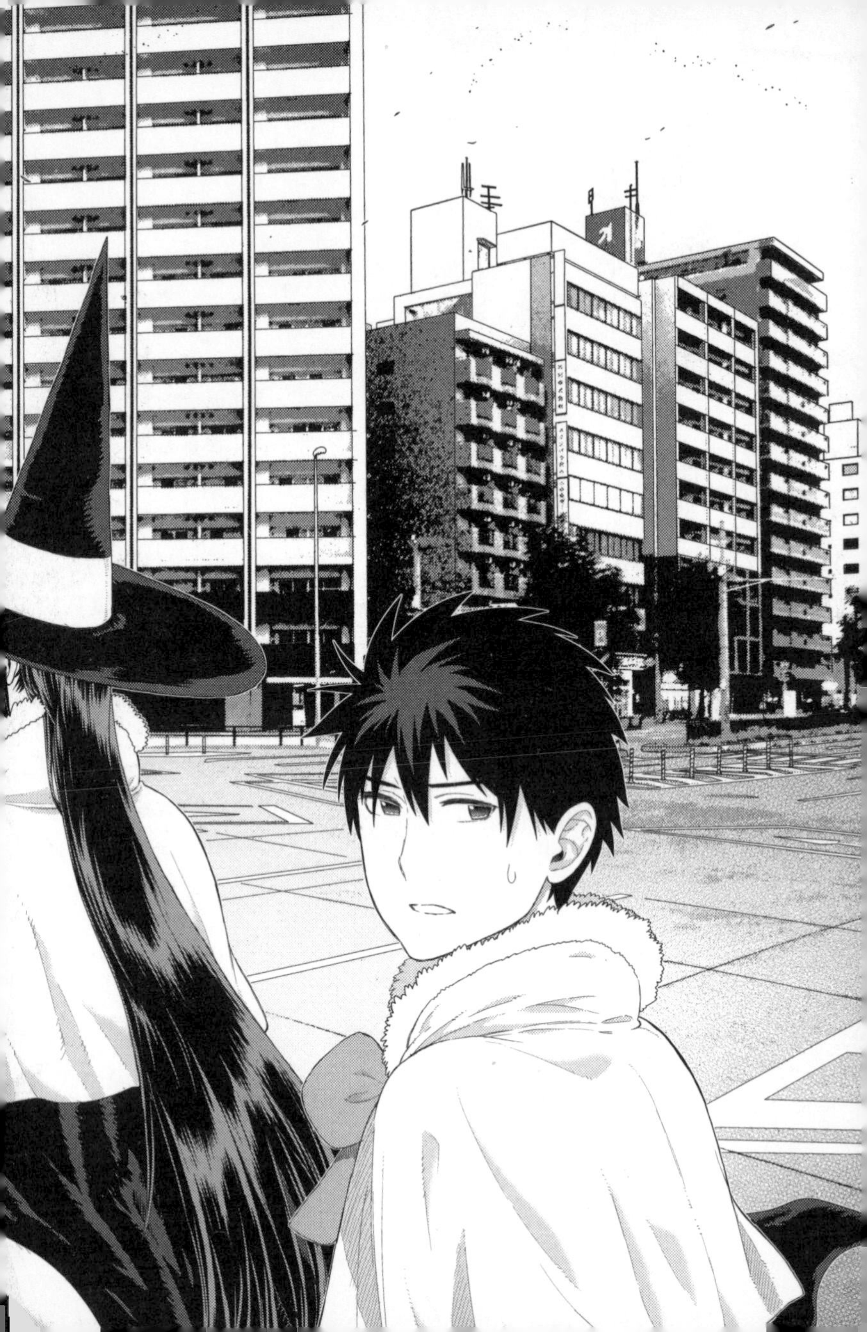

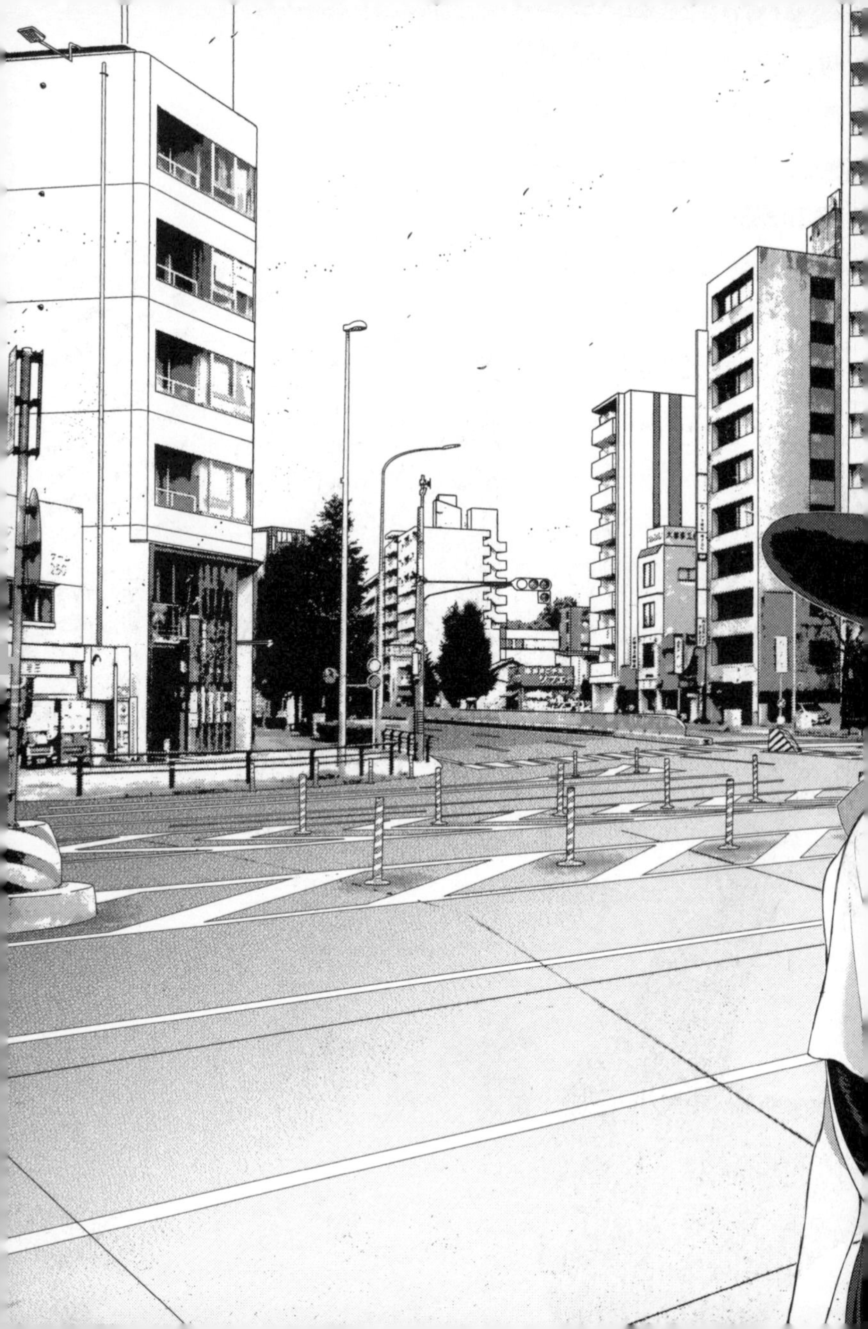

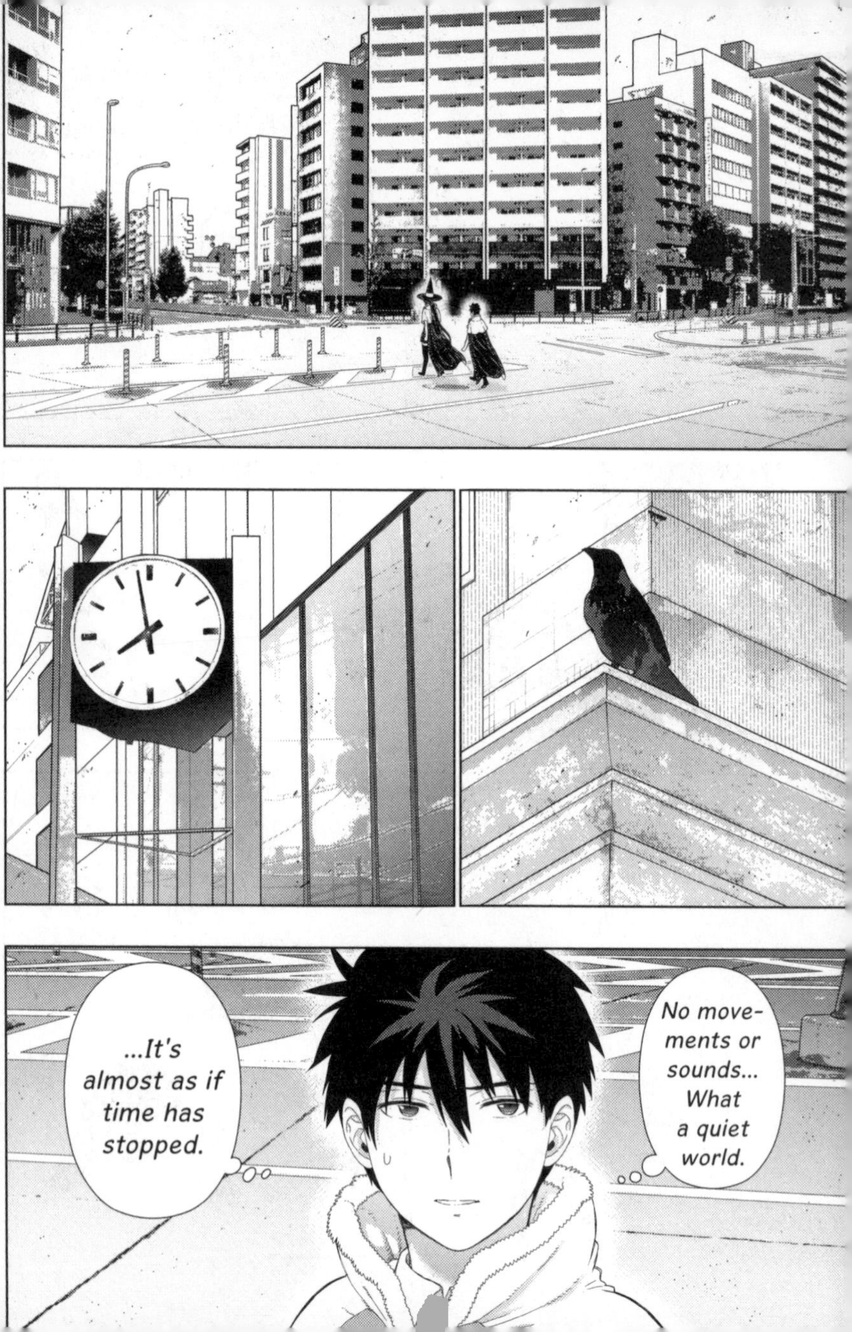
No move-
ments or
sounds...
What
a quiet
world.
...It's
almost as if
time has
stopped.

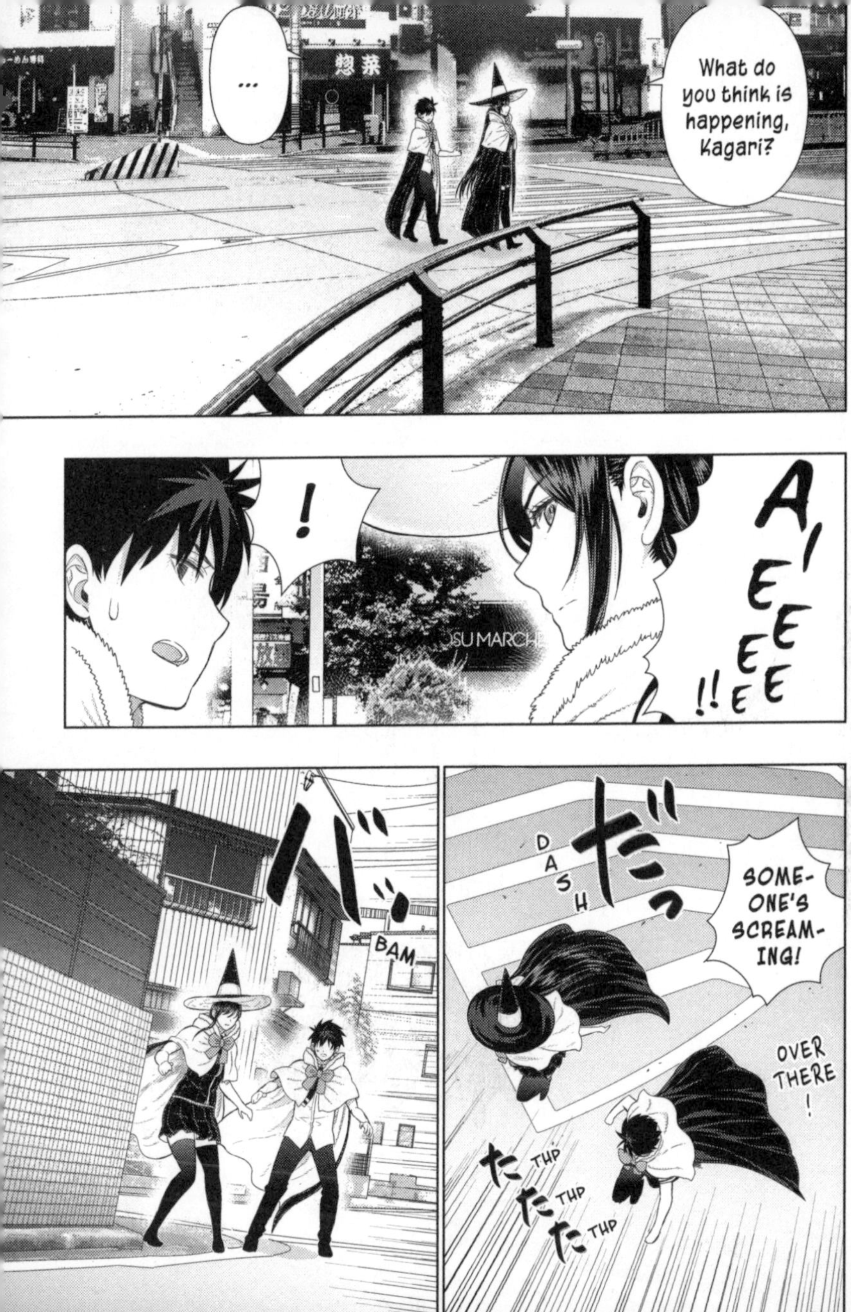
What do you think is happening, Kagari?
...
惣菜
AIEEEEEEE!!
!
SU MARCHE
だっ
DASH
SOME-ONE'S SCREAM-ING!
OVER THERE!
たたた
THP THP THP
バッ
BAM

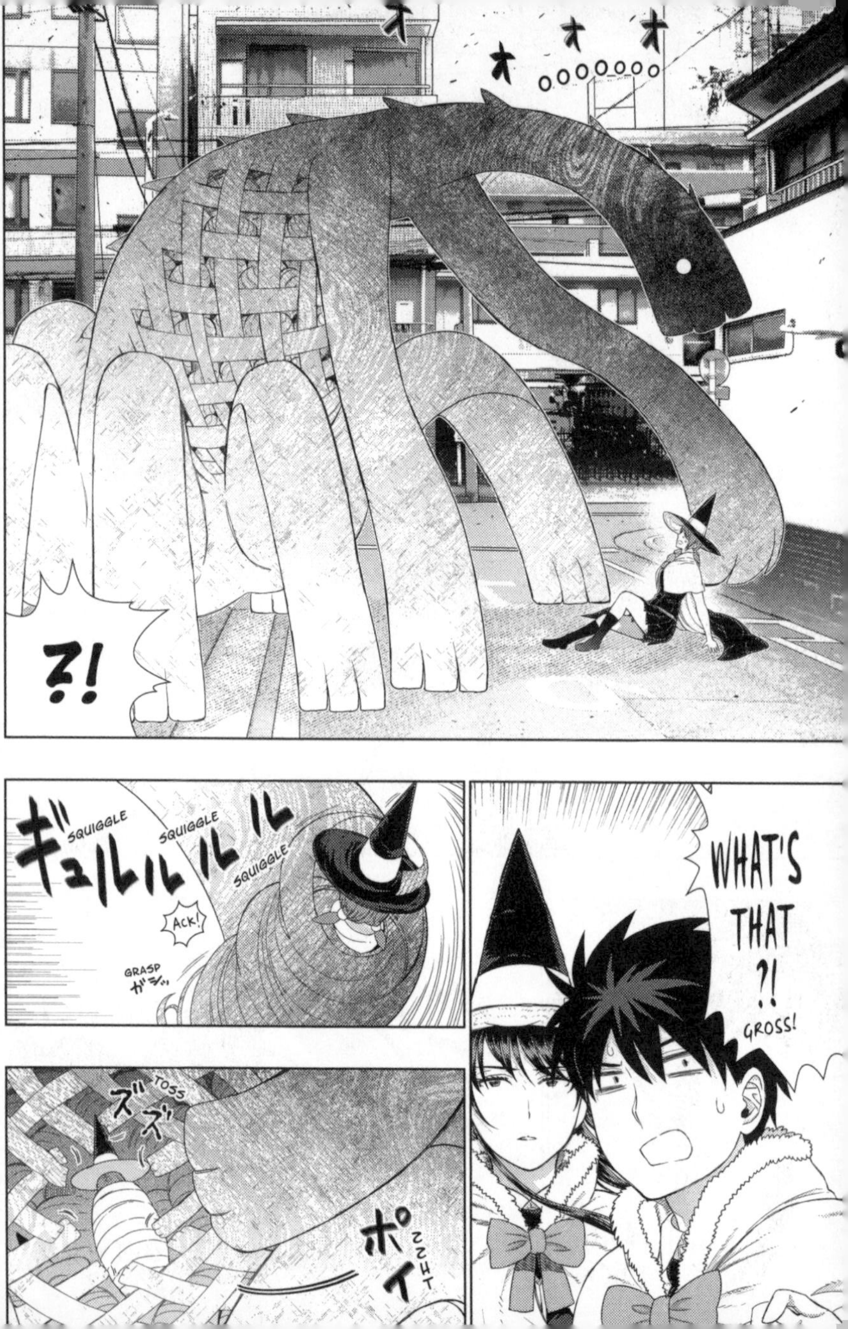
オオオオ
OOOOOOO
?!
WHAT'S THAT?!
GROSS!
ギュルルルル
SQUIGGLE SQUIGGLE SQUIGGLE
ACK!
GRASP ガシッ
ズズ
TOSS
ポイ
ZZHT

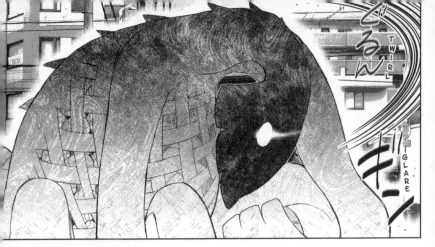

AH! IT NOTICED US!

Stay back.

!!
...MY MAGIC!

HUSH

RIGHT! WE CAN'T USE MAGIC RIGHT NOW, KAGARI...!

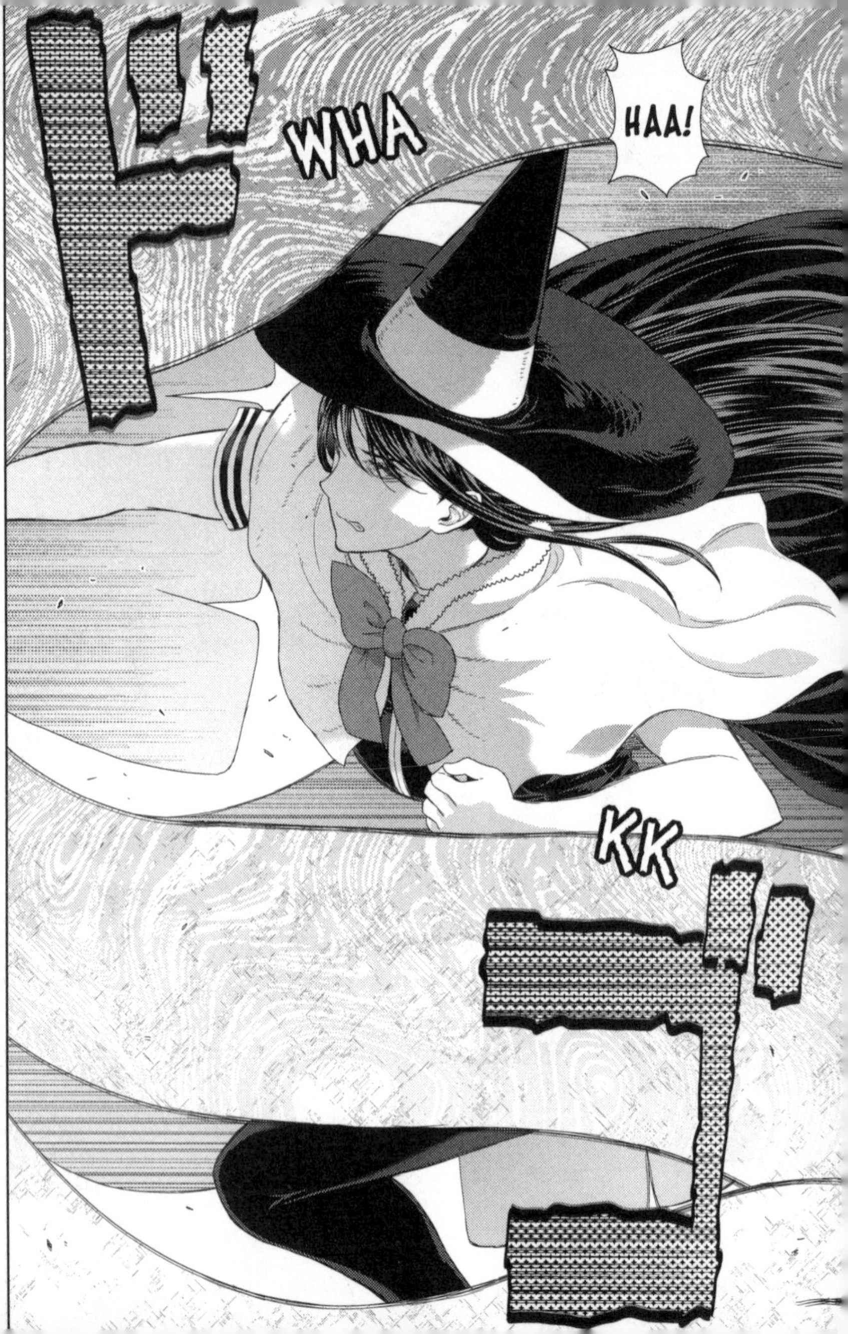
HAA!
WHA
ド
KK
ゴ

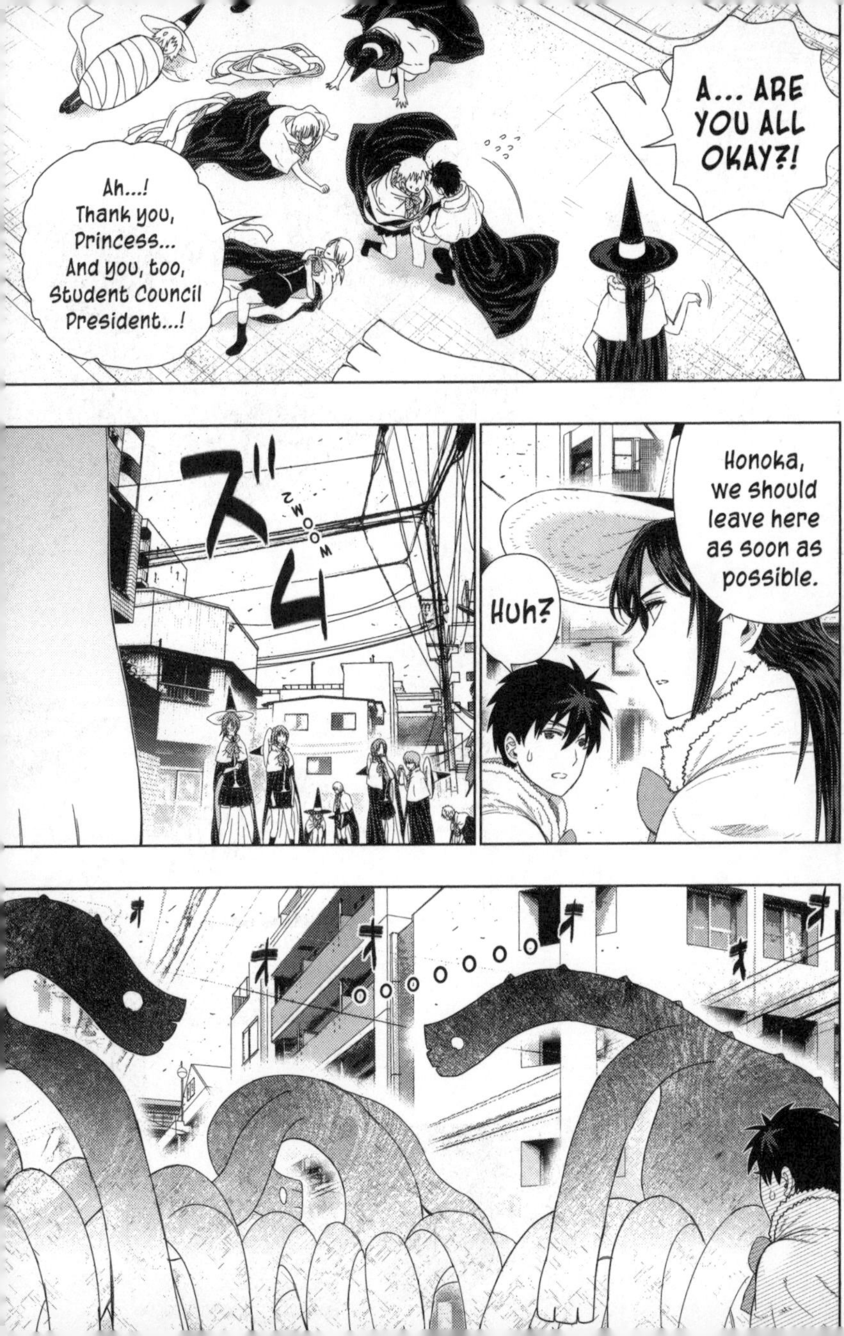
A... ARE YOU ALL OKAY?!
Ah...! Thank you, Princess... And you, too, Student Council President...!
Honoka, we should leave here as soon as possible.
Huh?
ズム
ZWOOM
オオオオオ
oooooooooo

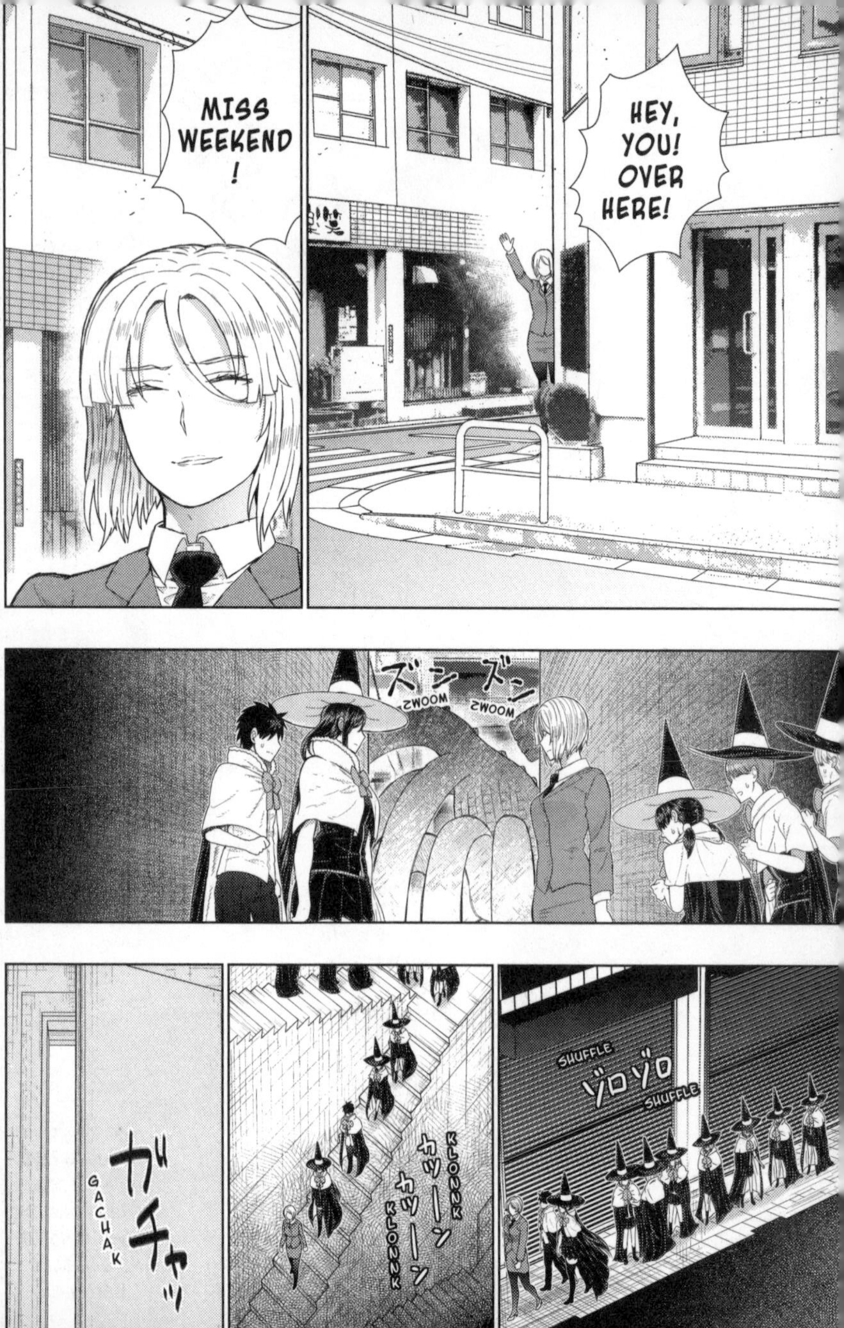
HEY, YOU! OVER HERE!
MISS WEEKEND!
ズンズン
ZWOOM ZWOOM
SHUFFLE
ゾロゾロ
SHUFFLE
KLONNK
カツーン カツーン
KLONNK
ガチャッ
GACHAK

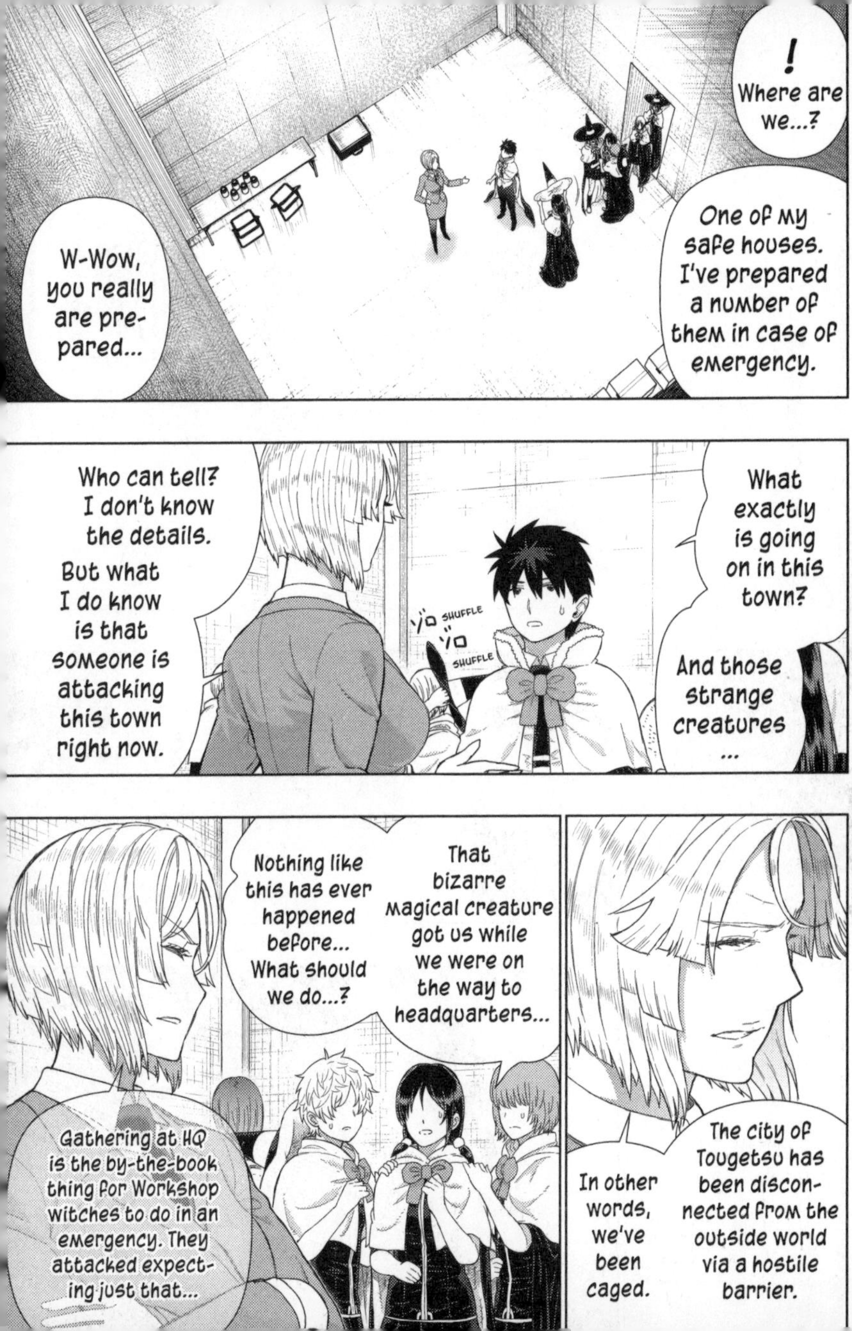
!
Where are we...?
One of my safe houses. I've prepared a number of them in case of emergency.
W-Wow, you really are pre-pared...
What exactly is going on in this town?
And those strange creatures ...
ゾロ SHUFFLE
ゾロ SHUFFLE
Who can tell? I don't know the details.
But what I do know is that someone is attacking this town right now.
The city of Tougetsu has been discon-nected from the outside world via a hostile barrier.
In other words, we've been caged.
That bizarre magical creature got us while we were on the way to headquarters...
Nothing like this has ever happened before... What should we do...?
Gathering at HQ is the by-the-book thing for Workshop witches to do in an emergency. They attacked expect-ing just that...

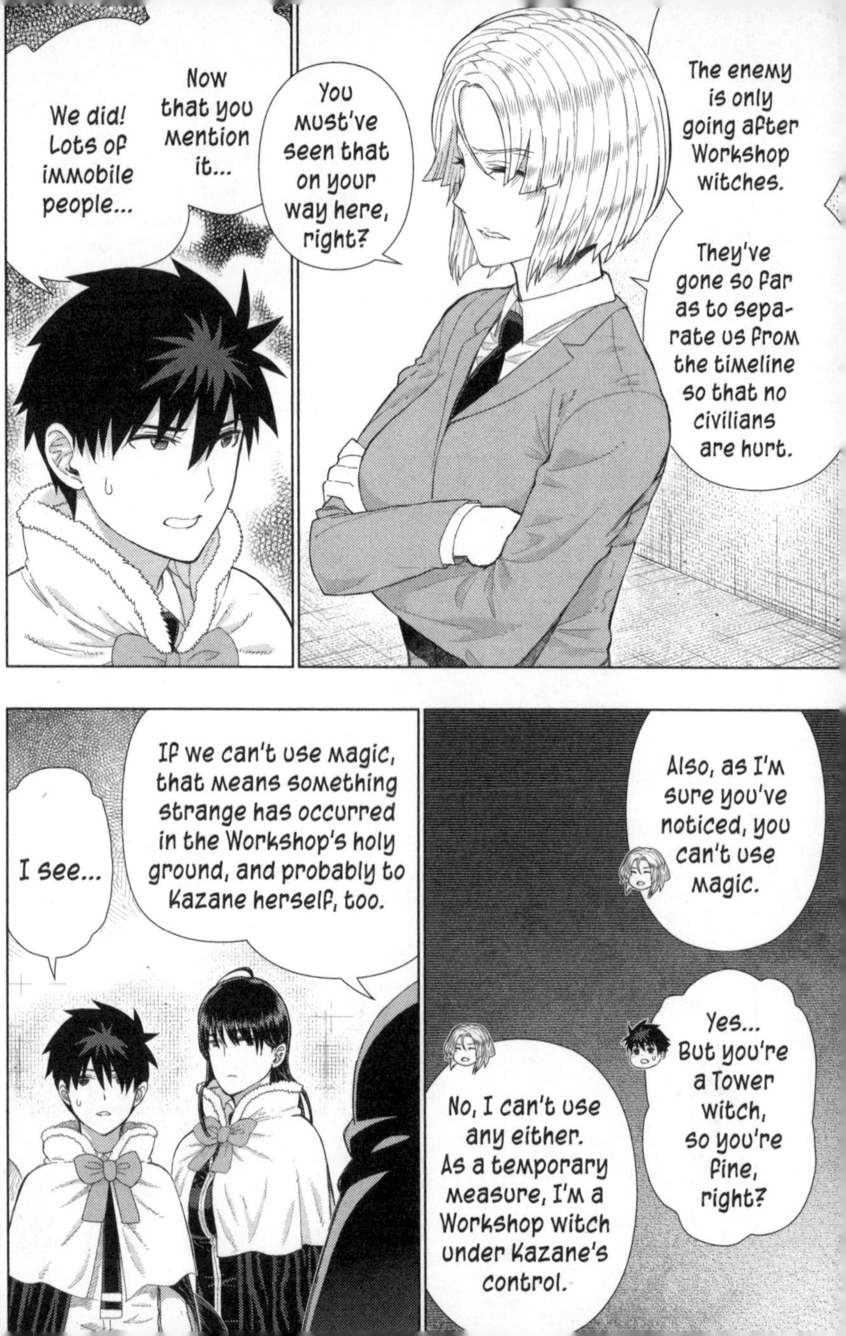

The enemy is only going after Workshop witches.
They've gone so far as to separate us from the timeline so that no civilians are hurt.
You must've seen that on your way here, right?
Now that you mention it...
We did! Lots of immobile people...
Also, as I'm sure you've noticed, you can't use magic.
Yes... But you're a Tower witch, so you're fine, right?
No, I can't use any either. As a temporary measure, I'm a Workshop witch under Kazane's control.
If we can't use magic, that means something strange has occurred in the Workshop's holy ground, and probably to Kazane herself, too.
I see...

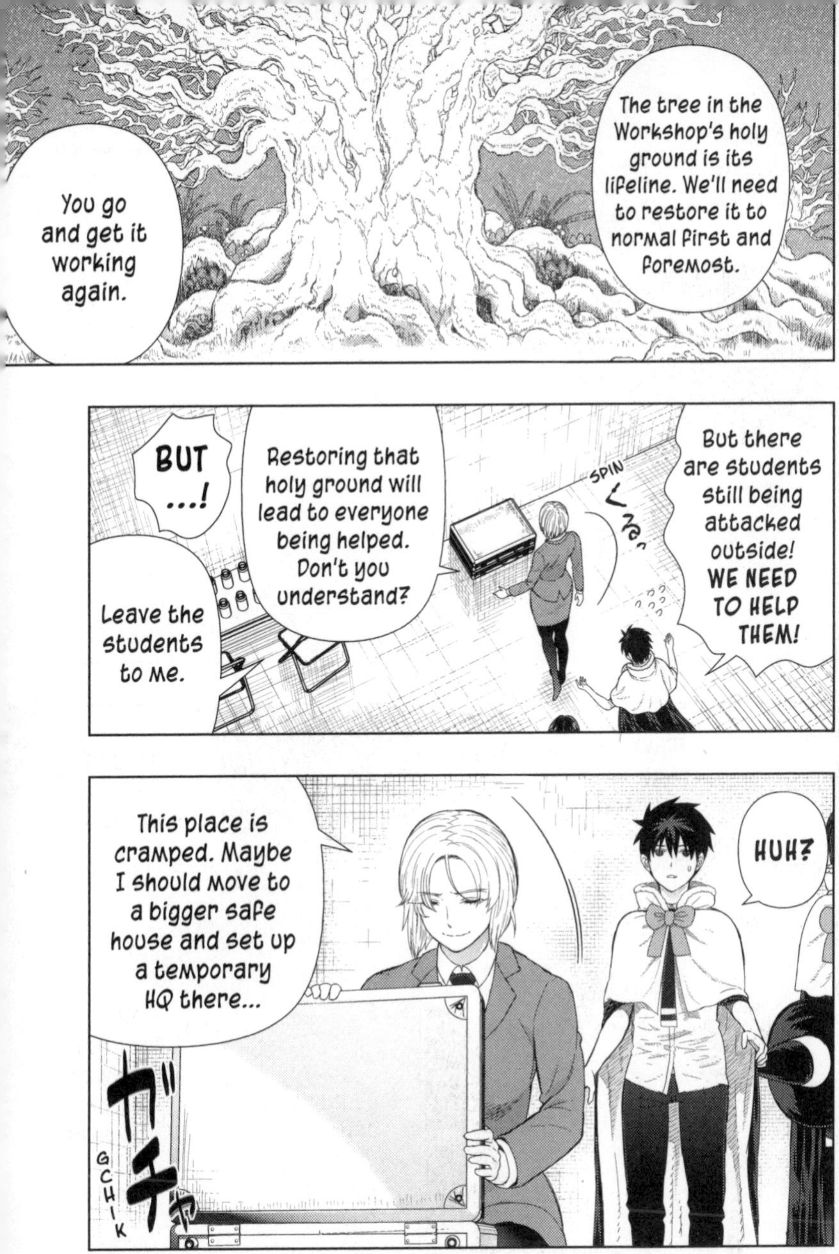
The tree in the Workshop's holy ground is its lifeline. We'll need to restore it to normal first and foremost.
You go and get it working again.
But there are students still being attacked outside! WE NEED TO HELP THEM!
SPIN
Restoring that holy ground will lead to everyone being helped. Don't you understand?
BUT ...!
Leave the students to me.
HUH?
This place is cramped. Maybe I should move to a bigger safe house and set up a temporary HQ there...
GCHIK

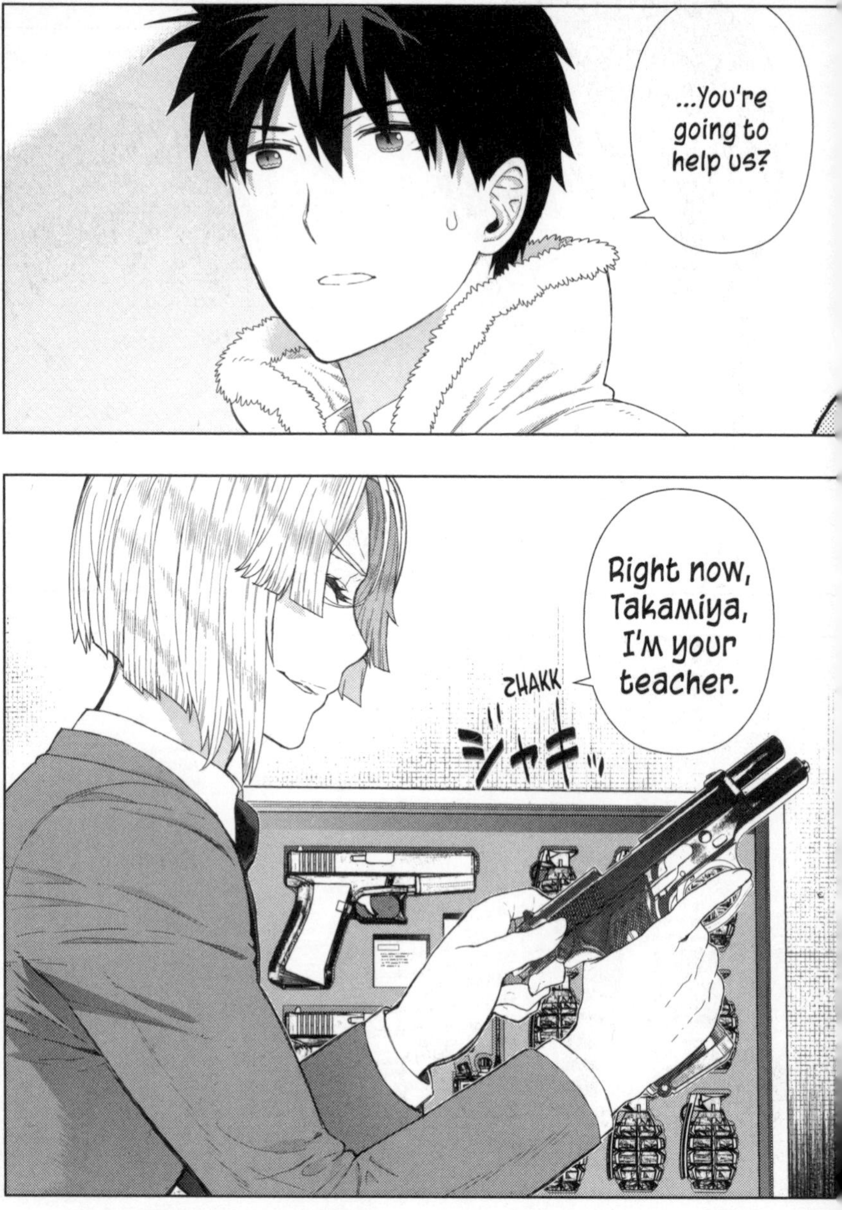
...You're going to help us?
Right now, Takamiya, I'm your teacher.
ZHAKK
ジャキッ

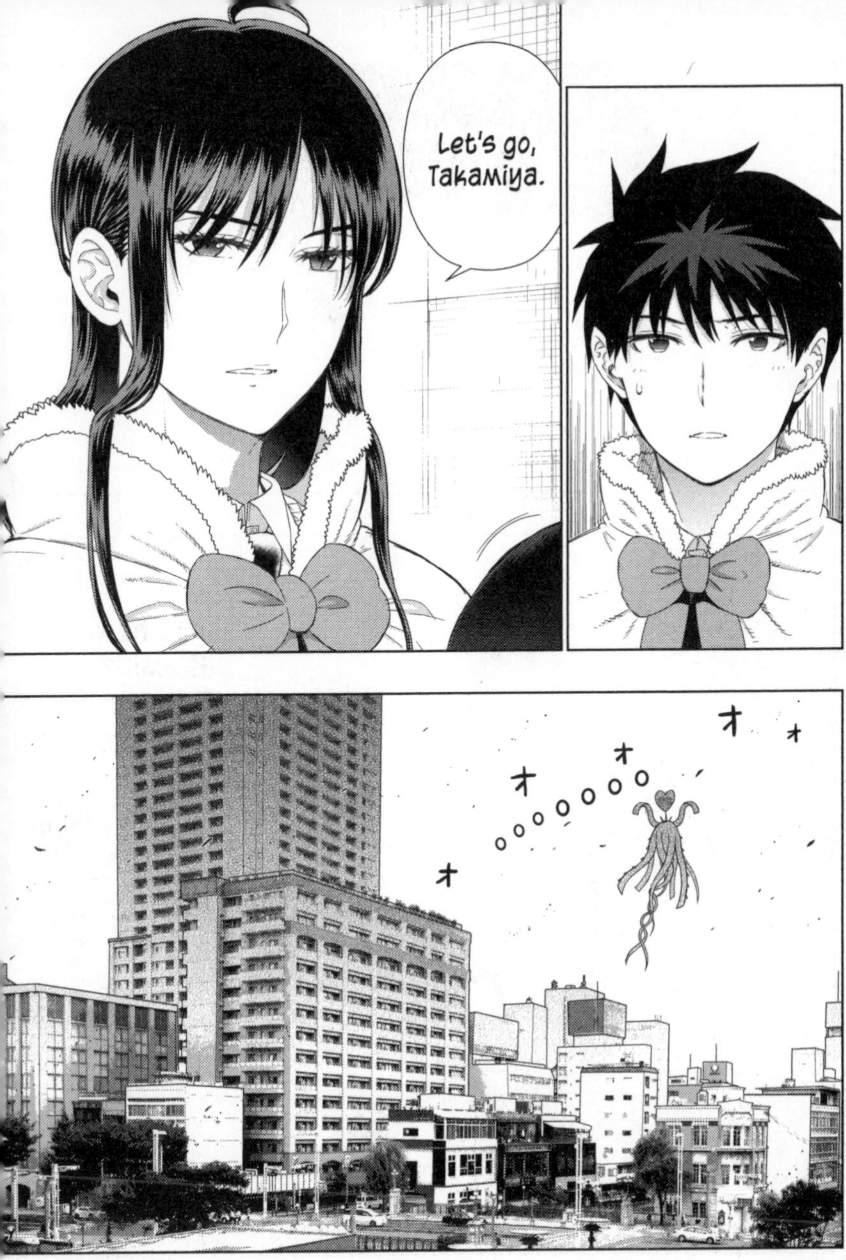
Let's go, Takamiya.
オ
オ
オ
ooooooo
オ
オ

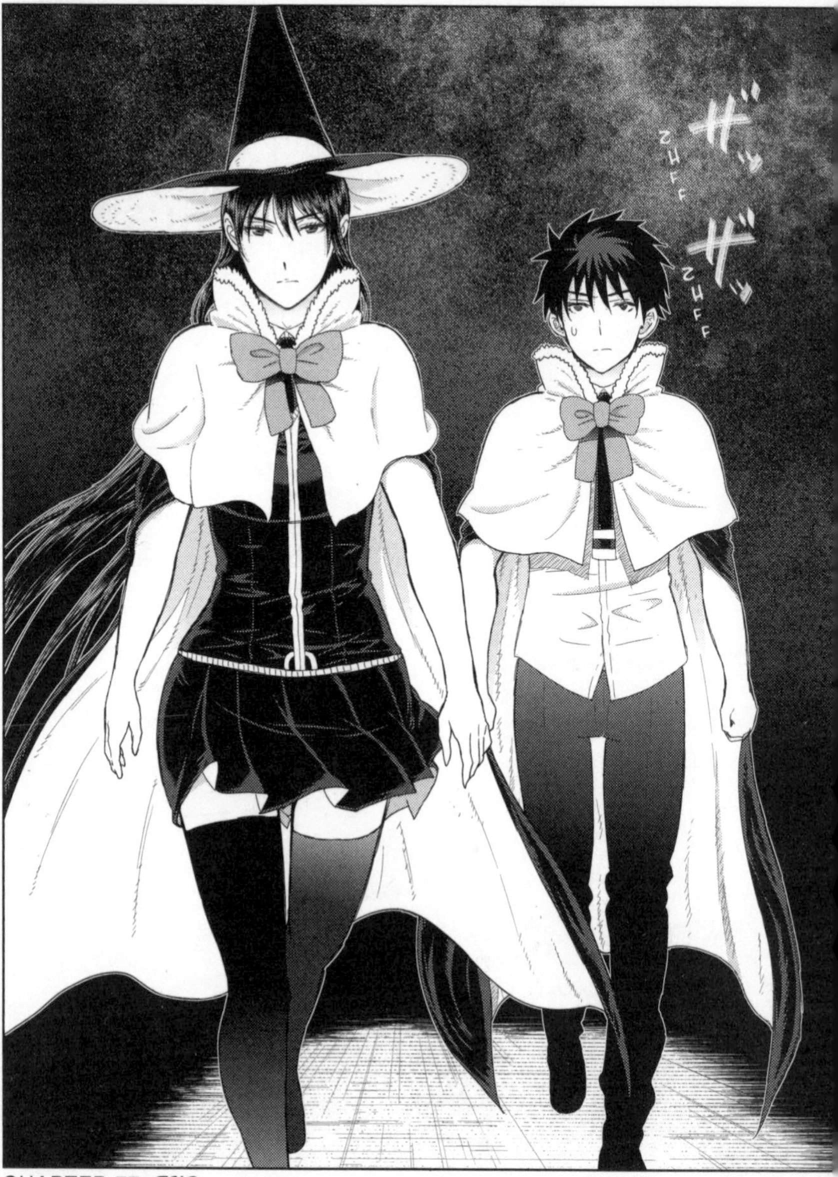
ザッ
ZHFF
ザッ
ZHFF

CHAPTER 77: END

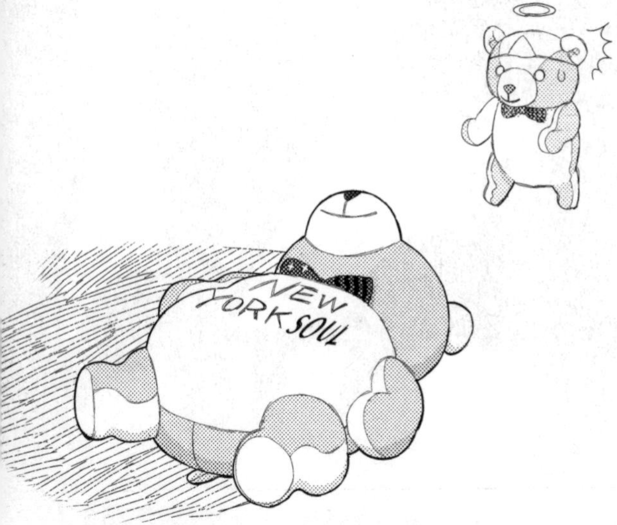
NEW YORK SOUL

Witchcraft Works

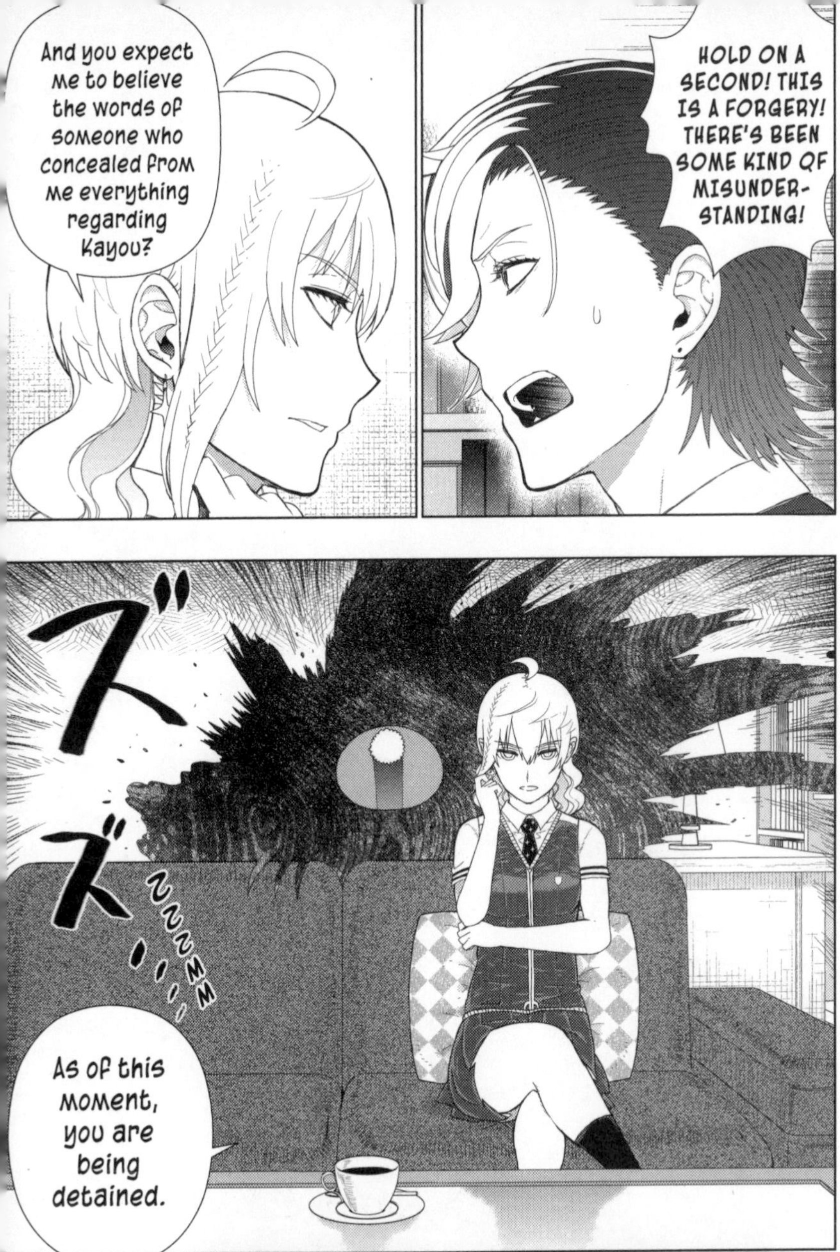
HOLD ON A SECOND! THIS IS A FORGERY! THERE'S BEEN SOME KIND OF MISUNDER-STANDING!
And you expect me to believe the words of someone who concealed from me everything regarding Kayou?
ズズ…
ZZZMMM
As of this moment, you are being detained.

CHAPTER 78 Takamiya vs. Alcina: Part 2

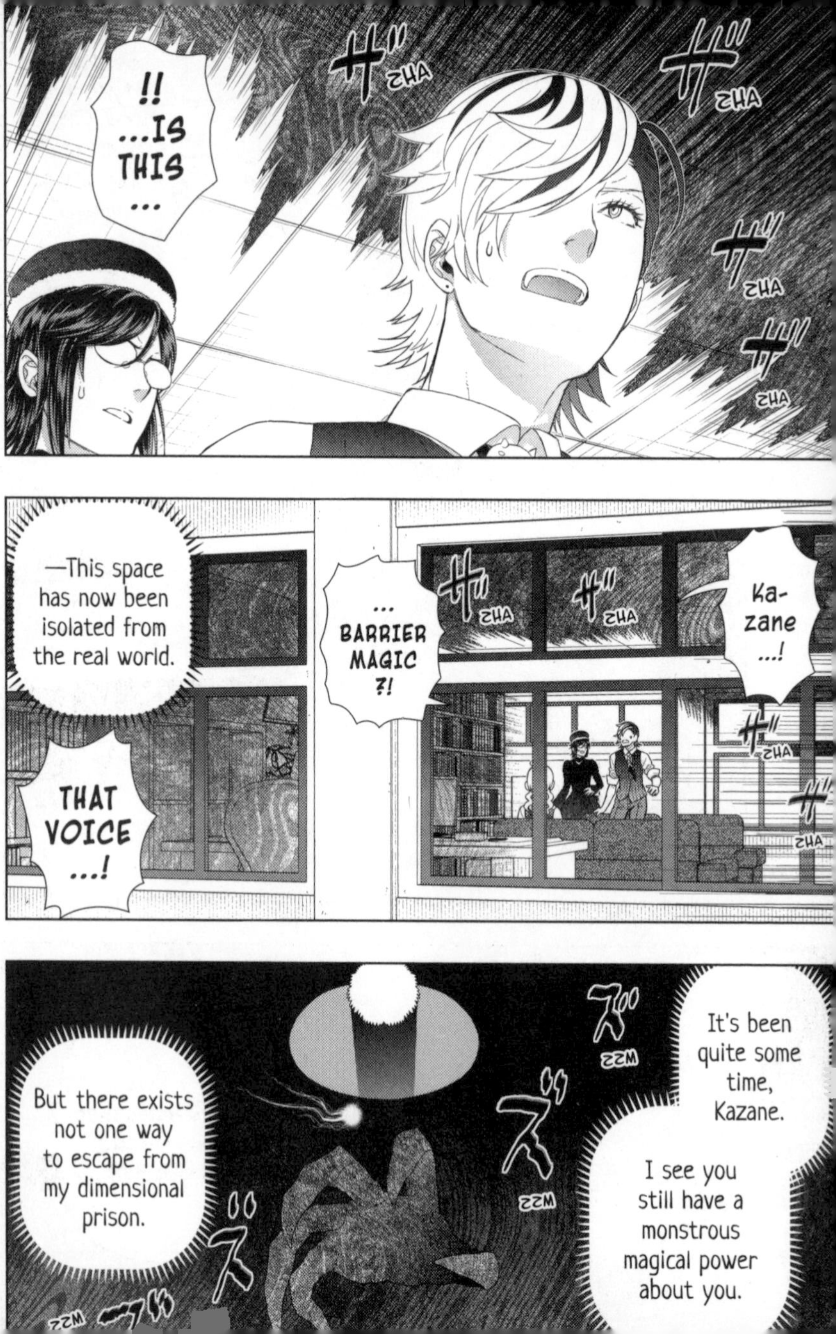

!! ...IS THIS ...
ZHA
ZHA
ZHA
ZHA
Ka-zane ...!
ZHA
ZHA
ZHA
ZHA
... BARRIER MAGIC ?!
—This space has now been isolated from the real world.
THAT VOICE ...!
It's been quite some time, Kazane.
I see you still have a monstrous magical power about you.
ZZM
ZZM
But there exists not one way to escape from my dimensional prison.
ZZM

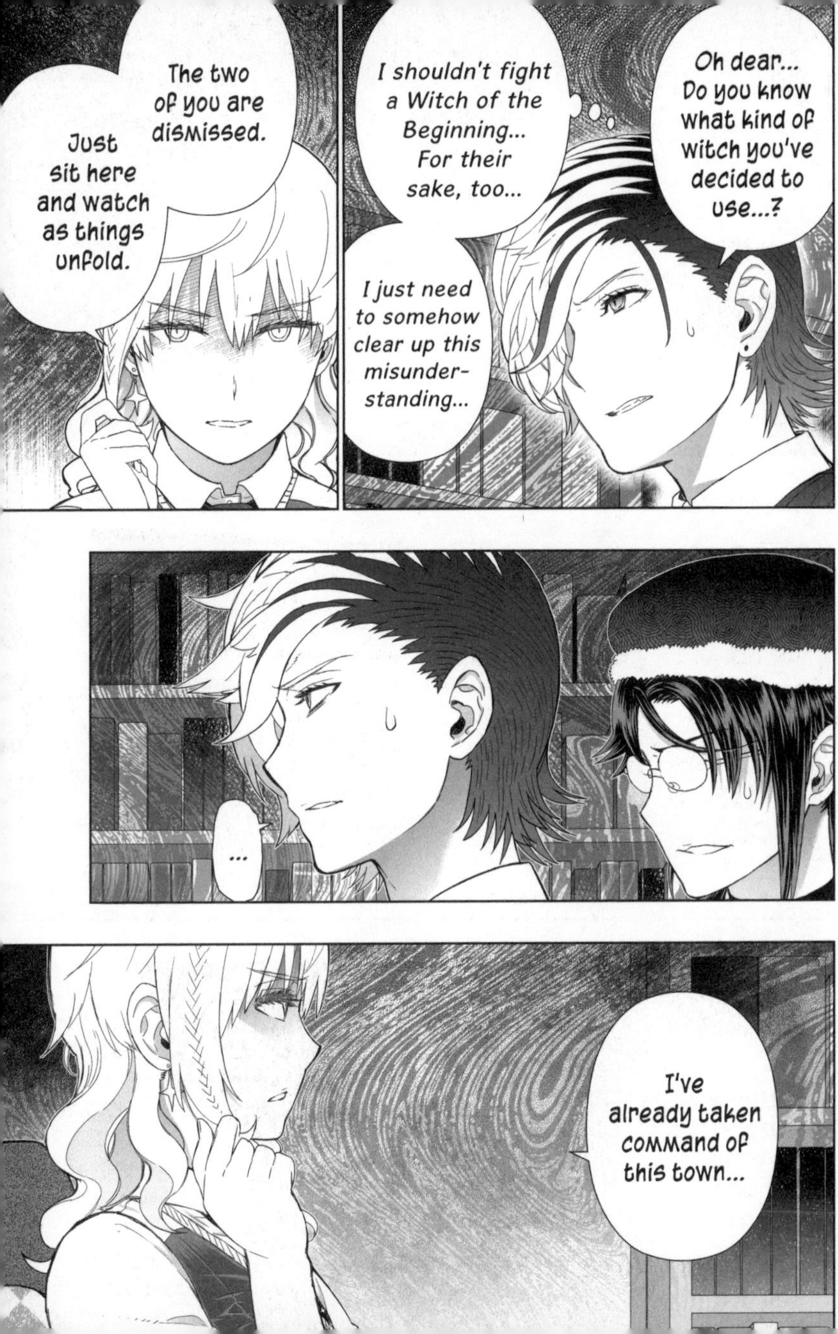
Oh dear... Do you know what kind of witch you've decided to use...?
I shouldn't fight a Witch of the Beginning... For their sake, too...
I just need to somehow clear up this misunderstanding...
The two of you are dismissed.
Just sit here and watch as things unfold.
...
I've already taken command of this town...

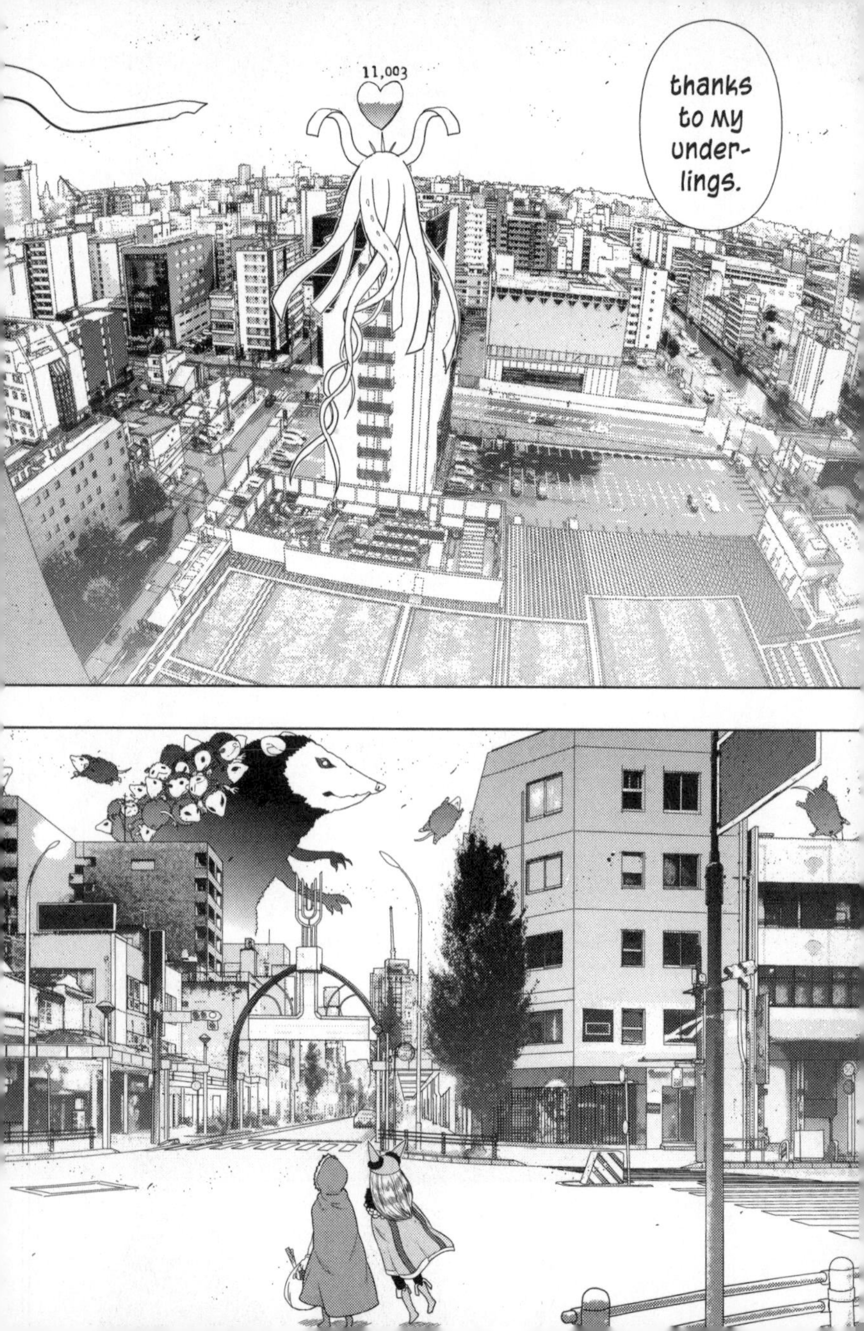
thanks to my under-lings.
11,003

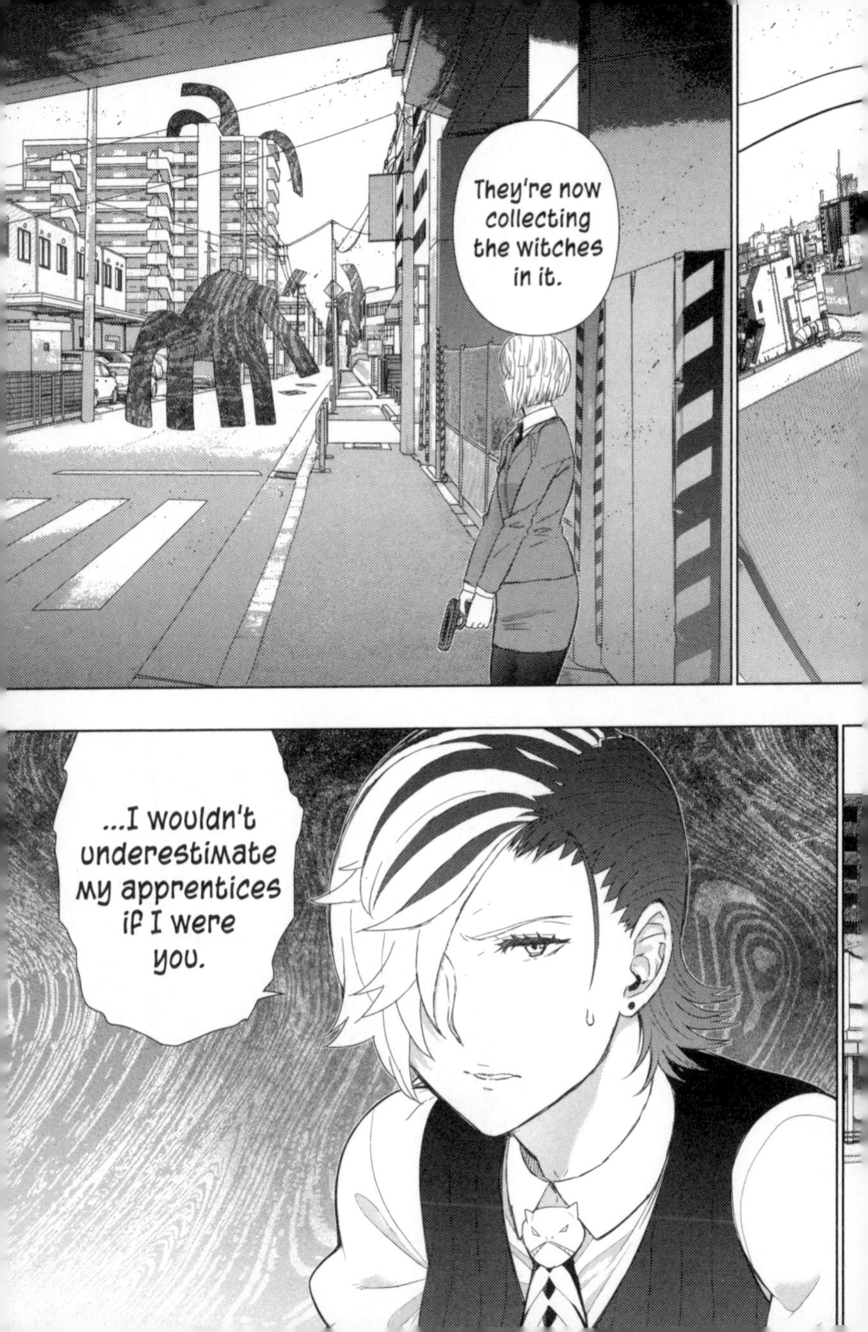
They're now collecting the witches in it.
...I wouldn't underestimate my apprentices if I were you.

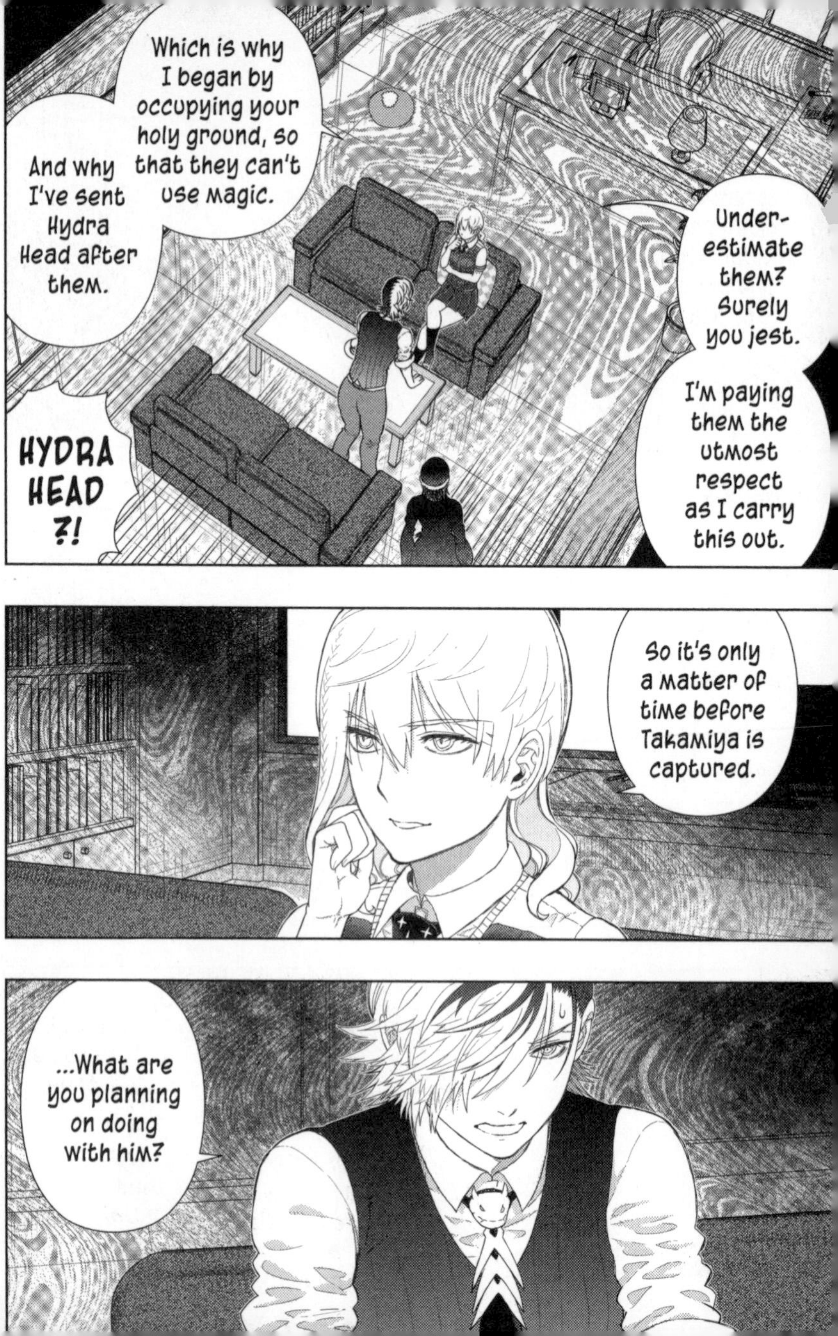
Under-estimate them? Surely you jest.
I'm paying them the utmost respect as I carry this out.
Which is why I began by occupying your holy ground, so that they can't use magic.
And why I've sent Hydra Head after them.
HYDRA HEAD ?!
So it's only a matter of time before Takamiya is captured.
...What are you planning on doing with him?

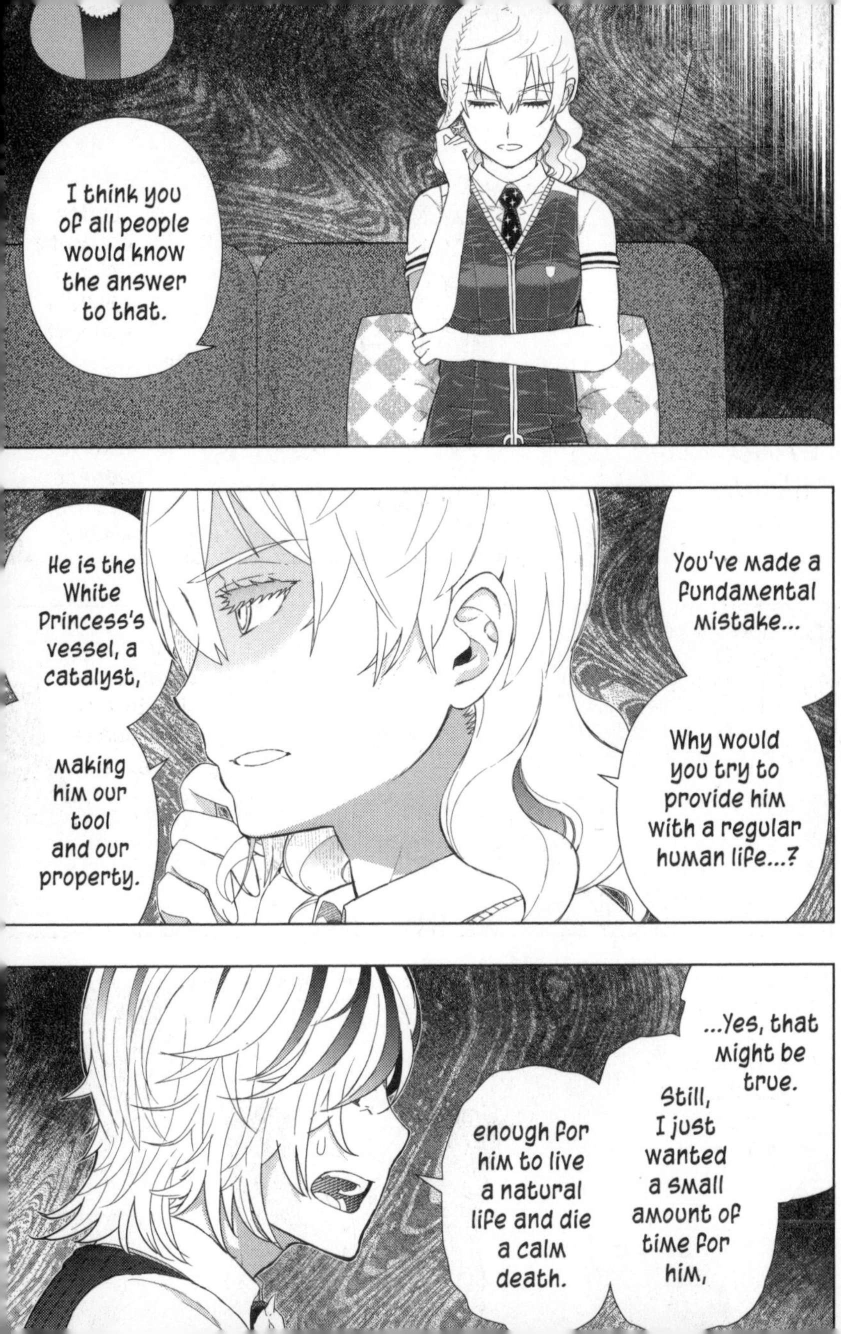

I think you of all people would know the answer to that.
You've made a fundamental mistake...
Why would you try to provide him with a regular human life...?
He is the White Princess's vessel, a catalyst,
making him our tool and our property.
...Yes, that might be true.
Still, I just wanted a small amount of time for him,
enough for him to live a natural life and die a calm death.

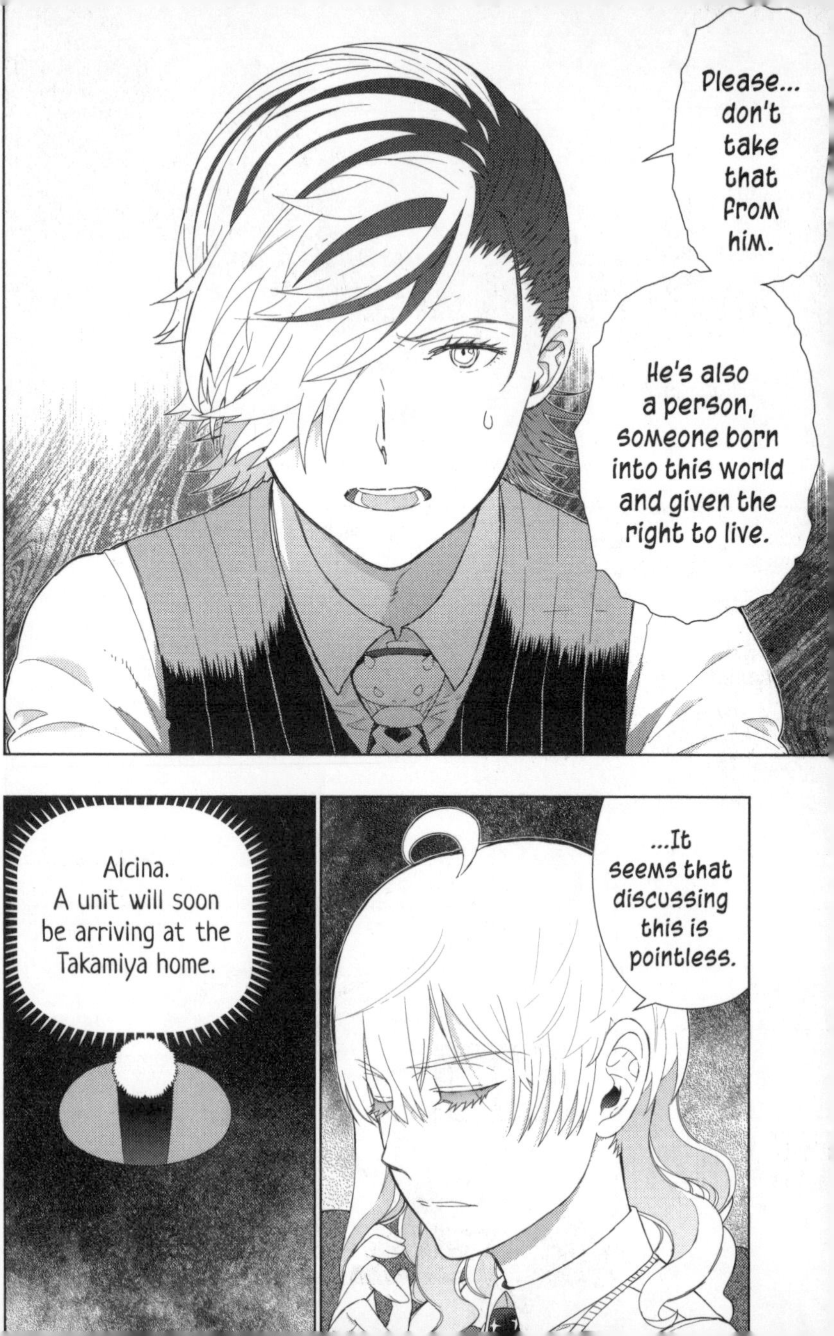
Please... don't take that from him.
He's also a person, someone born into this world and given the right to live.
...It seems that discussing this is pointless.
Alcina. A unit will soon be arriving at the Takamiya home.

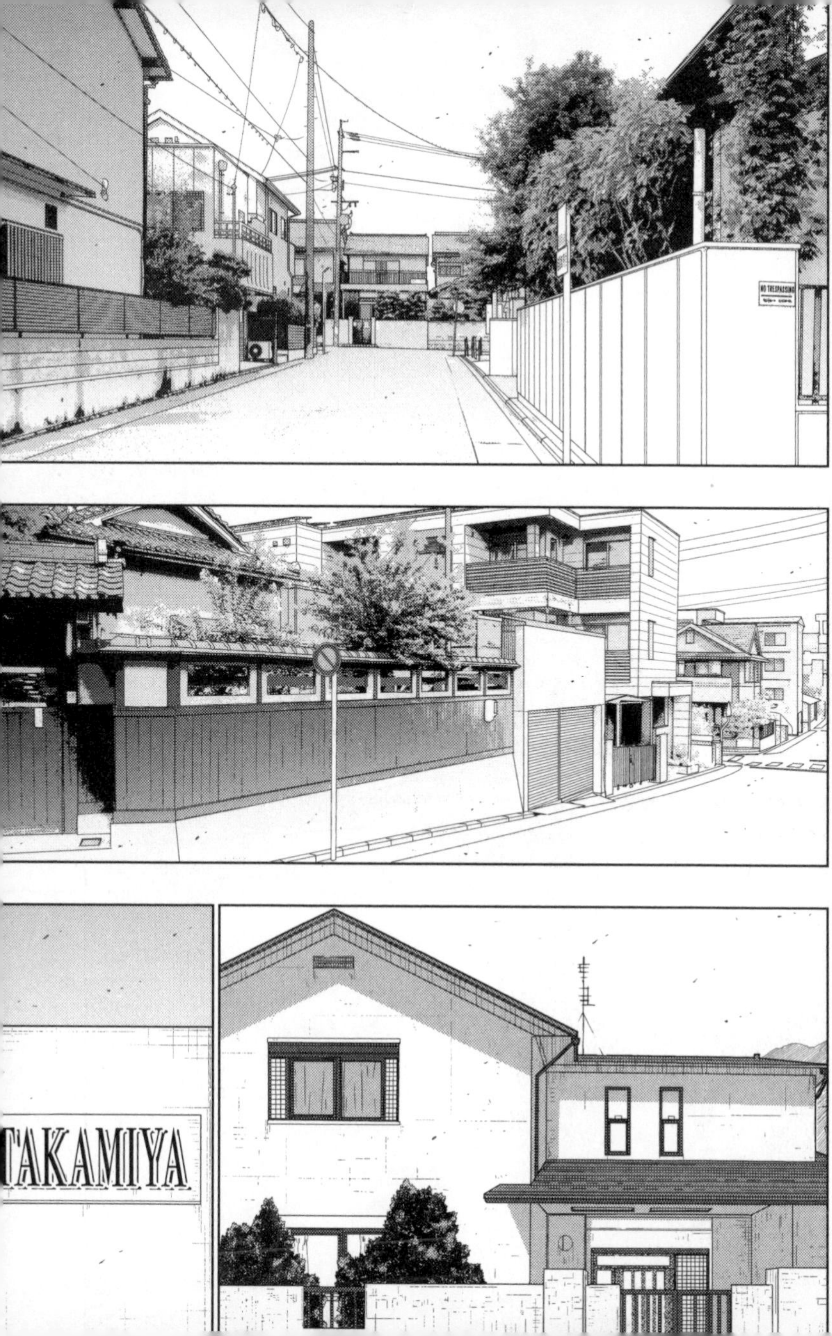
NO TRESPASSING
TAKAMIYA

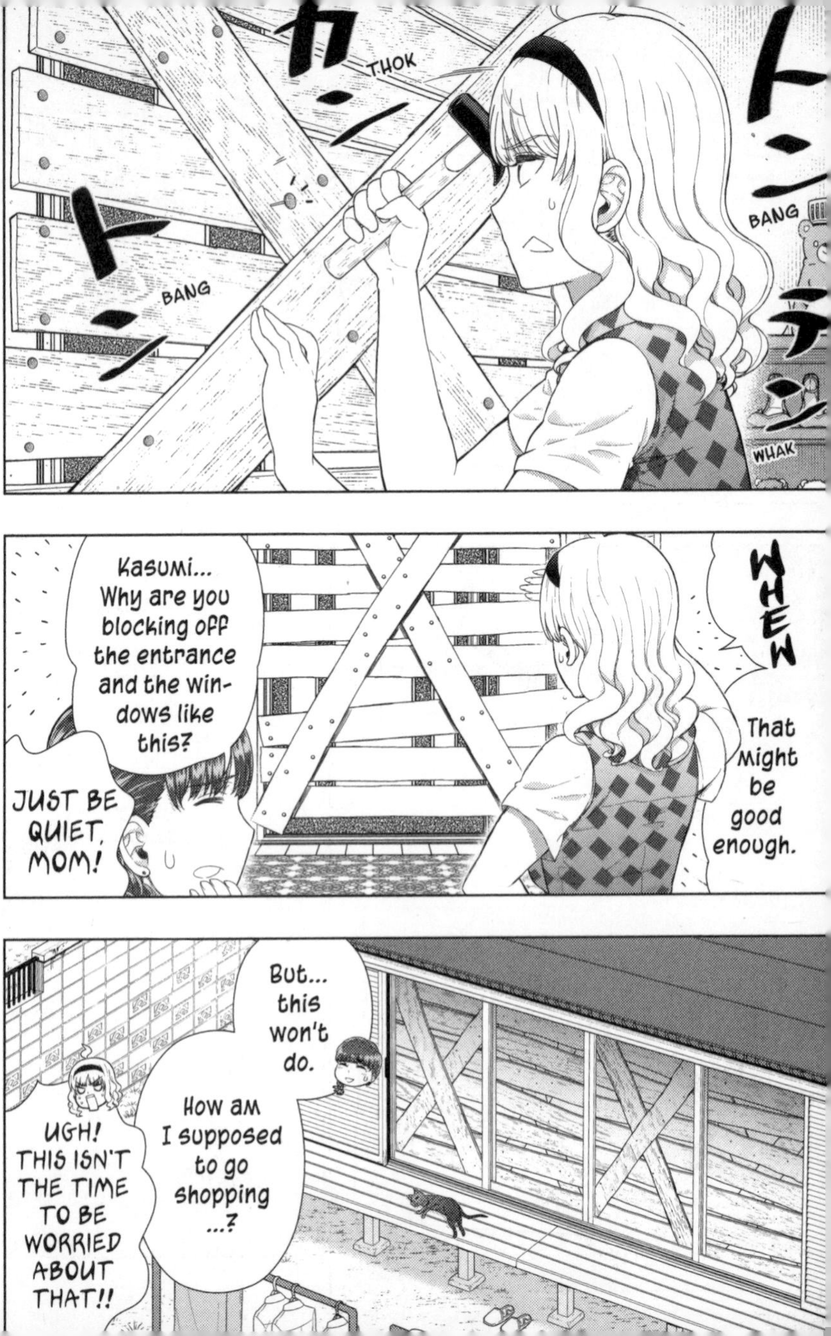
BANG
WHAK
THOK
BANG
WHEW
That might be good enough.
Kasumi... Why are you blocking off the entrance and the windows like this?
JUST BE QUIET, MOM!
But... this won't do.
How am I supposed to go shopping ...?
UGH! THIS ISN'T THE TIME TO BE WORRIED ABOUT THAT!!

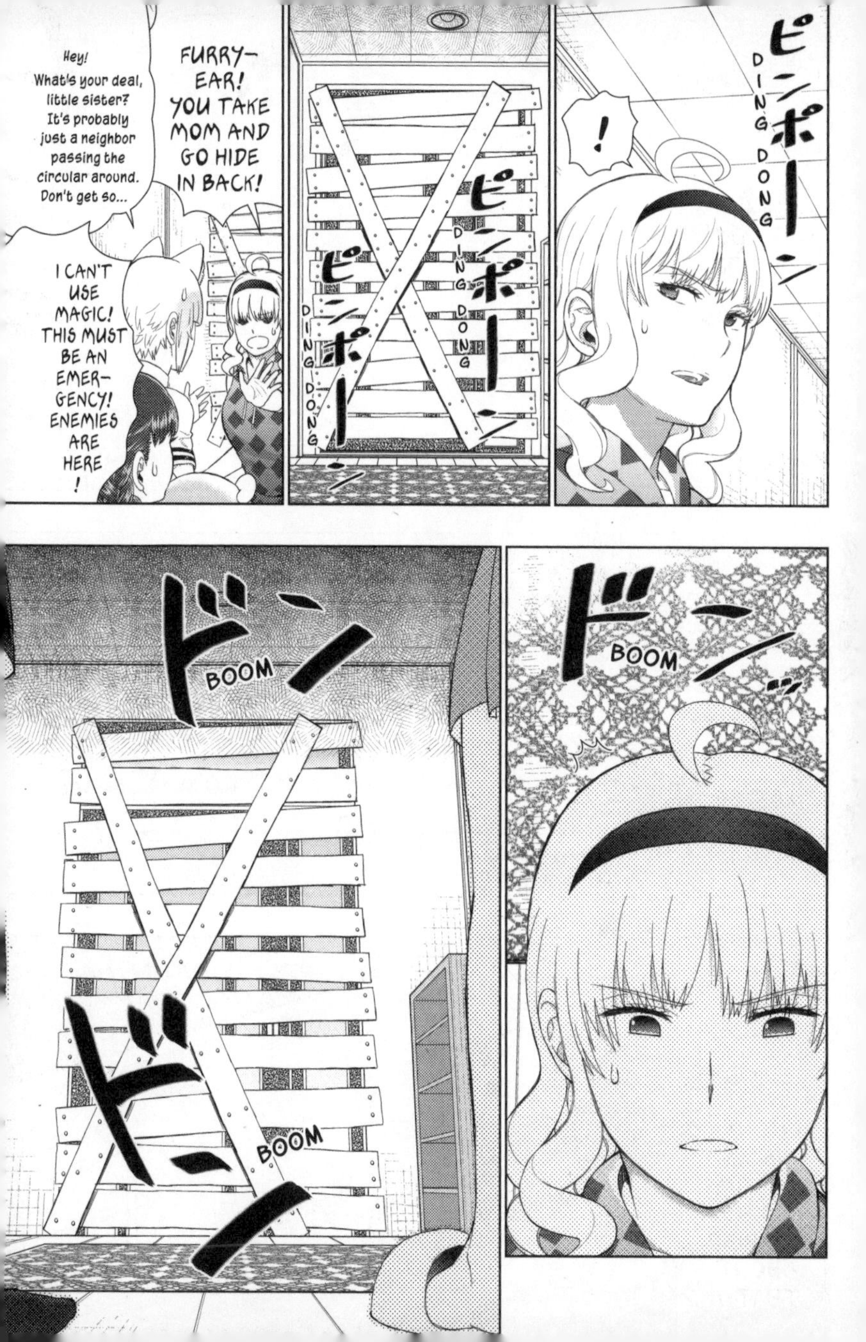
ピンポーン
DING DONG
!
ピンポーン
DING DONG
ピンポーン
DING DONG
FURRY-EAR! YOU TAKE MOM AND GO HIDE IN BACK!
Hey! What's your deal, little sister? It's probably just a neighbor passing the circular around. Don't get so...
I CAN'T USE MAGIC! THIS MUST BE AN EMERGENCY! ENEMIES ARE HERE!
ドーン
BOOM
ドーン
BOOM
ドーン
BOOM

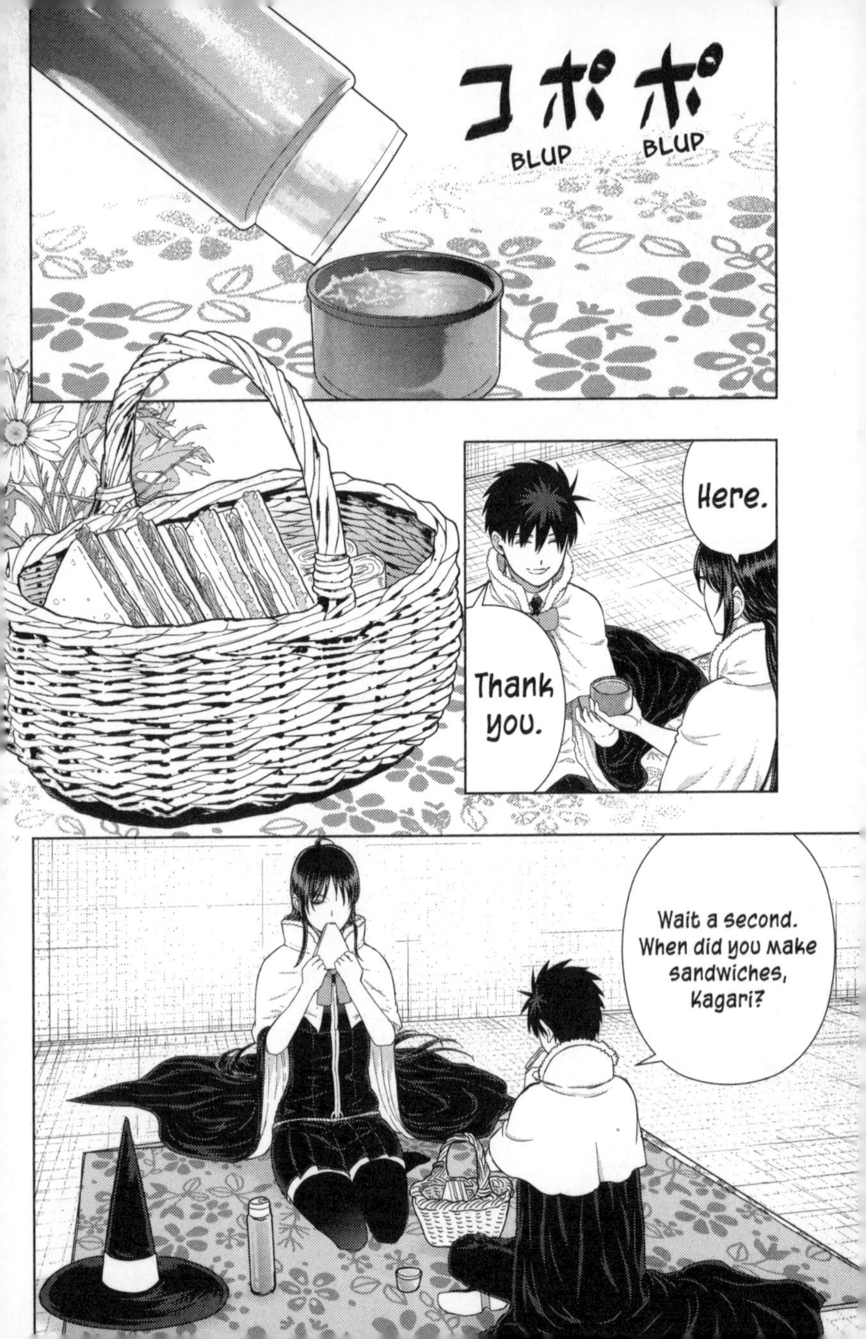
コポポ
BLUP BLUP
Here.
Thank you.
Wait a second. When did you make sandwiches, Kagari?

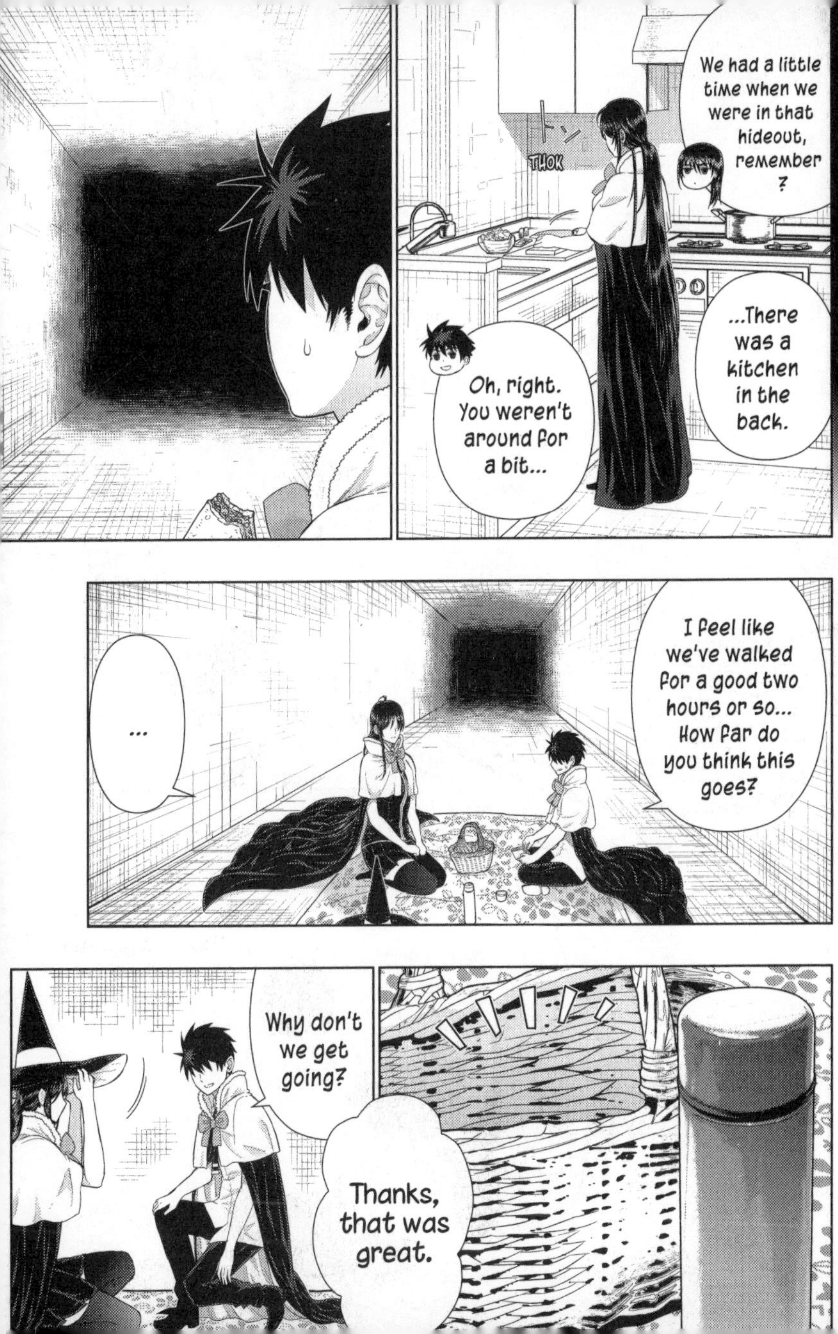
We had a little time when we were in that hideout, remember?
THOK
...There was a kitchen in the back.
Oh, right. You weren't around for a bit...
I feel like we've walked for a good two hours or so... How far do you think this goes?
...
!!!!!
Thanks, that was great.
Why don't we get going?

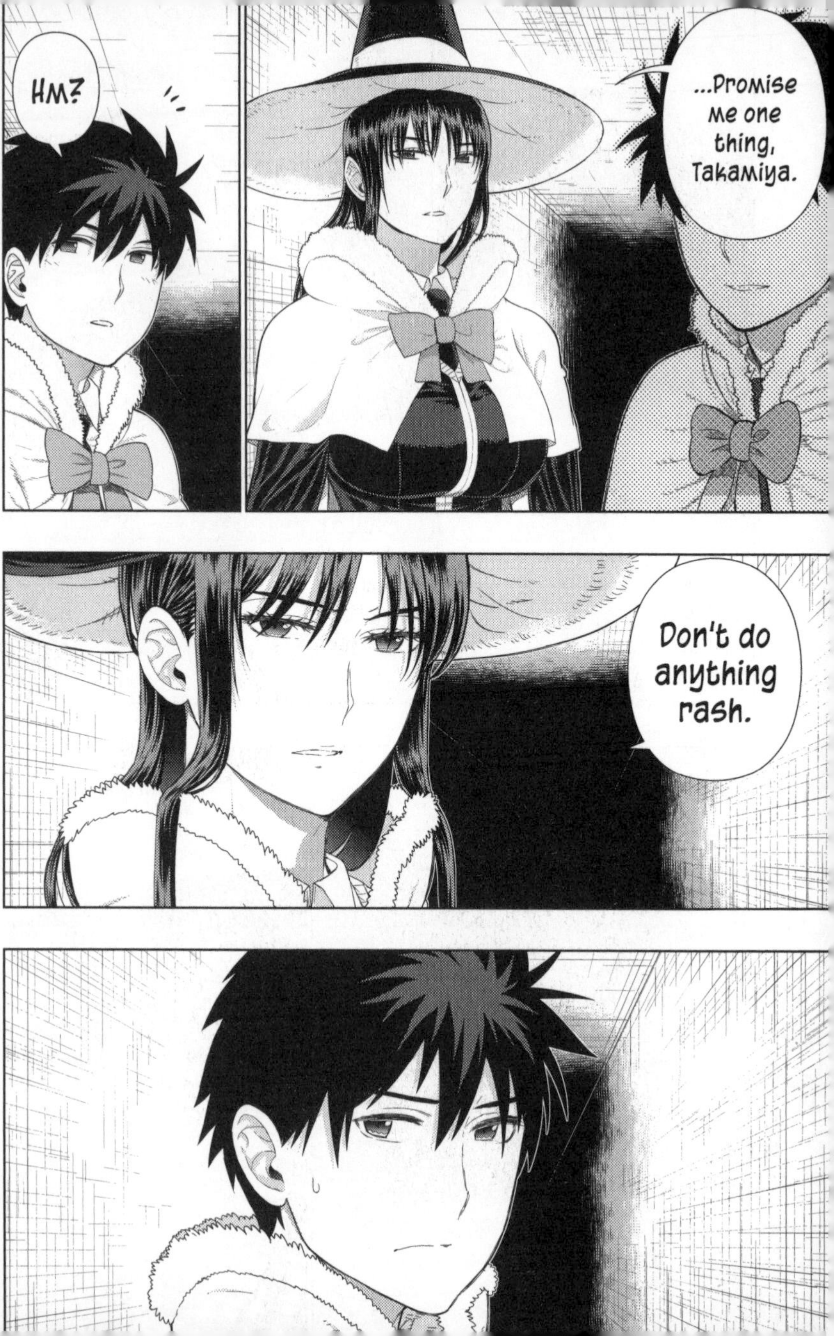
...Promise me one thing, Takamiya.
HM?
Don't do anything rash.

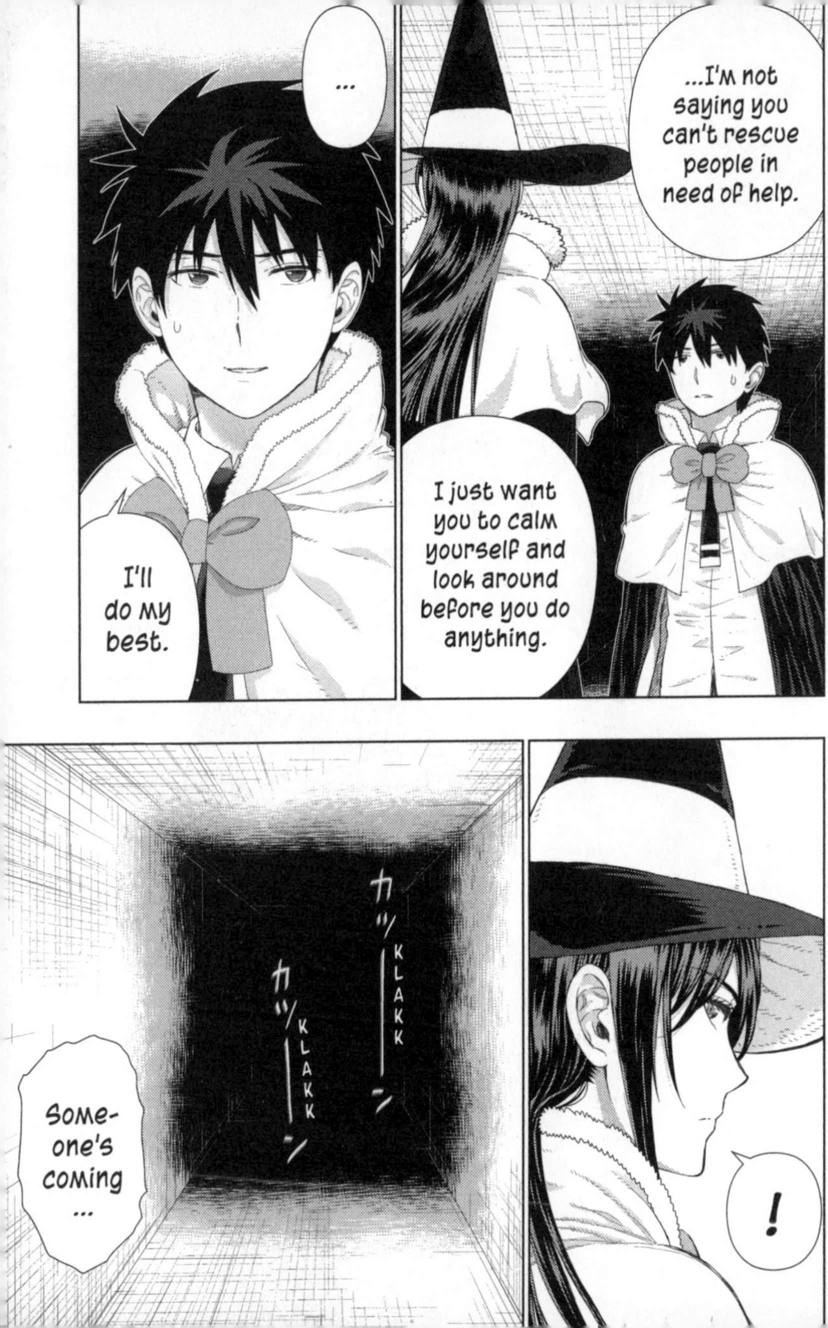
...I'm not saying you can't rescue people in need of help.
I just want you to calm yourself and look around before you do anything.
...
I'll do my best.
!
カッ KLAKK
カッ KLAKK
Some-one's coming ...

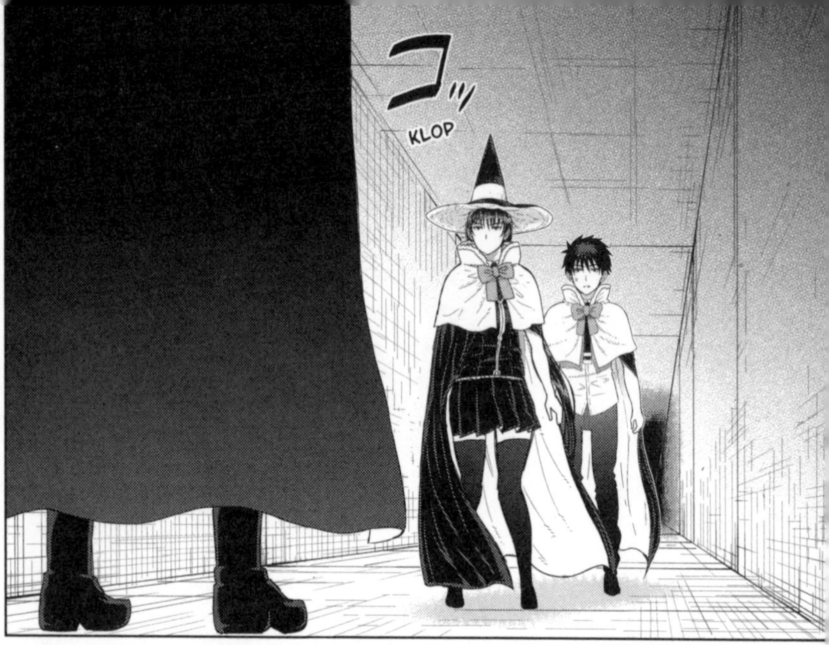
コッ
KLOP

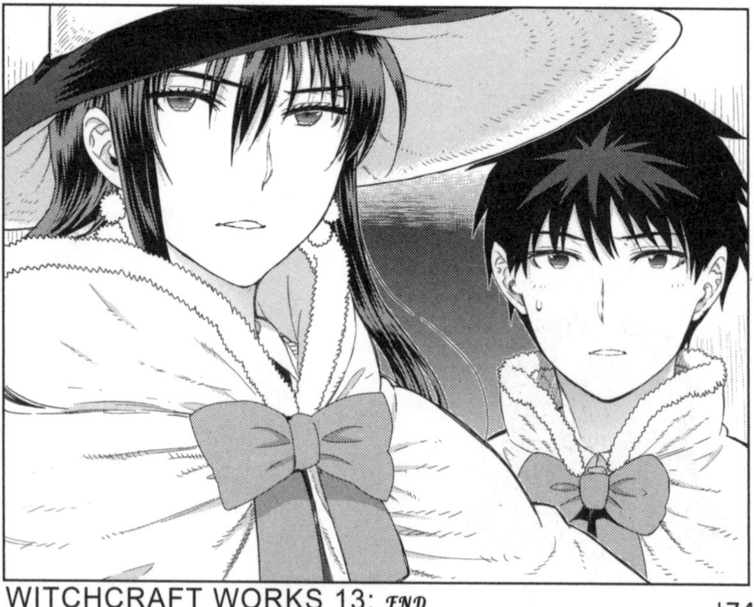

WITCHCRAFT WORKS 13: *END*

Witchcraft Works

Afterword

So, did you enjoy volume 13? This is Mizunagi. We're all the way into volume 13 of this title, and it seems like the moms are now quite active. My editor says that as well. Kagari's mother (Kayou) is the big boss, after all.

That being the case, I especially would like Komachi to take an active role out of all the moms. I think it'd be nice to put the spotlight on her for a bit, just as Kasumi had the spotlight. I don't know if there'd be any demand for that, though...

Well, please look forward to volume 14!

- Ryu Mizunagi

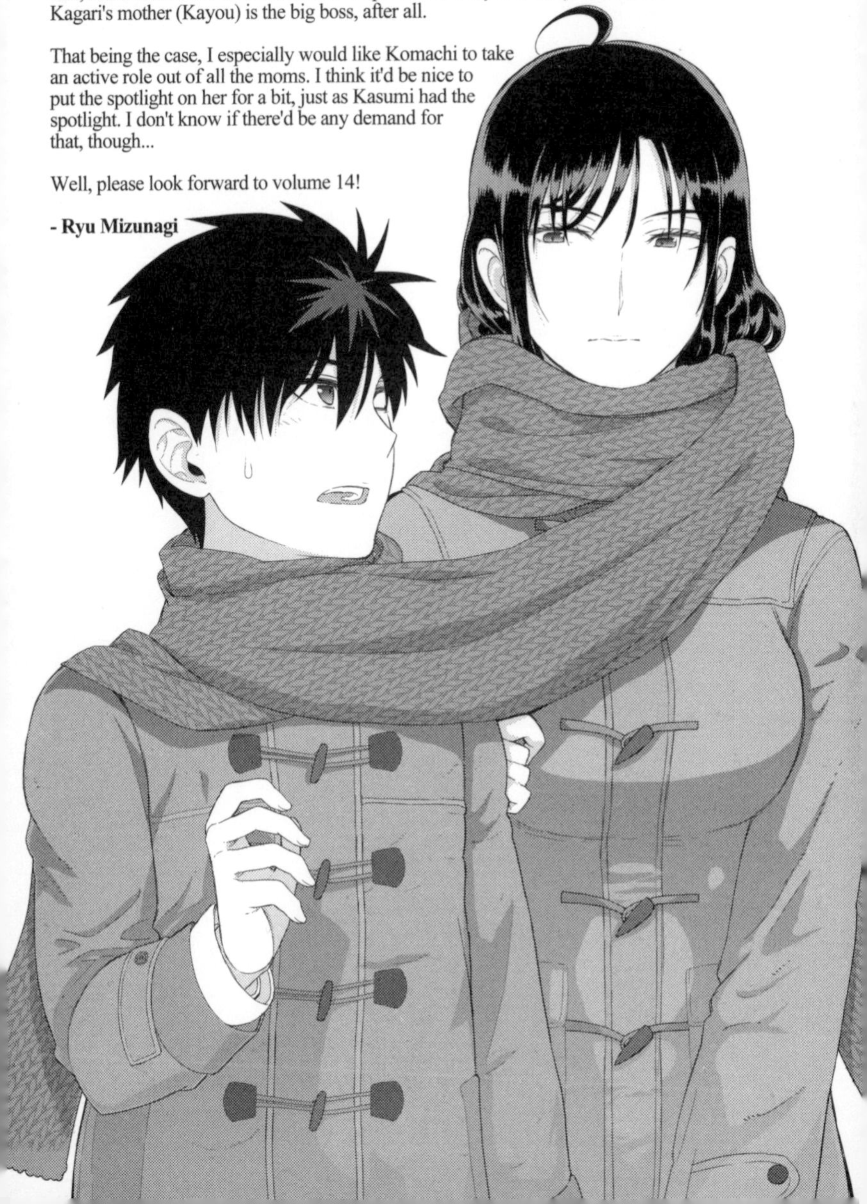

Witchcraft Works

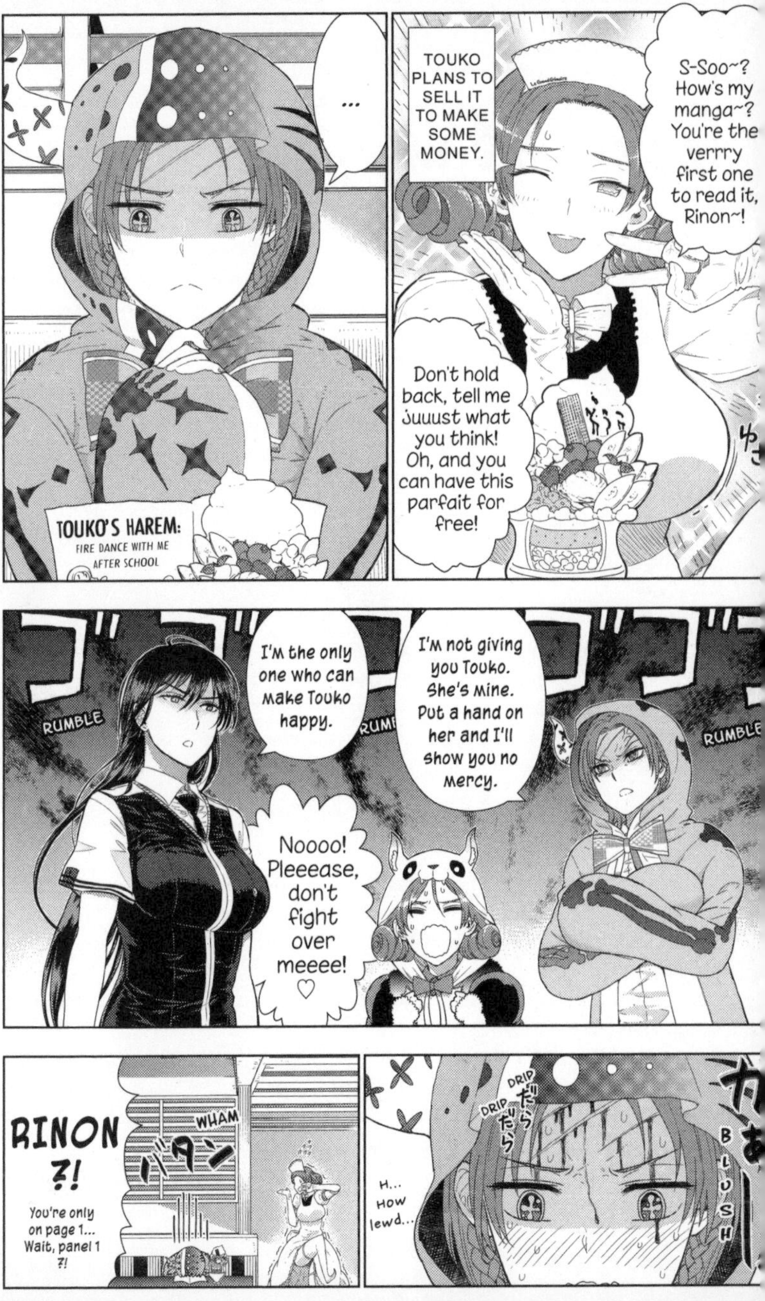

TOUKO PLANS TO SELL IT TO MAKE SOME MONEY.
S-Soo~? How's my manga~? You're the verrry first one to read it, Rinon~!
Don't hold back, tell me juuust what you think! Oh, and you can have this parfait for free!
...
TOUKO'S HAREM: FIRE DANCE WITH ME AFTER SCHOOL
RUMBLE
I'm not giving you Touko. She's mine. Put a hand on her and I'll show you no mercy.
I'm the only one who can make Touko happy.
RUMBLE
Noooo! Pleeease, don't fight over meeee! ♡
BLUSH
DRIP だら
DRIP だら
H... How lewd...
WHAM
バタン
RINON ?!
You're only on page 1... Wait, panel 1 ?!

IT TURNED INTO A BLOODY MESS.

Witchcraft Works | SETTING + SECRETS

This page is a collection of behind-the-scenes character and story elements that probably won't affect or appear in the main story, as well as comments by the author. If you finish reading the story and think, "I want to know more!" then we hope you enjoy the information here.

Chapter 71

Takamiya and Kagari cohabitate.

• Rinon
A chapter where Rinon shows us what a fraud she is. Just as we can see on the bonus manga, one of Rinon's weaknesses is her very limited knowledge when it comes to a certain subject.

   Of course, her underlings are also not allowed to have romantic relationships, and it seems that a very heavy penalty awaits anyone who breaks this rule.

• Touko
Shows up like nothing happened just one day after being blown to pieces as a firework. That's Touko for you. However, when considering the fact that she looks younger, it seems that a little more time will be needed for her to return to normal.

   It's to the point that Kagari now seems to suspect that she might be a magical creature.

Chapter 72

What is the nature of Kasumi's friendship with Alcina?

• Alcina

While Alcina collects magic-users and magical creatures she likes after turning them into furniture, we can see how disorderly she is when it comes to handling them by the fact that she tends to toss them all into cardboard boxes, and that she doesn't even know which ones are where. It may be that ownership is her goal, and that she loses interest in something once she possesses it.

The first household good she mistakenly dispels here is a tanuki tengu (goblin) captured a millennium ago. She only used it as a teapot twice.

• Kiora Pamera

A witch who floats through space-time, traveling between many worlds, and becomes a piece of furniture after making an agreement with Alcina in order to just barely keep a connection to this world. She has a special body that allows her to travel between dimensions without suffering any negative consequences, so she immediately flies off into other dimensions as soon as Alcina isn't around.

As far as her mind goes, though, it has no tolerance for traveling between dimensions, causing her to only grow madder as time passes. Now bored of conflict, she just wants to sleep in peace.

She was once the East Witch of the Zodiac.

• Furry-Ear

Alcina sees in Furry-Ear the talent to become a human chair. This is a great honor from Alcina's perspective, but, well...

• Takamiya

We can probably say that Takamiya's last words here are entirely to blame for the way Kasumi has turned out.

Chapter 73

A story about Takamiya and his dream with the White Princess.

• The White Princess

Evermillion appears in Takamiya's dreams in order to warn him once Alcina appears. She guides him in this dream, supporting him on his trip into the core.

She seems to like the way Takamiya looked when she first met him as a child, so she changes him to look this way.

• Alcina

Though Takamiya thinks the dream is his at first, it turns out that it's actually Alcina's. At its center is a sturdy, towering castle that protects its core, hiding Alcina's heart.

Chapter 74

Part 2 of the dream.

★ After sneaking into the heavily-guarded castle and descending deep down its corridors, they come to a pure-white plain of snow. After leveling the soldiers there, they arrive at a windowless tower.

• Evermillion and Alcina

It seems these two have some sort of history. Evermillion, who pursued extremes and became a god, and Alcina, who abandoned her research to live in this world.

What is important to Alcina is to continue living in this world. Evermillion has now lost sight of the person she was then, and can't seem to even remember how things turned out this way.

Chapter 76

Alcina vs. Kagari

• Kagari

While she sees Alcina as nothing but an enemy, Atori successfully advises her to try to settle things using persuasion. You could say that it's unusual for her to invite Alcina into her own private space. She seems to have grown in her own way through her many battles so far.

• Alcina

Alcina recognizes how much of a pervert Kagari is and considers trusting Takamiya, but she learns of his betrayal thanks to her underlings' investigation. She goes to meet Kazane and issues a declaration of war.

Chapter 77-78

The battle against Alcina begins.

• Alcina and Kazane

Alcina uses Kiora to make sure that Kazane is immobilized, sealing their current space with her inside, because Alcina is most concerned about how Kazane will act in this situation.

• Kagari

Kagari tries to go to the Workshop after noticing that something about the town is strange. She comes across a magical creature on the way there, and while she fights it off, she realizes that she herself cannot use magic.

• Miss Weekend

Weekend also is quick to notice that something about the town is off, and she guides Takamiya and the others to a shelter she had prepared in advance. Currently a Workshop witch, she cannot use magic either.

She thinks that it's a natural part of her job to protect her students, as she is now a teacher at Tougetsu High.

Prepare to be Bewitched!

Makoto Kowata, a novice witch, packs up her belongings (including a black cat familiar) and moves in with her distant cousins in rural Aomori to complete her training and become a full-fledged witch.

"*Flying Witch* emphasizes that while actual magic is nice, there is ultimately magic in everything." —Anime News Network

The Basis for the Hit Anime from Sentai Filmworks!

Volumes 1-7 Available Now!

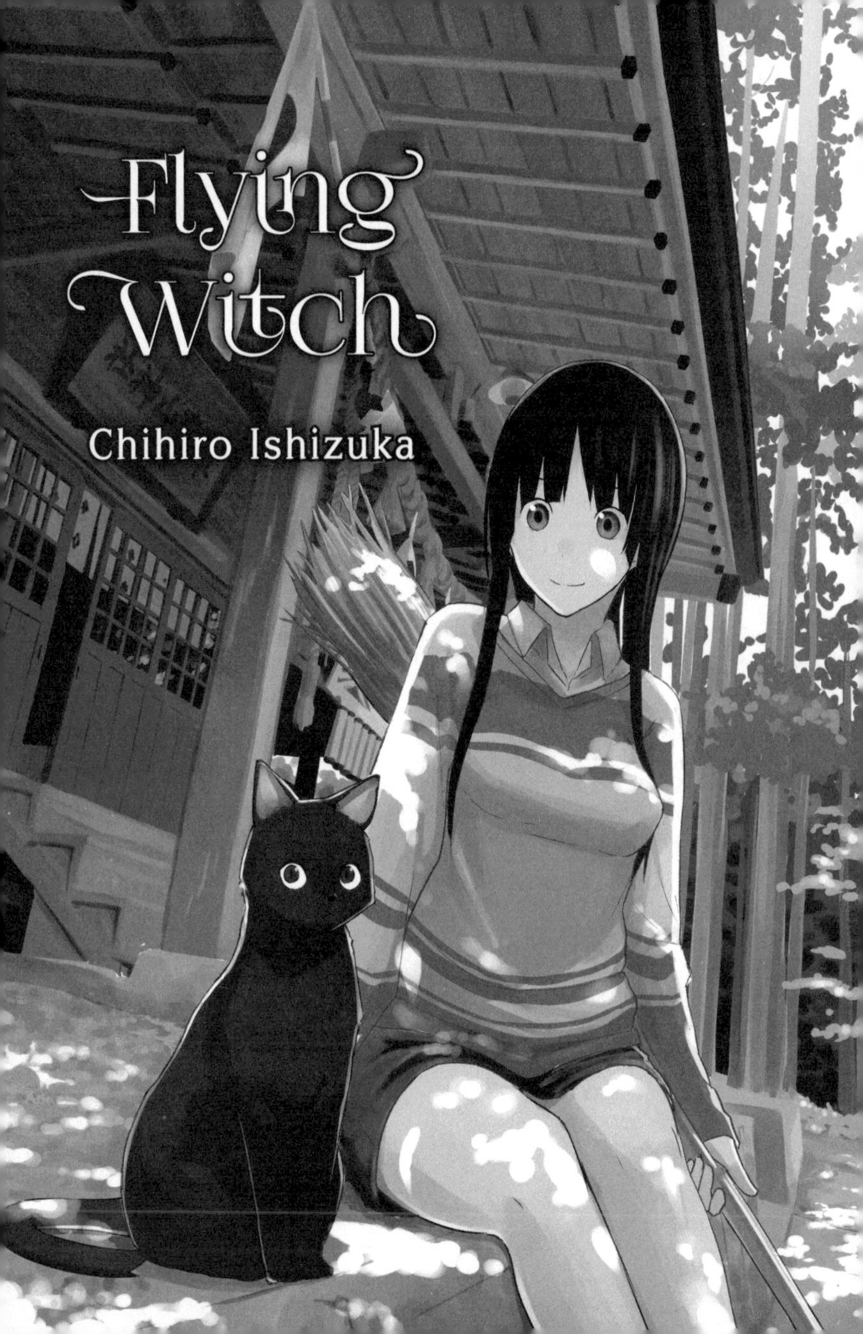
Flying Witch
Chihiro Ishizuka

Witchcraft Works, volume 13

A Vertical Comics Edition

Translation: Ko Ransom
Production: Risa Cho
Melissa DeJesus

First published in Japan in 2018 by Kodansha, Ltd., Tokyo
Publication rights for this English edition arranged through Kodansha, Ltd., Tokyo
English language version produced by Vertical Comics, an imprint of
Kodansha USA Publishing, LLC.

Translation provided by Vertical Comics, 2019
Published by Kodansha USA Publishing, LLC, New York

Originally published in Japanese as *Uicchi Kurafuto Waakusu 13* by Kodansha, Ltd., 2018
Uicchi Kurafuto Waakusu first serialized in *good! Afternoon*, Kodansha, Ltd., 2010-

ISBN: 978-1-949980-00-4

Manufactured in Canada

First Edition

Kodansha USA Publishing, LLC.
451 Park Avenue South
7th Floor
New York, NY 10016
www.vertical-comics.com

Vertical books are distributed through Penguin-Random House Publisher Services.